South Asian Education Policy, Research, and Practice

Series Editors

Radhika Iyengar
Earth Institute, Columbia University
New York, USA

Matthew A. Witenstein
Redlands, California, USA

Erik Jon Byker
Concord, North Carolina, USA

Aim of the Series
Tackling topics in education relevant throughout South Asia, the books in this series demonstrate the linkages between research, policy and practice. Titles employ varied methodological approaches (qualitative, quantitative, mixed) to address specific topics in policy and practice, such as teacher education, technology, educational planning, and globalization of education. Books have a regional scope, focusing on interactions and developments across the region as opposed to single-country case studies. The series developed out of the work of the South Asia Special Interest Group of the Comparative and International Education Society, which brings together policymakers, practitioners, and researchers to discuss pertinent issues, and welcomes work from non-SIG members and SIG members alike.

More information about this series at
http://www.springer.com/series/15224

Huma Kidwai • Radhika Iyengar • Matthew A. Witenstein •
Erik Jon Byker • Rohit Setty
Editors

Participatory Action Research and Educational Development

South Asian Perspectives

Editors
Huma Kidwai
Washington, District of Columbia
USA

Radhika Iyengar
Earth Institute, Columbia University
New York, USA

Matthew A. Witenstein
Redlands, California, USA

Erik Jon Byker
Concord, North Carolina, USA

Rohit Setty
Fairfax, Virginia, USA

South Asian Education Policy, Research, and Practice
ISBN 978-3-319-84043-7   ISBN 978-3-319-48905-6   (eBook)
DOI 10.1007/978-3-319-48905-6

© The Editor(s) (if applicable) and The Author(s) 2017
Softcover reprint of the hardcover 1st edition 2017
This work is subject to copyright. All rights are solely and exclusively licensed by the Publisher, whether the whole or part of the material is concerned, specifically the rights of translation, reprinting, reuse of illustrations, recitation, broadcasting, reproduction on microfilms or in any other physical way, and transmission or information storage and retrieval, electronic adaptation, computer software, or by similar or dissimilar methodology now known or hereafter developed.
The use of general descriptive names, registered names, trademarks, service marks, etc. in this publication does not imply, even in the absence of a specific statement, that such names are exempt from the relevant protective laws and regulations and therefore free for general use.
The publisher, the authors and the editors are safe to assume that the advice and information in this book are believed to be true and accurate at the date of publication. Neither the publisher nor the authors or the editors give a warranty, express or implied, with respect to the material contained herein or for any errors or omissions that may have been made. The publisher remains neutral with regard to jurisdictional claims in published maps and institutional affiliations.

Cover illustration: © Vivek Sharma / Alamy Stock Photo

Printed on acid-free paper

This Palgrave Macmillan imprint is published by Springer Nature
The registered company is Springer International Publishing AG
The registered company address is: Gewerbestrasse 11, 6330 Cham, Switzerland

Foreword

Participatory Action Research and Education in South Asia, edited by five educators, is a welcome addition to the knowledge base on how to bring about transformational change in the lives of marginalized people. One of its great strengths is its focus on one critically important basic service for poor people: delivery of education through government primary and secondary schools in South Asia. It is a great resource for researchers in the participatory tradition and also for those in other research traditions interested in collaborative and impactful research.

The focus on education in South Asia is important for several reasons. The region hosts some of the most spectacular failures of education as well as the greatest large-scale innovations in educational programs and research. Except in Sri Lanka, two generations of children have been cheated by a wrong-minded focus on measuring educational success by counting the number of schools built and school enrollment, without considering whether the children were learning anything at all. In India, for example, with the world's largest primary school program, the Annual Status of Education Report (ASER) showed that in 2014, only 48% of children in fifth-grade could read a second- grade text, and only a quarter could do simple math.

Systemic change is difficult, whether in power relations in one small community or in the institutional politics of an educational system of a whole state or country. This book recounts rich experiences particularly in the policy arena. It provides textured detail from a classroom in Bangladesh with children taking photographs to communicate their vision, to tribal and disabled children communicating their reality to policy makers, to the wrangling among stakeholders discussing alternative recommendations for educational policy reform in the Northern Province in Sri Lanka or in Nepal.

If the goal is transformational, ASER studies pioneered by Pratham, an Indian nongovernmental organization, are perhaps the best example of large-scale citizen mobilization in conducting research, creating a learning culture, and changing educational policy. Driven by the philosophy that every child can learn, Pratham launched the first ASER study in 2005. A teacher's job in this philosophy is to assess how much a child has learned so as to adapt and modify teaching approaches to fit the child's learning needs. It *empowers* teachers to bring about change. The ASER learning assessment tool is a very simple tool with a few learning indicators that can be used by ordinary citizens to assess whether a child can read or do simple math. And because it is so simple and understandable, it evokes great interest and discussion, which in itself starts the process of awareness, takes the mystique out of assessment, and increases the probability of change.

Each ASER survey includes 600,000 children sampled in order to be nationally representative. The survey is conducted over one weekend by an organization that has field presence, and it has been repeated every year for a decade. It is the continuity of ASER studies over time, their large scale, and the outreach and focus on a select few simple outcome statistics that have moved the thinking of policy makers from "enrollment" to "learning." After a decade of dismal news every year from these surveys, the government of India has just announced a major overhaul of the public educational system to realign the institutional systems to one goal: improving learning outcomes at each grade. And the methodology has inspired many other countries to do similar work.

All the researchers in this volume are deeply committed to bringing about change, if not transformation, in education. As highlighted in the conclusion, change is difficult to achieve. It may even be unfair to expect transformational change from small, one-time, time-bound participatory studies, no matter how well they are done or how committed, self-aware, and altruistic the researcher.

Many researchers in this volume would agree that handing over control to participants in research with a predetermined agenda is extremely difficult in practice. Most research is collaborative, and the choice of participants, the research problem, the tools, the methods, and even the nature of analysis are all primarily framed by the researcher, even though participants discuss, analyze, and present their lived reality. But even just this difference empowers participants, be it teachers or children, because the tools are evocative and easy to understand and tap into their knowledge. The critical difference from conventional academic research is that the process of engagement with selected participants builds their capacity to question, explain, and challenge and hence enhances their potential to bring about change.

This volume has several distinctions. Participatory action research is generally more commonly applied at the community level. This volume, however, is rich in case studies of policy dialogues between marginalized groups and government that have led to policy shifts, including in the difficult postconflict environment of the Northern Province in Sri Lanka. The volume also includes cases of collective action not in rural communities but by parents and marginalized youth groups that have also led to policy shifts. The challenge, as always, is to sustain these processes over time. Unusually, the book also includes use of participatory action research to improve implementation practice by providing timely feedback for continuous adjustment. Finally, the volume includes chapters in which researchers reflect on themselves and their own biases as researchers.

It is a mammoth task to change educational systems to improve learning outcomes for children. But without holding the *vision of change* as the primary goal, PAR efforts may fall short despite our best intentions. If we learn anything from the decade-long ASER studies conducted by Pratham and other examples in this volume, it is that research needs to be embedded and relevant to the local context and to use minimum tools that empower barefoot researchers, local people, and ordinary citizens; it also has to be repeated over time, until change takes root at local levels and captures policy attention. It is vital, therefore, for small studies with limited resources to link with other organizations that have long-term presence and that can function as conveyor belts to policy makers and implementers. When small, one-time studies are not linked to policy, they must work through local actors if they are to have any hope of altering the lives of marginalized people in their communities.

Those who try are courageous.

Deepa Narayan, Ph.D.

Acknowledgments

The editors of this volume of the South Asian Education series wish to thank the members of the South Asia Special Interest Group at the Comparative International Education Society. Members had multiple rounds of discussions to define the objectives of the series: South Asian education policy, research, and practice. Thank you to the authors for working on all the detailed comments from the reviewers and keeping to the timeline. The editors are grateful to the Comparative International Education Society for providing a platform for scholars, researchers, academicians, and practitioners based in South Asia and elsewhere to engage in enriching discussions, which resulted in the idea for this series. We would also like to thank Palgrave Macmillan Publishers for approaching the South Asia Special Interest Group for this series. Through this series, the group is attempting to bring the South Asian diaspora together to fill the gaps between policy, research, and practice.

Contents

Introduction: Participatory Action Research and
Education—Key Approaches and Debates   1
Huma Kidwai and Radhika Iyengar

1 Defining PAR to Refine PAR: Theorizing Participatory
Action Research in South Asian Educational Contexts   13
Rohit Setty and Matthew A. Witenstein

2 Utilizing "a Version of PAR" to Explore Children's
Voices on Inclusion: The Case of Two Primary
Schools in Bangladesh   49
Tahiya Mahbub

3 The ASER "Translating Policy into Practice" Toolkit:
From Participatory Action Research to Evidence-
Based Action   75
Suman Bhattacharjea and Erik Jon Byker

4 Northern Province Education System in Sri Lanka:
Participatory Review, Recommendation,
Implementation, and Monitoring   97
Meera Pathmarajah and Nagalingam Ethirveerasingam

5 Unpacking Participation: The Case of Child-Centered Pedagogy in India 129
   Neha Miglani, Jayasree Subramanian, and Vishnuteerth Agnihotri

6 Learning and Evolving in Hybrid Learning: A PAR Perspective 161
   Rajarshi Singh, Neha Sharma, and Ketan Verma

7 Reclaiming the Collective: Challenging Neoliberal Ideology Through PAR 185
   Shabnam Koirala-Azad

8 Applying Participatory Action Research to Program Evaluation in Education Policy 205
   Mary Vayaliparampil

Case Study 1. Photovoice and Girls' Education in Gujarat, India 229
Payal Shah

Case Study 2. Utilizing Memoing as a Reflexive Tool in Participatory Action Research 235
Tahiya Mahbub

Case Study 3. One Moment of Participatory Data Analysis 247
Meagan Call-Cummings

Case Study 4. Shikshagiri: Including Marginalized Children in Policy and Praxis of Education 255
Anusha Chandrasekharan and Pradeep Narayanan

Conclusion. Reading and Rewriting South Asia 271
Erik Jon Byker

Name Index	281
Subject Index	283
Place Index	289

Notes on Contributors

Vishnuteerth Agnihotri has experience of nearly 25 years in educational assessment, development of e-learning solutions, leadership training, consulting, business development, project management, and performance improvement. His last organizational role was with Educational Initiatives, a leading player in the field of educational assessments and e-learning, where he was employed for 10 years. He has worked on various educational research projects including assessment of values, school leadership, teacher assessment, and impact evaluations. Currently, Vishnu works as an independent consultant. His areas of focus include talent identification for middle and high school students, development of educational enrichment material for gifted students, sustainability education, and value education.

Suman Bhattacharjea has been Director, Research at ASER Centre, New Delhi, since 2008. ASER Centre is the research and evaluation unit of Pratham Education Foundation, responsible for facilitating the nationwide Annual Status of Education Report, among other research, assessment, and capacity-building activities. Suman has worked as a software developer, a high school teacher, an education specialist, and a researcher. She has extensive experience in the fields of education, gender, and women's rights and has worked with government, private, nongovernment, and international organizations in several countries, including India, the United States, Pakistan, and Mexico. She has taught courses on research design, gender, and education and has authored or coauthored numerous articles and books in these areas. Suman earned an undergraduate degree in Economics with Honors from Delhi University and master's and doctoral degrees in Education from Harvard University.

Erik Jon Byker is an assistant professor in the Department of Reading and Elementary Education at the University of North Carolina at Charlotte. Erik has a PhD in Curriculum, Teaching, and Educational Policy from Michigan State University and holds a M.Ed. degree in Curriculum and Instruction from the University of Virginia. His fields of specialization include curriculum foundations, educational technology integration, global citizenship education, and social studies. Erik's research agenda is comparative and international in scope. He has conducted ethnographic field studies in Cuba, England, Germany, India, South Korea, and South Africa and across the United States on how social actors in elementary school use and construct meaning for computer technology. Over the 2010–2011 academic year, he lived in Bangalore, India, and collected dissertation data on how an economic cross-section of Bangalore's elementary school teachers and students were using computer technology in their schools. Since then, Erik has returned to India to investigate the impact of volunteering for the Annual Status of Education Report on Indian young adults' perceptions of citizenship, schooling, and a future role in education in India. Erik teaches courses in culturally responsive pedagogy, instructional design, and social studies methods.

Meagan Call-Cummings has a PhD from Indiana University Bloomington and is an assistant professor at George Mason University, where she teaches qualitative research methodology. Her research interests center on methodological orientations and epistemological commitments that promote and build peace and social justice. Meagan's research tends to take critical, feminist, and participatory forms. Her most recent major project took place in rural Idaho, where she worked with 52 Latino/a high school students and their White teacher to collaboratively begin critical dialogue about race and racism at that school, in that community, and also in society. This project led to several opportunities to creatively showcase the group's research, including the website www.researchforempowerment.com. Meagan also has ongoing research projects in Jamaica that focus on critical approaches to peace education.

Anusha Chandrasekharan, Programme Manager, Communications, Praxis Institute for Participatory Practices, has worked as a print journalist with several leading newspapers before moving to communications in the development sector. She has facilitated participatory action research in different stages of development projects in contexts including gender and sexuality, women's rights, and children's development. She is a professional trainer in capacity building related to participatory methods and development communication and has facilitated use of participatory video and digital story telling as a tool to enable communities to make their voices heard.

Nagalingam Ethirveerasingam is a consultant to the Ministry of Education and Sports in Sri Lanka's Northern Province. From October 2013 to 2014, he served as Volunteer Coordinator of the Northern Education System Review. He is also a founding advisor to SERVE eLearning Institute, a Jaffna-based institute that develops and trains teachers to use e-lessons in science and mathematics. A former Olympian, he is an advocate and coach for young athletes in Sri Lanka. He completed his PhD in Education at Cornell University.

Radhika Iyengar has a PhD in Economics of Education from Teachers College at Columbia University. As the Education Director for the Millennium Villages Project for 10 countries in Africa and the Scale-up Operations at the Earth Institute Columbia University, Radhika provides guidance and leadership for over 15 education research specialists and coordinators based in the United States and certain other countries. She led the efforts to assess the use of technology for large-scale educational planning at the local level in Nigeria for Earth Institute's Nigeria Scale-up Initiative, a joint project between the Earth Institute and the Office of Special Assistant to the President of Nigeria on the Millennium Development Goals. Radhika also holds an Adjunct Assistant faculty position at Teachers College, where she taught a graduate-level course on Evaluation Research Methods and Data Analysis for Developing Countries. Currently she is acting as a Senior Special Advisor to UNESCO's Global Monitoring Report for 2016.

Huma Kidwai is an education consultant with the World Bank's Sub-Saharan Africa Division (Education–Global Practices). Over the last couple of years, she has worked on World Bank projects ranging from early childhood education, basic education, and skills development in East Asia and the Pacific region. In 2015 she graduated with a doctoral degree (EdD) from Teachers College, Columbia University; her research focused on the relationship between the state and madrassas in India. For her study, in 2013, she was awarded the American Institute of Indian Studies fellowship. Her other professional experiences include projects with the Poverty Reduction Group of the World Bank in New Delhi; projects related to health, education, and social equity at the Praxis Institute for Participatory Practices in New Delhi; and education programs and research at the Earth Institute's Global Center in Mumbai on their Model District Education Project.

Shabnam Koirala-Azad is Associate Dean of Academic Affairs and Associate Professor of International and Multicultural Education in the School of Education at the University of San Francisco. She is cofounder of the first degree program in Human Rights Education in the United States. Her teaching and scholarship focus broadly on the relationship between education and socioeconomic change and more specifically on issues of equity in access and opportunity. Her published works complicate traditional notions of educational research and outcome-driven models to highlight process. Using participatory research, she offers insights on democratic practices of research where the "researched" are integral to the both the process and the outcome of inquiry.

Tahiya Mahbub is currently working as an independent research and educational consultant based out of Montreal, Canada. Most of her work is focused on inclusive education, children's voices and rights, reflexive research methods, and indigenous knowledge. A passionate learner, Tahiya believes that education rooted in indigenous knowledge for any context is the best way to teach young people to lead more fruitful and meaningful lives in their specific settings. She has spent extensive time exploring the link between Rabindranath Tagore's educational philosophy and inclusion, especially in the context of her native country, Bangladesh. Tahiya completed her doctorate in Educational Studies at McGill University in June 2016. Prior to that she received her master's degree from the University of Cambridge (2006) and her bachelor's degree from Loyola University in Chicago (2004).

Neha Miglani is a PhD student at Rossier School of Education, University of Southern California. She is currently working on a Spencer Foundation grant that aims to understand the role of tutors in blended learning programs for disadvantaged students in India. Neha has worked as a researcher with Educational Initiatives, focusing primarily on the public education programs and government schools in India. She led and contributed to various research projects, including program evaluations, diagnostic assessments, and piloting a technology-based language learning program.

Pradeep Narayanan, Director, Research and Capacity Building, Praxis Institute for Participatory Practices, is a human rights activist and social development researcher who has been associated with many rights-based nongovernmental organizations and campaigns in India. Pradeep has more than 15 years of experience working in different capacities in government and nongovernment sectors. In the last decade, he has been involved in a number of projects in areas of monitoring and evaluation, policy advocacy, participatory research, and capacity building across various sectoral themes in India, South Asia, and Africa. While child rights has been a cross-cutting theme, in the last five years, he has worked extensively in the area of community mobilization with an overall focus on marginalized, vulnerable, and excluded communities.

Meera Pathmarajah is a part-time faculty member at the University of San Francisco and the University of California–Los Angeles. She teaches classes on gender, education, and development and has over 15 years of experience working in international education. She is the founder of Visions Global Empowerment, a nonprofit organization dedicated to youth education and empowerment. Meera also formerly served as Room to Read's Asia Regional Program Manager. Her research focuses on gender, development, pedagogy, and teacher education. She earned a doctorate degree in International Education Policy from Teachers College, Columbia University.

Jayasree S. received a masters degree in mathematics, after which she worked in the field of education in various capacities for about 15 years. She has taught secondary school and college students and worked on development of diagnostic assessments, teacher assessments, learning modules for an adaptive learning tool, and evaluation of educational programs at Educational Initiatives.

Rohit Setty is a recent United States–India Educational Foundation Fulbright–Nehru Fellow with the National Council of Educational Research and Training's Regional Institute of Education, Mysore, and a graduate of the University of Michigan. His work centers on the intersections of policy and practice as they relate to in-service teacher education in India and abroad. Currently his research explores the policies, the practices, and the possibilities of Indian teacher education. He has worked with faculty and research centers across India on textbook reform, teacher education curriculum reform, and the enactment of teacher education. He has written for the *Indian Express*, *Eklavya*, the *Annual Review of Comparative and International Education*, and several academic journals in the United States over the past few years. Rohit earned his bachelor's degree in Social Science and Secondary Education from James Madison University in 1998. He completed his master's degree in South Asian Studies at the University of Michigan in 2007, where he explored educational issues in India through the multiple perspectives of history, anthropology, economics, business, religion, and architecture. He completed his PhD in Teaching and Teacher Education at the University of Michigan in 2013. He has taught in Virginia, Japan, and New Zealand as a secondary school teacher and has worked with in-service and pre-service social studies teachers across Michigan and in India over the last 12 years.

Payal P. Shah (Ph.D., Indiana University–Bloomington) is Assistant Professor of Educational Foundations and Qualitative Inquiry in the Department of Educational Studies at the University of South Carolina. She conducts critical ethnographic research on gender, education, and development in India and has published across the fields of international and comparative education, qualitative inquiry, and women's and gender studies.

Neha Sharma has been associated with Pratham for two years and manages the Hybrid Learning Program. She has experience in digital content development and has worked as the content coordinator for information technology– based initiatives of Pratham. Before Pratham, Neha worked as a research scientist for two years at Ludwig Maximilians Universitat, Munich, Germany. She holds a master's degree in Biotechnology from the Indian Institute of Technology, Guwahati, and previously worked as an assistant professor at the National Institute of Technology, Jalandhar.

Rajarshi Singh is a consultant at Pratham Education Foundation's research wing, ASER Centre, New Delhi, India. His research focuses on social and cultural development with respect to educational practice and policy, discovering data-driven insights for outcome-oriented improvement of program designs and monitoring and evaluation. Rajarshi is currently working on discovering learning and content usage patterns of children in the Hybrid Learning experiment. He has a PhD in Computational Mechanics from Carnegie Mellon University, Pittsburgh, United States.

Mary Vayaliparampil is an educator and researcher. Her work lies at the intersection between education and peace building. She uses research, training, and education to develop programs for Nepal and Tibet at the Institute for Multi-Track Diplomacy in Virginia, United States. She also leads the research team in developing working papers for the Inclusive National Country Assessment dimensions at Sovereignty First, also in Virginia. She completed a dual-title PhD in Educational Theory and Policy—Comparative and International Education from Pennsylvania State University in the United States. Her dissertation is titled *Stakeholder Perceptions of the Education for All Campaign Effectiveness in Increasing School Enrollment in India*. During her doctoral studies, she had the opportunity to intern with UNICEF and examine the School Water and Sanitation towards Health and Hygiene intervention in Jharkhand, India. Mary also received an MS degree in Educational Leadership from the University of Oregon in the United States and a B.Sc. degree in Physics from Goa University, India. Mary has served as the cochair of the Ad-Hoc Committee for the Advancement of Early Careers in Comparative and International Education and the Chair of the New Scholars Committee within the Comparative and International Education Society. She is also a reviewer for the International Studies Special Interest Group with the American Educational Research Association. Prior to moving to the United States, she worked as a math and science teacher, English-language tutor, and program coordinator in the United Arab Emirates and India.

Ketan Verma leads projects related to learning assessment and program evaluation at ASER Centre. He is on the core team for the Annual Status of Education Report, the world's largest citizen-led assessment of learning outcomes. Ketan currently is working on expanding the scope of citizen-led assessments both geographically and thematically. He is also working to create new tools to measure gains in learning from Hybrid Learning and other technology-related interventions. He holds a master's degree in Development Economics from the University of Lancaster, United Kingdom.

Matthew A. Witenstein is a postdoctoral fellow in the School of Education at the University of Redlands in Redlands, California, where he helps coordinate the doctoral program. His research focuses on the student development (including academic and sociocultural issues) of immigrants in education, international student experiences, and international/comparative education issues about organization and governance, teacher training, quality, and the barriers impeding marginalized populations from persisting through the PK–20 pipeline. Matthew has worked extensively on projects throughout South Asia on the latter topics. His work has appeared in numerous journals, including *Teachers College Record, Ethnic and Racial Studies, International Journal of Intercultural Relations, Berkeley Review of Education, Asian Education and Development Studies,* and *Annual Review of Comparative and International Education.* Matthew has consistently presented work and provided active service at several North American–based organizations, including the American Educational Research Association, Association for the Study of Higher Education, Comparative and International Education Society, and Council on International Higher Education, and in international for a, including the World Congress of Comparative Education Societies, Comparative Education Society of India, and Global Conclave of Young Scholars of Indian Education. He is chair for the South Asia Special Interest Group and of the Book Awards Committee of the Higher Education Special Interest Group, both of the Comparative and International Education Society. He has been an invited speaker at higher education institutions and government agencies throughout South Asia and in the United States.

List of Acronyms

ABL   Activity-based learning
AL   Advanced level
ASER   Annual Status of Education Report
BRAC   Building Resources Across Communities
CAL   Computer-assisted learning
CCE   Continuous and Comprehensive Evaluation
CFLC   Child-friendly learning centered
DIET   District Institute of Education Training
EI   Educational Initiatives
EMIS   Education Management Information System
ICT   Information and Communication Technology
ILS   Internal Learning System
KGBV   Kasturba Gandhi Balika Vidyalaya Program
MDG   Millennium Development Goals
MOE   Ministry of Education
NESR   Northern Education System Review
NGO   Nongovernmental organization
NZA   New Zonal Administration
PALS   Participatory Action and Learning System
PAR   Participatory action research
PARI   Participatory action research and implementation
PGIS   Participatory Geographic Information Systems
PLA   Participatory Learning and Action
PSW   Psychosocial Wellbeing Committee

RIVER   Rishi Valley Institute for Educational Resources
RTE   Right of Children to Free and Compulsory Education Act
SSA   Sarva Siksha Abhiyan
TPP   Translating Policy into Practice
ZBE   Zonal Board of Education

List of Figures

Fig. 4.1	Sri Lanka Ministry of Education administrative structure	101
Fig. 5.1	Student learning outcomes by classroom organization	148
Fig. 5.2	Student learning outcomes by use of additional learning resources in classrooms	149
Fig. 8.1	Thematic map of the study's findings	211
Fig. 1	Process map of Shikshagiri	257
Fig. 2	Key questions raised by panelists	265

List of Tables

Table 2.1	Students at Schools "U" and "M"	58
Table 2.2	Written documents	63
Table 3.1	Teacher candidates' ratings of TPP module 1	88
Table 4.1	Number of schools and enrolment by type of school by zone—2015	105
Table 5.1	Sampled districts in the evaluation	136
Table 5.2	Key features of state ABL models	140
Table 5.3	Types of classrooms in the study sample	145
Table 7.1	Coresearchers	187
Table 1	Priorities evolved by children's panel from discussions	266

List of Photos

Photo 4.1	Jaffa Central College (a national school), established in 1816 by Methodists	103
Photo 4.2	A popular tutory in Jaffna	104
Photo 8.1	Midday Meal photographed by Parent 93	211
Photo 8.2	Dirty toilet facilities photographed by Parent 86	214
Photo 8.3	Caught in the Maoist conflict by Parent 17	216
Photo 8.4	Loss of income captured by Participant 68	218
Photo 8.5	Poor school facilities captured by Parent 102	219
Photo 1	Zooni's photo and voice	242
Photo 1	The Spectrum of Racism, as created by the research collective	250
Photo 1	Children interact with the public at Raahgiri as part of Shikshagiri	258
Photo 2	The five images reflect five cases, or scenarios, related to education that the children analyzed	259
Photo 3	Gandhi Talisman 1: Panelists draw Chotu, a child involved in labor at a roadside eatery. The employer asks him to come and wash the plates of the entire country. In the image, the children pledge to stop child labor	260
Photo 4	Gandhi Talisman 2: Panelists draw the photo of a snake charmer to represent extreme marginalization. The snake charmer belongs to a denotified tribe and does not have any means of alternate employment. Children from such families are exposed to poverty, according to the panelists	261
Photo 5	Exclusion. Panelists list different categories of vulnerabilities to identify the target of any policy	262
Photo 6	Nandkishor. Illustration by a panelist that explores the realities of India and its education system	264

Introduction: Participatory Action Research and Education—Key Approaches and Debates

Huma Kidwai and Radhika Iyengar

Participation has become a prominent idea in contemporary social change discourses. With the global popularization of democratic values and principles that support social and political structures throughout the world, it has become increasingly difficult to reject the idea of engaging different actors in deliberations on various aspects of life and desired change. Participation is now increasingly understood as a right held by all people to engage in society and in decisions that impact their lives (Institute of Development Studies 2016).

Participatory action research (PAR) is a processes concerned with developing "practical knowing" in the search of meaningful "human purposes," grounded in a "participatory worldview" and bringing together "action and reflection," "theory and practice," in participation with others "in the pursuit of practical solutions to issues of pressing concern to people, and more generally the flourishing of individual persons and

H. Kidwai (✉)
The World Bank, Washington, DC, USA
e-mail: humakidwai@gmail.com

R. Iyengar
Earth Institute, Columbia University, New York, USA
e-mail: iyengar@ei.columbia.edu

communities" (Reason and Bradbury 2008, p. 1). More specifically, as a process, PAR maybe defined as a "form of action research in which professional social researchers operate as full collaborators with members of organizations in studying and transforming those organizations. It is an ongoing organizational learning process, a research approach that emphasizes co-learning, participation and organizational transformation" (Greenwood et al. 1993, p. 175).

Localization of participatory development frameworks in different parts of the world and their application to diverse socioeconomic contexts and challenges have led to emergence of multiple interpretations of participatory methods (White et al. 2004). As a research process aimed at being conducted "*with* and *for* people rather than *on* people," it is obvious that PAR is in a constant state of evolution as an emerging paradigm of cooperative experimental inquiry (Reason 2004, p. 1).

To understand the increasingly complex and pluri-lateral field of PAR and its application to education in the South Asian context, this edited volume brings together some stories from the region on how PAR is currently being understood and practiced among the diverse communities of education practitioners and policy makers. In this process, this volume brings together an assortment of authors from the field of education and participatory development, with most being practitioners sharing their field experiences with PAR. We editors realized that while a lot has been written about the ideological and theoretical underpinnings of PAR, little has been documented about the field-based applications of PAR in education settings, particularly in South Asian countries. We noted that while PAR and other participatory development tools are quite widely practiced by civil society organizations in South Asian countries, writings on PAR are not proportionately representative of the region. Most documentation on PAR from the Global South tends to come from African and South America countries. Hence, we believed that a resource that specifically focuses on PAR, education, and South Asia would be a valuable contribution to each of the three areas of study. We circulated an open call for chapters through wide networks across the education development sector covering both practitioners and academics. This process allowed us to witness a range of PAR practices and interpretations prevalent in the region and to receive entries from field-based practitioners and scholars. This introduction provides a brief overview of key debates, actors, processes, and challenges presented by the various authors of this edition, in addition to laying out its organization.

PAR AND EDUCATION

Debates relating to poststructural and postdevelopment theory contributed significantly to increasing the willingness of development authors and practitioners to adopt elements from various trends and paradigms. The 1990s and thereafter saw several scholarly attempts to produce a new understanding of how development works and is transformed (Escobar 2006). Although such debates were ongoing since the 1970s, they became more popular after postdevelopment formalized as an approach during the 1980s and 1990s. With the rise of participatory development approaches emerged a family of methods and practices of engaging with stakeholder communities and forming an "endogenous intellectual and practical research methodology for the people of the Third World" (Peet and Hartwick 2009, p. 215).

Participatory development is driven by a belief in the importance of entrusting people with the responsibility to shape their own future (Chambers 2007). It requires recognition and use of local capacities and avoids the imposition of priorities from the outside. The belief is that participatory approaches to development increase the odds that a program will be on target and its results will more likely be sustainable. Participatory methodologies in development practice evolved in a sequence of various versions, all of which are continued to be practiced in various complementary ways. Common versions include rapid rural appraisal (RRA), participatory rural appraisal (PRA), and participatory learning and action (PLA). All three of these methods are "families of participatory methodologies which have evolved as behaviours, attitudes, methods, and practices of sharing" (Chambers 2007, p. 3). PRA/PLA took shape through a series of qualitative multidisciplinary approaches to learning local-level conditions and people's perspectives (Reitbergen-McCracken and Narayan 1998). Robert Chambers (2007) described several models through which PRA/PLA have been employed, such as Reflect, Stepping Stones, Participatory Action and Learning System, Farmer Participatory Research, Participatory Geographic Information Systems, Integrated Pest Management, the Internal Learning System, Community-led Monitoring and Evaluation, Integrated District-level Planning, and Community-Led Total Sanitation. Initially these approaches were adopted by local-level nongovernmental organizations and agricultural research organizations, but later they were adopted by international organizations, such as the World Bank and other donor agencies.

Action research has a long history, often traced to the work of Kurt Lewin in the 1940s, when he designed social experiments in natural settings. Other research movements that are often credited with strengthening the field of action research include the liberation thought (Freire 1970), feminism (Stanley and Wise 1983), pragmatism (Greenwood and Levin 1998), and critical thinking (Kemmis 2001) movements. However, as noted by Reason (2013) in his review of the history of action research, although many of these original forms of action research emphasized participation, the power to direct and shape the research often remained in the hands of the researchers. Recent developments in action research place greater emphasis on full integration of action and reflection and on increased collaboration between those involved in the research project (Reason and Bradbury 2008, p. 9). This integration has enabled researchers to develop a systematic inquiring approach to their own practices (Frabutt et al. 2008).

PAR is an attractive option for education researchers and practitioners. It may provide practitioners with new knowledge and understanding of educational problems and possible ways of addressing them through multiple windows. Teacher professional development and empowerment is one of the most commonly cited educational fields that benefits from action research (Osterman and Kottkamp 1993; Barone et al. 1996; Tomlinson 1995; Johnson 2012; Hensen 1996; Mills 2011). According to Hensen (1996), action research has the potential to help teachers develop new knowledge directly related to their classrooms, promotes reflective teaching and thinking, expands teachers' pedagogical repertoire, puts teachers in charge of their craft, reinforces the link between practice and student achievement, fosters an openness toward new ideas and learning new things, and gives teachers ownership of effective practices (reviewed by Hine 2013). Educators, schools, and policy makers have come a long way in extracting the benefits of PAR to education, albeit with numerous difficulties, mostly of which pertain to lack of clarity, time constraints, and holding a "presumed foreknowledge of a solution" (Hine 2013, p. 161). Over the years, PAR processes have been interpreted and new knowledge and solutions have been employed in an increasing number of ways. Chapters in this volume provide a snapshot of some of the emerging purposes and interpretations of PAR in education.

Overview of Chapters

In Chap. 1, Rohit Setty and Matthew A. Witenstein encourage readers to look beyond the definition of PAR, toward the processes that entail its enactment and the opportunities and challenges that frame the existence and potential of PAR to promote social justice, and transform the context and players. The authors explore the conceptual origins of PAR and highlight the unique positioning of an action researcher in dealing with tensions between "intervening" and "maintaining distance" as well as balancing objectives of activism and research." They also discuss an underlying risk of PAR processes—of filtering voices as researchers lend their voice to those of participants. This perhaps has been the most common critique of participatory methods, leading to questions regarding its true effectiveness in transferring power to participants. The authors argue that the uniqueness of PAR is conditional on effective handling of these tensions—the biggest challenge for PAR practitioners that is seemingly left unaddressed. Next, the authors delineate a rich historical account of PAR starting from its predominantly Western lineage to it's development in the Global South. Aligning their objectives with those of this book, the authors establish a clear distinction from several previously published discussions on PAR and education. In the second half of this chapter, the authors list questions and attempt to answer some. They remind us to critically examine the suitability of PAR methods to our contexts and to ponder how to overcome the multitude of challenges, such as different levels of literacy of many participants and implicit hierarchies between researcher and participants and within a group of participants, as well as the every-day logistical issues of effectively carrying out a PAR educational activity in South Asian context.

In Chap. 2, Tahiya Mahbub presents her journey as a diasporic scholar to locate her identity as a researcher in her country of origin and to adapt her research methodology, which she calls a "version of PAR," to the context of her study. The chapter mainly focuses on the field methods she used in her study to examine children's voices in two primary schools in Bangladesh. The author provides a view into her use of a combination of qualitative methods adapted for a PAR purpose. In doing so, she discusses the use of reflexivity as a form of methodological scrutiny, as a process through which a researcher engages in internal dialogue and detachment and inspects the process through which she constructs her questions and interpretations of field experiences. Mahbub advocates the benefits of using PAR and reflexivity together in contexts where researchers are faced with new and transitioning challenges of ethics and culture. She elaborates on her methodological struggle with researching children and childhood and the challenges associated with true representation of voice, which tend to increase greatly when the participants are children. She provides a rich account of episodes through which she has tried to resolve issues of losing children's voices in the process of negotiating access through gatekeepers, losing the quiet voices in the crowd, and eventually coming to terms with the situation when the participant voice begins to take over that of the researcher.

In Chap. 3, Suman Bhattacharjea and Erik Jon Byker draw on the PAR framework to examine trainee teachers' views of their training, the profession, and the national policies that impact education and schools in India. The chapter is a case study of a two-day workshop titled *Translating Policy into Practice* (TPP), by the Annual Status of Education Survey, at a District Institute of Education Training in the state of Haryana. The authors examine the effectiveness of participant engagement and action research tools by the Annual Status of Education Survey, called the TPP workshop toolkit, a toolkit that they argue it simple and adaptable. The "contextualizaton" component of the toolkit through instruments like village mapping, in which teacher candidates collect data about the schools in their community, is an example of a PAR process through which the community of teachers is empowered as colearners, coresearchers, and coactivists. PAR makes teacher candidates cognizant of the context for identifying their schools' and students' problems and prospective solutions, and connects the school's context within the larger community. The TPP toolkit is fundamentally an assessment tool intended to provide teachers with ways to assess in order to make informed decisions. Bhattacharjea and Byker strongly insist that "preparing teachers to assess is a key aspect of learning how to teach effectively in order for all children to learn." However, the chapter ends with an acknowledgment that although PAR helps facilitate reflection and enables teachers to become researchers, its effectiveness in bringing about change depends on the hope that it "reminds teacher candidates about the importance of teaching and moves them to act on behalf of children." The chapter concludes with a call for more research on the long-term impact of PAR approach to teacher education. The next chapter provides another context for raising similar concerns regarding the process of PAR and how contextual factors determine its connection with expected change.

In Chap. 4, Meera Pathmarajah and Nagalingam Ethirveerasingam propose the term "participatory action research and implementation" (PARI) to emphasize the importance of including implementation as a critical aspect of PAR. This chapter provides a comprehensive case study of the Northern Education System Review, a participatory exercise to give voice to hundreds of students, teachers, parents, and administrators in education planning, conducted by the Sri Lanka government. Although the Northern Education System Review was not particularly unique in its method or objective, the authors regard it as a rare example of participatory engagement for education planning and research where the PARI process seeks to transform the system in the process of investigating it. Most crucially, while emphasizing the importance of follow-up action and implementation in PAR, the authors propose reflection on the objectives and the postconflict environment of the Northern Education System Review. More specifically, they reflect on the challenges of implementation in the face of bureaucratic hurdles, limited human resources, and colonial legacies that continue to make the policy environment not conducive to participation. The authors raise relevant ethical concerns related to the failure of follow-up action to follow participatory research that may raise expectations for change.

Adding to the discourse and critical analysis of participatory methods in education, in Chap. 5, Neha Miglani, Jayasree S., and Vishnuteerth Agnihotri present their evaluation of the activity-based learning (ABL) program adopted as a pedagogical approach by seven states in India. ABL, a programmatic form of child-centered reform implemented statewide, represents a significant shift for Indian primary education, which has generally been characterized by instruction and rote-based, textbook-centered, and exam-oriented teaching and learning. The authors present the findings of an organized large-scale evaluation of the program on the ground. Critical to the process of this evaluation was the effort to seek participation of different stakeholders from research design to dissemination of findings. Through rich descriptions of findings on how ABL is applied in classrooms and how it impacts teaching learning practices as well as quality of material resources, the authors highlight the possibilities of the reform along with numerous limitations that restrict its potential. Over the years, as the implementation of ABL methods evolved through different program models, it has tended to move away from underlying principles of child-centered education, often resulting in partial and disjointed practices. The authors restate what has been asserted earlier (Hickey and

Mohan 2004): While the articulation of child-centered classrooms may seem ideal, an idealistic framework is only as good as its implementation. The chapter ends with a rich discussion of factors critical to the success of participatory and child-centered classrooms and emphasizes the role of teachers and their preparedness, insisting on establishing mechanisms for teacher involvement through various stages of program design and implementation. Furthermore, it points to the critical importance of consistency in implementation and alignment with other initiatives, reminding readers that several Indian states have witnessed the untimely downfall and dilution of ABL practices.

In another application of PAR framework to schooling, in Chap. 6, Rajarshi Singh, Neha Sharma, and Ketan Verma share their experience with the Hybrid Learning program, a large-scale digital learning experiment by Pratham, involving 26,000 empowered middle school children and their communities across three states of India. The program is based on a conviction that it is necessary to shift schooling strategies from "learning to read" and "reading to learn" to "learning to learn" if the country is to bridge the gap between schooling and learning outcomes. The program encourages discovery-based learning among middle school children. The Hybrid Learning experiment inquires into scalable solutions to overcome two primary barriers of quality learning across rural parts of India: "poor access to materials and the absence of a learner-centric learning environment." The authors describe ways in which the program helps children and their communities problematize education in rural India by recognizing that learning platforms in the modern world are not limited to pages and that multiple cultures of knowledge exist within society. Unique to the program were the dynamics of participation where children formed their own groups and memberships and fixed their own timetables and lesson plans. Not only were they seeking knowledge through the content available on their tablets, they went ahead, without prior facilitation, to create their own content. The authors evaluate the success of this program positively for its participatory design, which encouraged discovery-based learning and empowered children to realize the value of asking questions, working in groups, and selecting the pace of learning that works for them.

Chapter 7, by Shabnam Koirala-Azad, shifts the discussion to the use of PAR in engaging secondary- and tertiary-level Nepali students to identify problems facing their society and education institutions and to reflect on building participation and a collective voice to address some of these problems. This four-year long study focused on using an educational setting to develop a team of researchers (in this case, students) to use PAR for education research. In identifying with the underlying principles of PAR, the student research team recognized the value of collaboration, individual capacity (or agency), and nonlinearity of change for reclaiming of the lost sense of collective that they believe were the sources of various negative values plaguing their institutions and social interactions. The process, as described by the author, allowed student researchers, over time, to break away from the learned passivism that their educational upbringing had instilled in and to demystify the expert by building new knowledge. The author discusses the importance of local knowledge creation, especially in postdisaster context of Nepal and the country's continued reliance on foreign experts and aid. Through this exercise of PAR in understanding and presenting to the Ministry of Education educational challenges in Nepal, the team of student action researchers not only identified various discriminations based on student caste and class of students, they also challenged the pervasive neoliberal values by challenging their own assumptions about development and knowledge creation.

Mary Vayaliparampil, in Chap. 8, provides an example of PAR that can be used to examine the programmatic effectiveness of India's Education for All policy. In particular, the chapter illustrates the use of Photovoice as a PAR tool administered through 135 parents who were tasked with the mission of capturing photographs pertaining to the effectiveness of the SSA program (Sarva Shiksha Abhiyan) in their local school system. The author, based on her experience with Photovoice as a PAR application, explains that the tool not only enables a more inclusive and participatory process of policy development and implementation, it lends greater credibility and effectiveness to policy interventions. The photographs taken speak volumes and lend a voice to parents and other community members, potentially connecting them directly with policy makers. In this regard, Photovoice is particularly empowering for marginalized communities.

This view is echoed by Payal Shah in Case Study 1 on the use of Photovoice as a part of her study of a public residential school for girls in Gujarat, India. She highlights ways in which Photovoice empowers communities—school girls in this case—by equalizing power differences, building trust, and creating "a sense of ownership to bring about social justice and change." This case study discusses the process of carrying out Photovoice activities followed by a recall interview and concludes with brief discussion on the research and action implications of the tool.

The next three case studies also discuss PAR applications to education. They are included specifically to shed more light on the methods and their effectiveness for specific education contexts and research purposes. In Case Study 2, Tahiya Mahbub builds on her discussion on PAR and reflexivity in Chap. 2 by elaborating on the use of memoing to conduct reflexivity. She walks us through various memoing episodes during across milestones in her research process. This rich account of a PAR researcher's struggle with the biases inherited in her background, emotions, and ideological preferences is particularly relevant in demonstrating that "reflexivity and PAR go hand in hand" and that self-reflective inquiry allows researchers, as well as participants, to question the honesty and authenticity of their research process.

Case Study 3, by Meagan Call-Cummings, is an illustration of a PAR application to data analysis. This case is located outside South Asia, in rural Idaho, United States, but is included here for its focus on racism and the potential applicability of its PAR method to similar issues (other forms of discrimination based on caste, religion, tribe, and class) in other regional contexts. The author and her team drew from the Theatre of the Oppressed in carrying out data collection and data analysis with high school students on their experiences with and perceptions of racist practices. She points out the nature of the data collection process through PAR, a process that is often blurred with moments of data analysis. This account provides vivid descriptions of the process across different stages and concludes with a critical review of the logistical limitations in carrying out PAR research.

Case study 4, by Anusha Chandrasekharan and Pradeep Narayanan, provides an account of recent advocacy campaign led by Praxis Institute for Participatory Practices in New Delhi and a supporting consortium of civil society organizations to bring together a group of children from diverse backgrounds to discuss and provide comments on the draft New Education Policy 2016. The case study illustrates the various PAR activities that the panel of 16 students engaged with over the course of four days to share their experiences of education, identify key issues with the system and the draft National Education Policy note, and draft recommendations for the government. They used participatory tools, such as card sorting, root cause analysis, participatory theater, and illustrations, to explore the questions.

In the last chapter, Erik Jon Byker, concludes with a brief review of key themes and concepts pertaining to PAR and education that emerged during the course of the creation of this volume. The author identified and elaborated on three themes: (1) representation and exploration of identity through voice, (2) empowering of the collective, and (3) transforming the community. Byker highlights the need for further research and concludes with a brief set of recommendations for practitioners and researchers of education and PAR.

References

Barone, T., Berliner, D. C., Blanchard, J., Casanova, U., & McGown, T. (1996). A future for teacher education: Developing a strong sense of professionalism. In J. Sikula (Ed.), *Handbook of research on teacher education* (4th ed., pp. 1108–1149). New York: Macmillan.

Chambers, R. (2007). *From PRA to PLA and pluralism: Practice and theory.* Sussex: Institute of Development Studies.

Escobar, A. (2006). Post-development. In D. A. Clark (Ed.), *Elgar companion to development studies*. Elgar: Northampton, MA.

Frabutt, J. M., Holter, A. C., & Nuzzi, R. J. (2008). *Research, action, and change: Leaders reshaping Catholic schools.* Notre Dame, IN: Alliance for Catholic Education Press.

Freire, P. (1970). *Pedagogy of the oppressed.* New York: Seabury Press.

Greenwood, D. J., & Levin, M. (1998). *Introduction to action research, social research for social change.* Thousand Oaks, CA: SAGE.

Greenwood, D. J., Whyte, W. F., & Harkavy, I. (1993). Participatory action research as a process and as a goal. *Human Relations, 46*(2), 175.

Hensen, K. T. (1996). Teachers as researchers. In J. Sikula (Ed.), *Handbook of research on teacher education* (4th ed., pp. 53–66). New York: Macmillan..

Hickey, S., & Mohan, G. (2004). *Participation—From tyranny to transformation?: Exploring new approaches to participation in development.* Zed Books.

Hine, G. S. C. (2013). The importance of action research in teacher education programs. *Issues in Educational Research, 23*(2), 151–163. Retrieved from http://www.iier.org.au/iier23/hine.pdf

Institute of Development Studies. (2016). *Participation.* Retrieved from http://www.ids.ac.uk/team/participation

Johnson, A. P. (2012). *A short guide to action research* (4th ed.). Upper Saddle River, NJ: Pearson Education.

Kemmis, S. (2001). Exploring the relevance of critical theory for action research: Emancipatory action research in the footsteps of Jürgen Habermas. In P. Reason & H. Bradbury (Eds.), *Handbook of action research: Participative inquiry and practice* (pp. 91–102). London: SAGE.

Mills, G. E. (2011). *Action research: A guide for the teacher researcher* (4th ed.). Boston: Pearson.

Osterman, K. F., & Kottkamp, R. B. (1993). *Reflective practice for educators: Improving schooling through professional development.* Newbury Park, CA: Corwin.

Peet, R., & Hartwick. (2009). *Theories of development.* New York: Guilford Press.

Reason, P., & McArdle, K. (2004). Brief notes on the theory and practice of action research. In S. Becker & A. Bryman (Eds.). *Understanding research methods for social policy and practice* (pp. 1–6). Retrieved from http://www.peterreason.eu/Papers/Brief_Notes_on_AR.pdf

Reason, P., & Bradbury, H. (2008). *Handbook of action research: Participative inquiry and practice* (2nd ed.). London: SAGE.

Reitbergen-McCracken, J., & Narayan, D. (1998). *Participation and social assessment: Tools and techniques.* The World Bank: Washington, DC.

Stanley, L., & Wise, S. (1983). *Breaking out: Feminist consciousness and feminist research.* London: Routledge and Kegan Paul.

Tomlinson, C. A. (1995). Action research and practical inquiry: An overview and an invitation to teachers of gifted learners. *Journal for the Education of the Gifted, 18*(4), 467–484. doi:10.1177/016235329501800407.

White, G. W., Suchowierska, M. A., & Campbell, M. (2004). Developing and systematically implementing participatory action research. *Archives of Physical Medicine Rehabilitation, 85*(Suppl. 2), S3–S12.

CHAPTER 1

Defining PAR to Refine PAR: Theorizing Participatory Action Research in South Asian Educational Contexts

Rohit Setty and Matthew A. Witenstein

Participatory Action Research?

There are an astonishing number of ways to realize interpretations and knowledge. Researchers toil in diverse and multilayered contexts that often combine other forms of knowledge with an objective to shed light on multifaceted understandings. This infinite number of combinations offers researchers an array of means and methods from which to choose. If a researcher is interested in mapping an educational program or its effectiveness, quantitative methodologies can help. If the researcher is more interested in the social phenomena available to a community or how communities are influenced by them, then the researcher can leverage qualitative or mixed methodological resources. Sharing and borrowing ideas and tools is very common.

R. Setty (✉)
Setty & Associates International, Fairfax, VA, USA
e-mail: rohit.setty@setty.com

M.A. Witenstein
University of Redlands, Redlands, CA, USA
e-mail: matthew_witenstein@redlands.edu

Research, though, is rarely an individual endeavor. Even if an educational researcher works alone, as in teaching (Cohen 2011), there are trends to be aware of, ideas and notions that transit from multiple locations and times and usually those that are often deemed "research participants." Norms and standards coalesce through collaboration. Research is social, and as a result, consequences of influence cannot be overlooked. Participatory action research (PAR) is one such endeavor.

> PAR is rooted in principles of inclusion (engaging people in the research design, process and outcomes); participation; valuing all local voices; and community-driven sustainable outcomes. PAR is a process and a practice directed towards social change with the participants; it is interventionist, action-oriented and interpretive. PAR involves a commitment to research that develops partnership responses to developing purposeful knowledge (praxis); includes all those involved where possible, thus facilitating shared ownership of the development and outcomes of the research; uses innovative ways of consulting and working with local people and facilitates change with communities and groups. (O'Neill 2007, p. 214)

PAR has a rich and diverse history rooted in social contexts. What drives people to conduct PAR, as discussed later in this chapter, shapes what PAR is and what PAR will become. Action and participation are not enough for the capacity building required in industrializing South Asia. To omit the rigor of research as a constituent part risks isolating idiosyncratic activities and keeping PAR on the fringes of valuable academic research. PAR researchers who attempt to generate inquiry and data in South Asian educational contexts, in particular, may benefit from following the path laid out by the PAR advocates of the 1970s. They recognized that their new raw methodology needed to respect all people's knowledge while simultaneously pursuing the validity of critical methodology and scientific investigation (Fals-Borda 2001.) A combination of mutual commitments, however, seems to pervade the more regarded characterizations of PAR. These definitions have proven to be touchstones, resources, and mobilizing forces for the PAR researchers showcased in this volume. The progress of PAR can be seen through the important practical work, theoretical development, and critical commentaries laid out in the various portrayals of PAR. And while more and more meaningful work emerges, the divisions are increasingly less evident.

As we worked on this project, we read many articles and chapters concerned with framing PAR. Over time, we learned that in spite of the mountain of academic arguments, few dealt with doing the work of PAR. Very few asked the fundamental questions: What is the work involved in enacting PAR? What kinds of opportunities might researchers face and what kinds of problems will they need to solve? What would it take to solve the problems and leverage the opportunities in a way that promotes social justice and transforms the context and the players? These three questions frame the task that we assigned ourselves. What follows are our responses. Our hope is that readers will not only come to know about what informs PAR but begin asking their own questions about what it takes to pull off PAR in the contexts and countries they seek to support. We also ask these questions because in spite of the great appeal of PAR in qualitative research, these ideas have not been sufficiently unpacked. Before discussing these driving questions more directly, this chapter discusses the terms used in the discourse of PAR and examines some historical markers that may underlie the enthusiasm for the research methodology.

Conceptual Contexts of PAR

PAR research work originated in traditionally exploited or oppressed communities and populations. Those communities may face challenges and seek to alter their own circumstances. The methodology works to address the specific concerns of the community and the primary causes of oppression. This is mostly because researchers with intellectual curiosity and drive to effect change in contexts in which they have witnessed or have felt injustice. For many, PAR is simultaneously a process of research, education, and action in which all participants contribute, learn, and are transformed (Hall 1981; Fals-Borda and Rahman 1991). If these aims seem ambitious, so is the labor involved. In spite of the difficulty involved, researchers utilize PAR to improve the human condition.

Orlando Fals-Borda, a seminal figure in the advent of PAR, defined the methodology in the 1970s as "research that involved investigating reality in order to transform it" (Fals-Borda 1977). When he used the term "participatory action research," he was describing his efforts to work with and support farmers in Colombia. Rather than posing a singular intellectual question, his efforts constituted a long-term engagement focusing on areas of adult education, agricultural development, and economic reform emanating from the needs of a victimized community. At approximately the same time, Rajesh Tandon was distilling a congruent approach to conduct community-based research in northern India (Hall 1997, p. xiii). Both actors were promoting participation in their inquiry and seemingly were driven by a Freirian critical consciousness, believing that all people have a right to participate in the production of knowledge that ostensibly shapes their world (Freire 1997, p. xi).

Efforts to improve PAR have grown considerably since its beginnings, as have the knowledge base, its important capacities, and its sophistication. Doubts about its utility have risen as well. As with any effort to improve the human condition, advocates of PAR grapple with the paradoxes of expertise and engagement differently from those who campaign for other research methodologies. Researchers in the PAR framework relegate their expertise as secondary to the deep knowledge of the participants. It is the groups' questions, issues, and concerns that drive the agenda, and it is through their actions and reflections that the aspirations of the human condition are fought. The efforts of PAR practitioners to balance engagement, expertise, and participation led them to encounter a set of intellectual challenges and methodological tensions. In what follows, we discuss some of those core tensions within PAR.

Distance and Intervention

The first of such tensions is the pull between intervening and maintaining distance. Distance and detachment are requisites of academic research (e.g.: Silverman 2016; Patton 2005), but most advocates recognize that all research strikes a balance between detachment and involvement. In a PAR endeavor, the social arrangements are different. Practitioners often need to supplement their own understandings with participant expertise. Engendering a psychological and somatic closeness is beneficial. Fals-Borda (1999) articulated what Agnes Heller termed "symmetric reciprocity" as a key PAR requirement. In order to arrive at what \Heller calls a "subject–subject horizontal or symmetric relationship" (Fals-Borda 1999: 13), researchers likely need to manage participants' level of commitment. This may involve reporting or communicating results/findings in ways that are understandable to participants. The participants' knowledge and commitment are critical path items and often can wholly replace practitioners' preexisting notions. Additionally, recognizing this symmetry involves developing what Gramsci called "good sense" and is a route to achieving authentic participation. The inevitability of researchers' influences on the research setting, and vice versa, is not one that can, or should, be avoided from a PAR worldview. However, it is a tension that needs to be recognized and articulated in the conceptualization and articulation of PAR work. Since PAR openly seeks to understand the world from participants' perspectives via closely working with them, the vigilant distance often espoused as a standard for research would fail in PAR contexts.

Activism and Research

The stance on distance and intervention leads us to the second tension that PAR researchers encounter: Is this activism or research? Brydon-Miller and her colleagues (2011) pointed out that PAR requires the *participation* of not only those who are formulating the inquiry but those who are intended to go on informing it; *action,* which anchors the research methodology, as it is the manifestation of the social justice necessary to PAR; and of course *research,* indicating the social process of inquiring, constructing data/insight, and making warranted assertions with data to aid in the struggle for social and economic justice (Hall 1981). As Brydon-Miller and colleagues noted: "PAR is distinct [from other forms of action research] in its focus on collaboration, political engagement, and an explicit commitment to social justice" (p. 388). PAR has an agenda typically focused on societal or local change and an interest in altering unjust situations.

PAR practitioners may be pulled in divergent directions when balancing their activism with research, and it can be difficult to merge the directions. It is exhilarating, though, when they do. Typically, an academic researcher's goal is to articulate and publish documentation and analysis of conducted research. This may serve a professional purpose, a need to contribute to the discourse, or a desire to share local experiences with an audience. Conversely, PAR is concerned greatly with effecting change for a historically victimized or vulnerable community. One way to view how to balance the tension between activism and research is through setting and revisiting goals. It is risky for practitioners to perceive that they will achieve dramatic change, and conducting PAR is unnecessary if the sole goal is publication. Both ambitions diminish the possibilities of PAR.

PAR is about mobilizing social change over time. To be more than activism, though, such change needs to come at a discourse level and at a practical—on-the-ground—level. Fals-Borda (1999, p. 7) posited that "popular knowledge has always been a source of formal learning.

Academic accumulation, plus people's wisdom, became an important rule for our movement" (in O'Neill 2007, p. 216). The combination of popular knowledge and academic knowledge is the crux of PAR. It is the practitioner's responsibility to find ways where outcomes and deliverables can be used at not only the community level but also to expand the curiosity and knowledge of those not present. Tiered feedback and publication, then, become crucial to the success of a PAR endeavor. Outcomes, interpretations, and findings, for example, can be print-based or performance-based, or even art exhibition–based. They can be taken to a broader audience and distributed within the local community. Although there is little consensus on acceptable results, all of the above and many more can stand uniformly as products of social change. We claim, though, that practitioners can avoid the risks of total failure if their aims are calibrated for multiple levels and media.

Alterity and Recognition

Academic research often situates practitioners in the role of authority and the putative participants in a position of alterity. Alterity can be understood as the contrast between the lived identity and the constructed identity. This can be a hallmark of the necessary distance that can provide the space to offer insight. However, in providing that insight, there is a positioning of practitioners as narrators and participants as the narrated. The inherent risk in such positioning is that practitioners become the participants' voices and, as such, the filter. Spivak (1989) argued this in her treatise, challenging the masculine orthodox and colonizing nature of historical writing. She emphasized that socially constructed histories run a risk of keeping histories and historical behaviors covered and that authentic experiences intuitively illuminated the histories being written about. PAR practitioners can manage this tension by keeping in context, through linguistic choices, intersectional identities such as race, gender, ethnicity, and class. Language is an important resource in considering how to narrate the PAR outcomes and interpretations for larger audiences. For example, a PAR researcher needs to be highly attuned to the linguistic choices that are made as the research unfolds and also in the representations of it.

The changes that practitioners seek through their research can be grounded in changes not only with respect to the community but also within the practitioners themselves. Fals-Borda (2001) enhanced his initial characterizations of PAR from the 1970s in recent years by arguing that

PAR provides "a transformation of individual attitudes and values, personality and culture, an altruistic process" (p. 32). Altruism is a defining quality for PAR and is useful to recognize in the research process. Critics of PAR projects may argue that researchers regularly omit their own lived experiences and evolution, narrowly focusing on participants. Keeping this narrative in the frame can help to make the experience for readers and audiences coalesce.

Several organizing tenets and principles attempt to define PAR, such as the very concise definition of critical feminist theorist Maggie O'Neill, who claimed that "PAR is a social research methodology, which includes the stereotypical subjects of research as co-creators of the research. It creates a space for the voices of the marginalized to become involved actively in change or transformation" (O'Neill in Kellner 2007, p. 213), and the characterization of Brydon-Miller et al. (2011) of PAR being like jazz—a collaborative process requiring diverse experiences and capitalizing on those experiences in its performance. A spectrum of definitions and characterizations frame PAR's discourse, and it is impossible to analyze them all in this chapter. Yet it is important to recognize the indirect discourse that is present in PAR and to highlight what can often be omitted.

The three tensions noted earlier are manageable for PAR practitioners, but in our reading of PAR research, we often find that they go without recognition. Our claim is that PAR is distinctive from other research methodologies but not necessarily unique. PAR shares common frameworks on participation and engagement with other phenomenological traditions. It shares a common agenda with Marxism and social psychology. It provides deep meaning and interpretations, but doing so requires balancing different conceptual tensions. Cultivating an ability to manage these tensions, not necessarily resolve them, is a challenge for PAR practitioners. Attending to them and worrying about them in such a way that allows them to run through the research is a useful way to build momentum on the leading features of PAR.

HISTORICAL CONTEXTS OF PAR AND ACTION RESEARCH

Although we can delineate the leading features and possible gaps in PAR, it seems reasonable that readers might appreciate some discussion on the historical groundings of PAR to better understand how they connect to its past, current, and future usage in South Asian educational contexts. It may be helpful here to share a proposition about PAR based on the concepts of Kurt Lewin, one of action research's forerunners. Argyris and Schön (1991) posited that PAR is "based on the Lewinian proposition that causal inferences about the behavior of human beings are more likely to be valid and enactable when the human beings in question participate in building and testing them" (p. 86). Therefore, those participating in the study are coresearchers/coparticipants, creating a more synergistic approach to the research in which all participants (instead of a single researcher or research team) carry the responsibility for theorizing and making meaning of information obtained to guide action (Baskerville 1999).

Dewey's Historical Connections to Action Research Methods

Although the history of action research methods in general dates back to the 1930s, it would be remiss to not include some of Dewey's philosophies on educational research, which clearly have a footprint on these methods (Hinchey 2008). Dewey argued that traditional inquiry methods and theory development were valuable in education; he also called for theory development and methods grounded in practice (Noffke 1997). Additionally, Dewey called for the active participation of teachers in the research process. Hinchey (2008) shared that Dewey was a progenitor of educational research occurring in practical settings. In fact, Dewey proposed that: (a) research findings should be tested out by teachers, particularly since classrooms and teachers' positionalities differ and are contextually bound; and (b) findings were incomplete without teachers testing and adapting them to their respective milieus. In other words, Dewey aspired for teachers to have the agency not only to be familiar with research but to consider and apply new concepts and findings relevant to their classroom in a reflective manner (Noffke 1997). Interestingly, Dewey's (1916) conception of scientific method, applied in classroom contexts, was close to action research methods, as it called for an improvement-oriented action plan to be utilized in a real-world environment.

The Beginnings of Action Research: Collier and Lewin

The literature largely points to the work of John Collier in the 1930s and Kurt Lewin in the 1940s as the beginnings of action research methodologies (McNiff and Whitehead 2011). Ottosson (2003) claimed that the term "action research" was first coined by Collier in 1945. Collier and Lewin's work addressed important social inequities including in work, in daily life, and in promoting a more democratic approach to education as well as prejudices encountered by marginalized populations (Noffke 1997). As PAR does, they viewed action research as collaborative, dynamic, and concentrated on social issues.

Collier's work as Commissioner of Indian Affairs was highly influential on action research and particularly toward PAR. His work there highlighted the unjust actions taken against Native Americans by the dominant culture and the US government. Collier criticized government policies that viewed all tribes as the same when in fact there was incredible diversity (as one find in classroom settings) (Hinchey 2008). He used the terms "action" and "research" to describe a cyclical and reflexive research process (Corbett et al. 2007). Collier (1945) used the term "action-research, research-action" to explain how both administrators (researchers) and laypeople could work together (p. 294). He aimed to improve the lives of Native American tribes through this integrative research approach (the key word being "integrative"), which one also finds in the collaborative nature of PAR (Collier 1945). The goal was to devise solutions to common problems collaboratively (Corbett et al. 2007).

Collier's work also extended into the educational realm. According to Noffke (1997), Collier and his wife established a progressive school, and his action research work with the Bureau of Indian Affairs focused on developing educational initiatives, such as developing self-sufficient education rooted in local culture and language. Collier proclaimed that freedom through knowledge was possible via addressing local issues through educational programming. Similar to how PAR involves researchers, Collier was not averse to outside researchers supporting knowledge building in educational programming, yet he maintained that administrator and lay involvement was critical to the success of improving respective communities (Hinchey 2008).

Lewin, like Collier, also cared about the integrative process of both experts and participants as well as how the process impacted group change (Noffke 1997). Furthermore, although Lewin deemed basic research to be important, he found research in everyday, natural contexts critical (Hinchey 2008). Similar to Collier's (1945) axiom, Lewin stated that there is "no action without research; no research without action" (Lewin as quoted in Marrow 1969, p. 193).

Lewin's first foray into action research commenced when he arrived in the United States after fleeing Nazi Germany in 1933 (Adelman 1993; Hinchey 2008). His experience facing oppression as a Jew may have impacted his interest in social justice. In one of his earliest articles on action research, Lewin (1946) explained that social research has two different question types—the first examines group life's general laws and the second diagnoses a precise situation. Type 1 questions related to "possible conditions and possible results ... expressed in 'if so' propositions" and type 2 questions related to those who engage the "specific character of the situation ... determined by a scientific fact-finding" (pp. 36–37). He posited that for action to take place, both types of research are needed. Lewin further explicated the steps or cycles of research (commonly seen in action research) that related to the contexts of ordinary people collectively participating in research related to a common problem. In conjunction with his interest in social justice, he used these propositions to foster greater self-esteem of marginalized groups so they might achieve greater independence and obtain a more level playing field with the dominant culture through action research (Adelman 1993).

Lewin's most renowned work may have taken place in industrial settings, yet he also made his way into the educational realm, particularly with teachers and teacher educators. He accomplished much of this work through the Horace Mann-Lincoln Institute of Teachers College, Columbia University (Kemmis 1980). The institute was involved in collaborative programs with schools, districts, and teachers; therefore, action research was a natural fit to study issues in schools, stimulating various projects on curricula, teacher supervision, and the practice of teaching (Kemmis 1980).

Corey: Action Research in Education

Lewin heavily influenced the work of the Horace Mann-Lincoln Institute, and by the late 1940s, Stephen Corey (dean and professor at Teachers College and executive director of the institute) became the best-known proponent of action research in education (Hinchey 2008; Kemmis 1980). Corey worked diligently to legitimize action research as a viable form of educational research and to describe the process itself (Noffke 1997). Herrick's (1953) review of Corey's seminal text, "Action Research to Improve School Practice," still cited in recent literature, found this text to be "timely" for all educational stakeholders who were concerned about improvement in educational contexts and had heard about this new methodology. Herrick (1953) emphasized Corey's concept of involving multiple stakeholders in the research process for a particular problem as the best means to strengthen the issue. This view was highly congruent with

PAR, which is not a surprise, considering that the institute Corey directed included multiple stakeholders (e.g., teachers, administrators, students, community members, etc.) as research participants. Corey (1954) further strengthened this participatory nature of action research by adding:

> The cooperative efforts of all of these people will tend to result in better problem definition, a more realistic consideration of the numerous possible action hypotheses, easier translating of these hypotheses into action, and a more adequate understanding of the meaning of the evidence that is procured to test them. (p. 378)

Corey's diligent work promoting and engaging in action research impacts current practices of action researchers, particularly those components related to collaborative efforts and teacher engagement in this research to improve their practice (Hinchey 2008). Despite Corey's valiant efforts, the popularity of action research faded for seven reasons:

1. Criticism of action research as unscientific
2. Criticism that the process was not meaningful
3. Evolving interests heading into the Cold War and McCarthyism
4. Shifts in school populations
5. Shortage of teachers
6. Decreased interest by the US federal government in funding action research
7. The ever-increasing notion that matters of educational policy and curriculum should be in the hands of teachers. (Hinchey 2008; Noffke 1997).

1970s Revival of Action Research and Emergence of PAR

During the 1970s, action research was revived on a global scale. Stenhouse's work was particularly influential in this movement as he reacquainted teachers and researchers with the concept of teachers pursuing practitioner-scholarly pursuits to improve classrooms and schools through disciplined self-study (Hinchey 2008). This was accomplished through Stenhouse's heavily cited 1975 book, *An Introduction to Curriculum Research and Development*. His work spread throughout not only England but globally and left a notable mark by developing engaging, supportive action research networks and communities worldwide.

While Stenhouse was facilitating notable progress in action research in education, parallel movements occurred across the globe that helped build PAR (Minkler 2000). Many of these scholars returned to the roots of Collier and Lewin regarding the utility of action research as a mechanism for improving the lives of the marginalized (Hinchey 2008). In 1970, several of these scholars became dissatisfied with their status in academic institutions because they desired a new orientation toward social theory and its practice (Fals-Borda 2001). Some left the academy during this time and created their own institutions and procedural methods, honing in on "local and regional problems involving emancipator educational, cultural and political processes" (pp. 27–28). Among the projects that Fals-Borda (2001) shared that profoundly impacted the PAR movement included work in Mexico, Tanzania, Colombia, Brazil, and India. Minkler (2000) noted the important influences of Freire (i.e., the notions of colearning and critical reflection–based action) and Fals-Borda's work (i.e., his Latin American–based work employing and refining PAR methods) during this time, which helped develop the theoretical and practical components of PAR. Hall credited Swantz with coining the term "participatory research" through her early 1970s work in Tanzania, which drew on the insight and expertise of the local community to develop locally managed projects; Fals-Borda used the term "participatory action research" in Colombia to describe similar work that emphasized the social change component of community projects; and Tandon was working on similar approaches in India conducting community-based research (Brydon-Miller 1997). Efforts coalesced during the decade through respectful exchanges across disciplines and cultures in what was termed "vivencia" (or life experience) (Fals-Borda 2001). These exchanges and amalgamations of PAR principles and theoretical underpinnings resulted in the first World Symposium of Action Research in 1977. From this meeting forward, the notion of vivencia permeated the soul of PAR and its offshoots and emerged as a worldwide movement combining research methodology and life philosophy (Fals-Borda 2001).

Some Temporal Markers on the Articulation of PAR in SA and the World

Kaluram and the Bhoomi Sena

Predating the PAR movement of the 1970s, Bhoomi Sena was formed in the Indian state of Maharashtra through numerous community meetings in 1945 as a mechanism for *adivasis* (indigenous, tribal society members) to protect their rights (Szal 1979). The adivasis had lost their land to an outsider group (*sawkars*), which turned them into tenants (Islam and Nag 2010). This tenancy parlayed into a number of protective outcomes between 1945 and 1947 including ensuring that community members received pay for their work and organized efforts to suppress phony rents and suspicious back payments (Szal 1979). Although there was some initial resistance and violence in reaction to the movement, officials warmed up to it as they monitored evidence of positive accomplishments (Szal 1979). Laws in 1957 overturned tenancy; therefore, the adivasis became owners of the land upon which they toiled; however, high debt levels drove them to significant land loss once again, and control of much was returned to the sawkars (Islam and Nag 2010). Interestingly, Szal (1979) mentioned that interest in Bhoomi Sena had been revived due to the movement's focus on local problem solving.

The revitalization of Bhoomi Sena in 1970 was one of the projects Fals-Borda (2001) Mentioned as heavily impacting PAR, Kaluram, a social scientist who had not finished school, led this effort (Fals-Borda 2001). He was instrumental in leading the land-grab movement in 1970 to return control of the land to the adivasis. After leaving jail, he investigated the illegal sawkar land ownership and educated adivasis through a grassroots effort via small community meetings in numerous villages (Islam and Nag 2010; Nilsen 2012). This led to hundreds of crop seizures, which sawkars contested but was upheld by the law. Although there were stumbling blocks following the land takeover, central leadership encouraged villages to engage in proactive measures germane to their own local issues while relying on the central leadership for support. These collective actions at the village level created Tarun Mandals (local advocacy organizations composed of adivasis) to support the local struggles, which spread to over 120 villages (Islam and Nag 2010). This example of PAR in a South Asian context exemplifies important concepts from Freire (1970) such as colearning, critical reflection–based action and liberation from oppressors.

Building on the success of Bhoom Sena's efforts, PAR has been utilized throughout South Asia in a variety of contemporary contexts including these five representative PAR examples:

1. Rammelt (2013) worked with communities in rural Bangladesh since 2005 to develop safe drinking water programs.
2. Braun and Saroar (2012) engaged with four villages susceptible to oversalinity of local water and soil due to flooding.

3. Gibbon (2002) outlined her PAR study with two volunteer organizations in Nepal with the goal of promoting awareness of women's health issues.
4. Aziz et al. (2011) used PAR in Sindh, Pakistan, to promote women's empowerment (utilizing the notion that empowerment is derived from one's own agency) with the end goal of mobilizing action and social transformation.
5. Ariyadasa and McIntyre-Mills (2015) employed PAR as a mechanism for ensuring that vulnerable, institutionalized children in children's homes are properly supported while also addressing social justice issues impacting them.

Teacher education experiences in regard to work of teaching and developing skills in judgment, discernment, and the practice of teaching are reported only rarely. (See Setty 2016 for more details.) We argue here that such professional skills are characteristic of PAR and that engaging educational practitioners in South Asia in the work of PAR can be a mechanism for bolstering teachers' education and practice.

This chapter articulates the discourse on the practice of PAR, exploring PAR not as an ideology but as a methodology. However, the ideological drive for rigorous methodological research cannot be easily disaggregated. Therefore, although this chapter does discuss how PAR is framed, it is more concerned with how to *deploy* PAR in South Asian contexts rather than why one may choose to do so. Before delving specifically into these points, we first provide more context on PAR as a methodology of educational research.

Doing the Work of PAR

When considering PAR, it may be better to ask whether PAR is the best methodological choice than "what it takes to do the work of PAR." How can the different levels of literacy ever present with possible coresearchers be overcome? How would you foster an organic relationship with your grassroots collaborators and overcome the implicit hierarchical relationship that collaborators would come to expect and know? How will you build symmetry in the relationship, or, as McTaggart (1991) proposed, how will you authentic participation ensue? How will you leverage the oral tradition? Will you privilege your researchers' notes or the collective memory? What forms of records will you deploy and which will you value?

Will you translate local-language data into your own first language or leave data as constructed? How will you employ quantitative measures? Will you make use of ethnographic descriptions and critiques? In what ways and to what extent does your project—or my phenomenon of interest—warrant an inquiry through PAR? Does it require deep and respectful interaction? Will the knowledge gained be enhanced by an empathetic position or hindered? What will you do with the knowledge generated? What is the phenomenon you are trying to understand, and whose interests are you trying to serve? Who will benefit the most from it? Who will construct the questions? Who will write up the interpretations? Who will decide on how to disseminate the research? How long can you commit?

Method Selection and the Drivers of Selecting PAR

If your research inquiry is motivated by a focus on the concrete, such as a particular practice, a mode of operation, or a government program, then PAR may help create meaning. To study teacher practices or student uptake, for example, requires two conditions: proximity to practice and cases to examine. Leaning toward proximity tends best to evolve through a qualitative research tradition and raises questions about whether what is desired to be known would be accessible from an outside research position. Research methods influence what can be seen and what can be imagined for the improvement of teaching and teacher education. Therefore, to imagine and see practice effectively, some researchers gravitate toward first-person research methods (Ball 2000); PAR arguably could be categorized as such a method.

First-Person Research

First-person research is one way to characterize the work of educational researchers such as Lee (for a specific example, see: Lee 2007), Lampert (for a specific example, see: Lampert 2001), and Ball (2000), who classified her early work as first-person research. Ball (2000) argued that a first-person research perspective helps to "probe beneath" the boundaries of practice, through researchers' careful tracking of adjustments, decisions, role shifts, and struggles; and it can also "transcend above" the boundaries of idiosyncratic practice by aiming to produce knowledge for the profession. In her classification, Ball made a distinction between first-person research and other inquiry types that collapse teacher and researcher roles (e.g., action research, narrative inquiry, teacher research, etc.). She pointed out that first-person research shares with these models a focus on practice; what distinguishes first-person research is the deliberate use of the educator's position to ground questions, structure the analysis, and represent the interpretation (p. 365). And these methodologies are not intended to consider the production of insights that can be shared broadly and theories that can be expanded to inform the profession. Moreover, she argued that first-person research allows the researcher to understand local meanings, languages, norms, and practices in a grounded manner.

First-person research, though, does not come without hazards. In her explication of the research approach, Ball (2000) flagged three special questions of which to be mindful when conducting this type of work.

1. "Does the researcher think he or she is particularly well-equipped to be designer, developer, and enactor of the practice, or would an experienced practitioner be a more reliable partner in the construction?" (p. 391).
2. "How can the researcher gain alternative perspectives and interpretations of his own and others actions and thoughts in the session, while also seeking to use the intimate and personal as resources?" (p. 393).
3. "Is the question at hand one in which other scholars have an interest, or should have an interest, and if so, will probing the inside of a particular design offer perspectives crucial to a larger discourse?" (p. 391).

    With so much bound up in the psychologizing the researcher's position in PAR studies, his or her stance could be a cause for concern, as it is with many first-person research studies. To mediate this terrain, Ball's second question urges first-person researchers to thoughtfully create distance between their practitioner-selves and their researcher-selves (as one of the authors of this chapter did: Setty 2013). In his research report, Setty highlighted how Ball pointed to Ruth Heaton's work (1994), where Heaton used the methodological device of "multiple Ruths." Heaton invented a Ruth 1, a Ruth 2, and a Ruth 3 to help her separate her vantage point at different time points. Ruth 1 was Ruth as the teacher; Ruth 2: Ruth as the teacher reflecting on Ruth 1's efforts; and Ruth 3: the third "self," three years removed from the teaching and reflecting, looking back with conceptual distance.

In his own work, Setty created this necessary conceptual distance in a slightly different way. As the teacher educator, he kept his own journal of the instructional experience that focused on the challenges and struggles of teaching teachers in India. This reflexive work inevitably focused on his failings and missed opportunities as the instructor. As a research informant, he kept a separate journal to collect data on his core phenomenon of inquiry—explicit modeling practice. This journal had a specific protocol of questions that he responded to immediately after each session. And as an analyst, he kept a third journal. The intent of maintaining these three sites to collect his thoughts was to have a deliberate way to keep distinct his thoughts as a teacher educator, research informant, and research analyst. These ways of framing his roles helped condition him to see the work that he had done as if it were the work of another. Developing this tripartite way to create intellectual space for himself and from himself was necessary for him to understand the phenomenon on multiple levels. Also, during analysis, he adopted the convention of referring to his work as a teacher educator in the third person.

Such efforts may seems excessive for PAR, but to be able to warrant claims and push past natural observation, maintaining structured means of documentation and analysis can help to yield defensible claims. Ball's third caution was one of warrants and claims: What can be warranted from the study of a single teacher educator's practice? First-person research, it should be noted, is a genre of qualitative case studies. Case studies have achieved routine status as a viable method of educational research (Yin 2009). The viability of case-based methods is based on two conditions. First, are the research questions trying to address descriptive or explanatory issues, or are they concerned with causality? Second, is the researcher interested in illuminating a particular situation through a close understanding of it? Your study may not pursue causality or effectiveness; rather it may be concerned with how a particular practice unfolds and operates. Furthermore, you may want your study to unfold in authentic learning situations with the aim of producing firsthand understandings of the work involved in a practice and illuminating facets of a local environment. By that token, a main objective of your research may be to contribute to local practices.

Although a focus on a particular practice may seem narrow, such an inquiry more than anything is concrete. It is through this lens of the concrete that first-person research can help create meaning. Erickson (1986) described the kind of research on the concrete that can surface relevancy for a larger audience:

> Mainstream positivist research on teaching searches for general characteristics of the analytically generalized effective teacher. From an interpretive point of view, however, effective teaching is seen not as a set of generalized

attributes of a teacher or of students. Rather, effective teaching is seen as occurring in the particular and concrete circumstances of the practice of a specific teacher with a specific set of students "this year," "this day," and "this moment." The search is not for *abstract universals* arrived at by statistical generalizations from a sample to a population, but for *concrete universals*, arrived at by studying a specific case in great detail and then comparing it with other cases studied in equally great detail. ... The task of the analyst is to uncover the different layers of universality and particularity confronted in the specific case at hand—what is broadly universal, what generalizes to other similar situations, what is unique to the given instance. This can only be done, interpretive researchers maintain, by attending to the details of the concrete case at hand. Thus the primary concern of the interpretive research is particularizability, rather than generalizability. (p. 30)

Studying a teacher's efforts anchored in authentic practice, for example, creates a valuable opportunity for researchers to arrive at and readers to derive "universals" that can be applied and appropriated to their own educational efforts. What is needed, though, is a convincing argument arrived at by confronting concrete circumstances of practice and an interpretive perspective that values the particular. If these two conditions exist, then there is viable power in what Erickson refers to as "concrete universals." Such a PAR study makes no attempt to claim probabilistic generalization; however, the PAR study raises theoretical generalizations. In particular, involving and eliciting voices from South Asian classrooms or South Asian teacher education settings could contribute crucial perspectives necessary to comprehending larger discourses of classroom teaching and teacher education (Iyengar et al. 2014).

Civil Resistance

The advocacy of participation and engagement in research has increasingly gained traction in mainstream educational research. In what follows we discuss some of the factors that potentially could have influence on this current agenda. In part, this may be due to a pushback against psychoanalysis and a developing understanding of the affordances and limitations of what Robert Chambers has called the "vertical transfer of reality" (Chambers 1997) and an interest in decolonizing methodologies; that is, a press for dialogism (Bakhtin 1981).

Challenging the Vertical Transfer of Reality—A Pushback Against Psychoanalysis

In his critique of the advantages and privileges of the privileged class, Chambers (1997) argued that powerful professionals maintain their authority through their social standing and lengthy training, as in the case of psychoanalysts and doctors. These professionals have specialized knowledge and experiences, helping carve out space as informed others. Chambers contended that this power(s) can be misused and misconstrued, and the reality often held can be flawed.[1] Chambers reasoned that the issue in such situations is that the supposed authority stems from a conditioning of the mind, and individuals who undergo professional training often internalize the beliefs, constructs, and systems of interpretation of the profession. Although there are benefits to such training, the inherent risk with the professional study of practices such as psychoanalysis, medicine, teaching, and research is that there are impediments to hearing and discerning the realities of those they serve. Chambers (1997) wrote:

> The vertical transfer of reality occurs with all development bureaucrats and professionals through their education, training and socialization; and many then seek to transfer their reality in turn to the poor and the weak. While the conditioning can rarely be as intrusive or radical as that of psychoanalytic training, the imprinting can be deep and strong, leading to the internalization and adoption of normal professional concepts, values, beliefs, methods and behaviours. (pp. 78–79)

The training and socialization of researchers can generate frames of reference for students becoming researchers and practicing researchers whereby they unknowingly appropriate their frame of reality onto their research subjects. Such concerns typically are managed through validity checks or even third-party reviews. However, those checks and reviewers are conditioned by similar realities. Researcher socialization is not much different from teacher socialization (Lortie 1975). Ostensibly, PAR, when deployed, can mediate this concern by bringing to bear the realities of the participants—researcher and researched—through the active engagement of participants as action researchers at every step of the process (McTaggart 1991). In its idealized form, PAR is an endeavor where patterns of control are recalibrated and flows of information are rerouted; thus, it seems to be a method that researchers can apply profitably in South Asia.

Academic Lag Time—Accelerating Change

Classic academic research can lag behind real-time—or proximity to the experience—issues and endeavors. Take, for example, our own research used later on in this chapter. The fieldwork—conducted in 2012 and 2013—is being represented and used for data several years later and is being read (we hope) even years after that. Published government statistics and data, because of the mechanics required to capture macro-level data, often are years behind research publications. These statistics can drive academic arguments and even be used for future data analysis. Chambers (1997) pointed out that even the *Economic and Political Weekly* regularly uses statistics published 10 or 20 years ago. The nature of research and its dissemination requires swaths of time for research to be conducted; data to be analyzed; and interpretations to be written up, reviewed, rewritten, and published. Compounding this academic lag time, educational researchers increasingly run the risk of being isolated from the field. Doctoral students in the field of education bear the brunt of field practicums as faculty are more and more tied up in committee meetings, admissions reviews, and recruitment. As a result, their confinement to bureaucratic commitments marginalizes their time and ability to distill new knowledge and understandings from the field and apply them through their own teaching in proximity to the experience.

There are ways and means, however, to minimize academic lag time, and PAR practitioners may have opportunities to make headway on this problem just as design researchers have (Cobb et al. 2003; Design-Based Research Collective 2003; Edelson 2002). In its ideal form, PAR allows for research and findings to inform each other concurrently. As participants undergo and conduct research, they constantly adapt and revise practice simultaneously while building insights and drawing understandings.

Feyerabend and "Against Method"—A Challenge to Gadamer (1960)

Conceptually, PAR also differs from other educational research in its approach. In its ideal form, PAR eschews universalizing scientific method, and therefore there is no single way to approach its enactment. However, PAR is not just an experiential form of research and analysis either. Moreover, the struggle with conducting PAR successfully is that it is neither wholly inductive—based on natural interpretations—nor does it run completely counter to deductive research. It is, and can be, on a spectrum between the two.

Bacon argued that natural interpretations were limited by a priori suppositions and therefore that "serious" examination was unlikely to proceed unimpeded (Feyerabend 1975). The Baconian framework guided academic research for decades, and in some ways an argument can be made that a Deweyan perspective on learning from experience corroborates this perspective. For Dewey, not all experiences were equal; some can be "educative" and others "mis-educative" (Dewey 1938). For Dewey, a miseducative experience is an experience that has one of two effects; it either "arrests" or "distorts" growth in future experiences. By "arrest," Dewey pointed out that miseducative experiences slow growth; by "distort," he said that miseducative experiences give a false impression of growth. These two broad banners constitute the effects of miseducative experiences. Dewey deepened the definition by offering four characterizations to help contrast the two types of experiences.

Dewey first characterized miseducative experiences as ones that "engender callousness" (Dewey 1938, p. 13). Callousness, for Dewey, entailed a lack of sensitivity and of responsiveness. Callousness, he pointed out, by its very nature needs to be conditioned—calluses develop to protect our skin from a relentless irritant. Callous individuals may be thick-skinned and uninterested in another's feelings, concerns, and pain. According to Dewey, this lack of sensitivity limits one's ability to learn and apply that learning in a future situation; thus, it is "arresting." Dewey's second characterization considered how certain experiences may land an individual in a "groove or rut." A rut is a fixed course and is unpromising. For Dewey, when one obtains proficiency in a particular skill, it becomes automatic. Once this level of automaticity occurs, however, the ability to leverage that skill in innovative ways becomes lost. The effect is an "arresting" of future growth. His third characterization is that experiences, when only immediately enjoyable, promote the formation of "a slack and careless attitude." A slack attitude dulls perceptions. When this occurs, researchers could be limited in what they can carry off from the experience into subsequent experiences, thus "arresting" their future growth. Dewey's fourth characterization is that miseducative experiences are "not linked cumulatively to one another." An individual who encounters disconnected experiences may struggle to bring the experiences together or may do so artificially. The result is that "energy is dissipated" and the individual becomes "scatterbrained." When energy is dissipated, it is frittered away and less generative. When an individual is scatterbrained, he or she is disorganized and unable to focus. Thus, when experiences are disconnected, learning for future experiences is "distorted."

Miseducative experiences continue to plague schooling (which Dewey was explicitly illuminating) but raise concerns for research as well. The distinction between educative and miseducative experiences in research—explicated through the two effects and four characterizations—offers those interested in PAR a way to consider the obstacles to conducting PAR, without the necessary rigor.

Ensuring that the PAR research experience is an educative one requires moving beyond simply an experiential level of academic inquiry, yet it cannot elide the importance of experiencing situations, as they can indeed be educative. In contrast to Bacon's ideas, Feyerabend (1975) argued "Against Method" and wrote "eliminate all natural interpretation and you eliminate the ability to think and to perceive" (p. 50). There is value to the natural interpretations, just as there is value to the distance that helps researchers see what is difficult to see when inside the maelstrom of experience. Feyerabend explained that natural interpretations orient us and allow researchers to become aware and tune their senses so that they can begin the business of scientific investigation. Bacon, in fact, also argued that natural interpretations can be explored through a method of analysis that peeled off the sensory observations until the core observation was exposed. Finding the balance between the perspectives, however, is a complicated undertaking.

The participatory nature of PAR pushes against a Baconian interpretation of deductive research, but the action-oriented nature of PAR runs counter to a purist perspective of inductive research. When researchers engage with their research setting by participating in the activity framework, they enter themselves into a different inquiry mode. They are decreasing distance between themselves as observer and increasing the likelihood that their perceptions lead to natural interpretations. By bringing other participants into the inquiry, activities, and interpretations, researchers also increase the spectrum of perspectives and a priori assumptions. These myriad perspectives require negotiation and constant interpretation so that no one perspective takes priority over others. By acting on these interpretations and leveraging them for further action and inquiry, PAR pushes past static versions of inductive inquiry that seek solely to generate new theories from the data. Dewey (1916) wrote: "Knowledge results if the mind discriminates and combines things" (p. 59). It is the dynamism of taking experience and deploying it back into the research setting while simultaneously maintaining the rigor required to constitute educational research that defines PAR. This point is where educational research distances itself from research in the humanities—art, history, philosophy—where truths cannot be verified by science but rather by modes of experience. (Gadamer 1960, p. xxi)

In his treatise on method and the discernment of truth, Gadamer (1960) explored how research is conducted in the fields of art, philosophy, and history. He noted that for these fields, there is limited value in universal application of scientific method that could be used to understand and come to deeply know certain aspects of the inquiry. Therefore, investigations in art, history, and philosophy begin with a critique of the experience and consciousness—aesthetic or social—and move quickly into mapping a social topography. The strong value, however, of academic analysis in art, history, and philosophy is that there are struggles over how to share critiques. Truths may be experienced in these genres, as Gadamer noted, but sharing that experience with others is a necessary requirement to bolster one's own interpretations and also to extend the knowledge and ideas developed beyond the initial experience.

What Gadamer (1960) revealed is that a social dynamic in research can bring in external measures of comparison and can yield new ways to relate concepts and interrogate perceptions. It can also promote an aspect of strangeness that aids in the discovery of ideas and rounds out concepts. Therefore, researchers seeking balance between social organizations of research rather than individual ones, which leverage experiences of others while also retaining a method of inquiry that strips down those sensory observations, may be attracted to PAR. In what follows, we discuss some ways to maintain rigor in the deployment of a PAR methodology that seeks not only to marshal the resources of those leading the inquiry but to maintain structure and thoroughness that can bolster utility of such research.

"Decolonizing Methodologies"

Increasingly, doctoral students carry out dissertation research in their native countries, focusing on local and national issues that they deem critical to address or that others have steered them toward (Wilson 2001). In doing so, many novice researchers are striving to retrieve spaces and narratives that have been marginalized by predominant hegemonic research.

Thus, a fourth potential driver for selecting PAR as a research mode of inquiry is an interest in decolonizing methodologies.

Tuhiwai Smith (1999) posited a rejection of the dominating forms of "Western"—that is, colonial/postcolonial[2]—research by arguing that the history of research has been monopolized by the West. Smith's argument echoes that of Said (1979) in his monograph *Orientalism*, where he described how travelers and observers represented indigenous peoples as the other. The narratives of those travelers and observers were taken as authoritative representations and thus framed the discourse toward indigenous peoples for centuries.

Tuhiwai Smith (1999) expanded on this foundational argument critiquing the cultural assumptions behind more contemporary research. She contested the inability of such research to provide valid indigenous knowledge and epistomologies. Anchored by her own narratives of Maori research in New Zealand, she argued that assumptions, motivations, and values inform research practices and that decolonized methodologies are those concerned with having "a more critical understanding of the underlying assumptions, motivations and values that inform research practices" (p. 20). Therefore, existing methodologies, theories, and writing styles are exclusive and insufficient. An inherent risk in her position is that researchers potentially can universalize the experiences of indigenous peoples or groups, which can be as equally damaging in trying to develop ways of knowing and distilling concepts. There are ways, however, to manage this risk.

Dialogism

One such way to manage totalizing experiences is to find ways to frame the research inquiry, methodology, and written narratives with dialogism in mind. Our use of the term is not simply about dialogue and is not an attempt to identify the superficial feature of who is talking or that talk is involved. Rather, it is a conceptual marker facilitating attention to the co-construction of the work involved, where the participants in a PAR research project—researcher, researched, and external guides—are all co-constructors of the research narrative and facilitate its unfolding, unpacking interpretations together.

An account of dialogism can draw from Wells (1999) or even Shor and Freire (1987), yet we found Bakhtin's work (1981) most relevant to this argument for PAR. Bakhtin's conception of dialogism refers to the dual functions of communicating through text. In a written text, both writer and reader convey and generate meanings. These meanings develop through words or, as Bakhtin proclaimed, utterances. Both writer and reader, through thoughts, perspectives, points of view, shared meaning, individual understanding, judgments, and particular emphases, qualify every word. He claimed that each word is connected to another that is also laden with the *same* qualifications, which is connected to another word (and so forth). Dialogism entails writers' words being incorporated into readers' discourses where words house ideas, which are fitted in with—or rejected by—existing conceptual understandings. Such a process helps to develop relationships between readers' and writers' conceptual frameworks. Dialogism, for Bakhtin, also meant that the discussion informs, and is informed by, what has come before. Dialogic literature, for example, is in communication with multiple works that may span time and space, potentially informing readers' perspectives on them all.

The theory of dialogism (Bakhtin and Holquist 1981) can contribute to developing a common language about how to do PAR. All participants' values, ideas, and comments are required and need to be considered in subtle ways. PAR places a premium on dialogism from the provision of research questions through to the dissemination of research write-ups. According to Bakhtin (1981), every dialogue, whether text or spoken, is qualified by both writers' and readers' thoughts, perspectives, points of view, shared meanings, individual understandings, judgments, and particular emphases. There is a great deal of value in fostering environments where such a conception can take shape. Discussions that ensue throughout a PAR project can help plant seeds of particular interpretations, but only if all individuals accommodate rather than dispute the ideas put forth. Negotiating the numerous interpretations in a PAR research project is complicated and may take researchers into unfamiliar territory. However, this concept, if grounded in PAR, can help coordinate the myriad views that emerge over the course of PAR studies and press participants toward locally relevant, valuable, and usable knowledge.

Data Construction and Its Limitations

Selecting a methodology is essential for a sound research project; however, knowing why you have selected a methodology is not enough. Your choice becomes relevant when it merges with research practices that organize and leverage the ever-evolving technologies of communication. As with teaching (Cohen 2011), social organization and communication technologies are important because they can help shape the participation and activity structures from which practitioners can construct data. From ethnographic methods to interviews, certain data construction tools can constrain and cultivate the data; others can restrict it. In what follows, we discuss tools and practices that can create connections that facilitate edification of warrants and claims.

As discussed earlier, first-person research methods can provide proximity to practice and generate cases yielding rich data. Studies of practice occur in the concrete situations of social interactions. There are moment-to-moment nuances that are complex and elusive. Erickson (2006) noted, "Interaction face to face is so complex that it can be monitored only in highly selective ways, by participants during the course of its conduct, and by researchers who study that conduct after the interaction has taken place" (p. 179). Being in the interaction helps attend to these moments, but deriving meaning from these interactions for research requires a mechanism to record the details. Therefore, to gather the concrete and fine-grained information about what goes on requires multiple ways to collect information that can be used for descriptions and analyses. Several data construction tools, often associated with ethnographic methods, can be used to gather information that can then be converted into data. Video records, journals, ethnographic field notes, and stimulated recall interviews can be primary sources. Additionally, PAR practitioners can leverage a variety of other approaches, including popular theater, political action, group discussions, community seminars, educational camps, intercultural exchange programs, video productions, and storytelling (e.g., Arratia and de la Maza 1997; Brydon-Miller 1993; Debbink and Ornelas 1997; Tobias 1982 in Brydon-Miller 1997, p. 661). Next we describe these tools in more detail and discuss how pilot studies can benefit the design of these tools.

Pilot Studies

Many qualitative researchers have expressed the importance of a pilot study in qualitative inquiry (Patton 1990; Maxwell 2013; Creswell 2012; Kim 2010). Maxwell (2013) shared that pilot studies can foster an understanding of the concepts and theories held by the individuals one intends to study. For Maxwell, these exploratory studies provided opportunities for researchers to engage with the meaning and perspectives that can inform their conceptualization of the phenomena. Furthermore, Creswell (2012) asserted that pilot studies can refine and develop research instruments and assess degrees of bias. Kim (2010) wrote about other important affordances of pilot studies. She carried out pilot work in preparation for her dissertation on Korean American family dementia caregiving, describing the specific practical and methodological issues that emerged and the modifications she made for the main study resulting from her pilot work. Implementation of her pilot was essential in four ways. Like Maxwell and Creswell, Kim found that pilot studies helped her reflect on the research process and potential difficulties in conducting a phenomenological inquiry, and she was also able to modify her data collection tools, such as her interview questions. Moreover, the pilot helped her find out about issues and barriers related to recruiting potential participants, and she sensed what it meant to carry out research in culturally appropriate ways.

Pilot studies offer researchers opportunities to test data collections tools, organization and logistics, and modes of communicating the research agenda with practitioners. They can help PAR practitioners formulate a number of realizations. First, what is involved in the labor of conducting first-person research? Designing and developing the settings, let alone enacting the research, requires time management. Moreover, such work requires systematic modes of generating information relevant to the research. Second, what are the ways in which participants' skepticism can be overcome? Finally, pilot studies inform one's thinking about the conceptualization of the phenomenon of inquiry and how it might unfold in the contexts of consequence.

Video Recording

Video recordings play two parts in PAR studies. First, they aid in constructing data about the groups' social interactions. And second, records can be used for stimulated recall interviews. The choice to use video devices to record and generate data reflects an interpretation of what qualitative research on social interactions can afford. Erickson's (2006) writing is helpful in considering this position.

> Interaction face to face is a social ecology, a system of relations of mutual influence among participants that is sustained "online" in real time. That is, interaction is not usefully to be regarded as a succession of isolated acts, a ping-pong match of successive moves between speakers and hearers, and

> interaction involves nonverbal as well as verbal behavior. Everybody in the scene is continuously active—and interactive—that is, speakers are continuously doing verbal and nonverbal behavior and so are listeners, all addressing one another in varying kinds of ways. Thus social interaction involves not only talk by speakers but also the reciprocal attention behavior of listeners, who influence the speakers (continuously) during the course of their speaking. In recording for research purposes it can be analytically useful to document through picture and sound the continuous influence of speakers on listeners and also that of listeners on speakers (p. 178).

Understanding the practice PAR practitioners are interested in requires inquiry into what the practitioners and participants do together to push forward the agenda and phenomenon of inquiry. For this reason, video records help to present everyone involved, who, by their very presence, influence the practice. Participation is not linear; nor is it all verbal. Instruction, for example, is a constant flow, as Erickson (2006) noted, and is composed of details and distractions. The nonverbal behaviors of speakers and listeners continuously inflect meaning into the interaction as well, and any exploration of practice would be deficient without a way to attend to these nuances.

Video recording, though, no matter how fine-grained and directed, can be incomplete. For one thing, placement of the video camera can narrow what can be gained from video records. Also, the video operator's attention can shift, and pertinent information can be missed. If poorly directed, the operator may zoom in and out or from one speaker to the next. Thus, the video footage would be filtered through the video operator's lens. Also, the presence of the video operator would be more noticeable and potentially influence behaviors. Taking the videos is only part of the journey. Elsewhere (Setty 2013) we discuss how the information derived from videotapes can be prepared, packaged, transcribed, and coded for analysis.

The two tools discussed here are just samples of the myriad tools available for a PAR researcher. They are emblematic, however, of tools that are defined and can assist in constructing data. Working with that data becomes the critical part of PAR and, in a way, overemphasizing the "R" can provide appreciable gains. In short, analysis of PAR data should in the least entail proto-analytic work, generation of empirical packages, analytic work—including various analytic trials—and a coalescing of themes and warrants. Doing so can support PAR practitioners in making claims and arguments and in "verify[ing] their sturdiness" (Miles and Huberman 1994, p. 16).

In terms of carrying out a PAR process from start to finish, Maguire (1987) offered an outline. The process of conducting PAR begins with the establishment of relationships with participants. A period of relationship building may predate any analytic data gathering, as the success of the project depends on the reflexive depth of trust between participants and the practitioner. Following the period of relationship building, participants may request support to conduct a research project. In PAR, participants and researchers together take responsibility for research design, data collection, data analysis, and development and implementation of plans for change. Typically, this phase of the research concludes with reflection and consolidation of the learning that has ensued. In many cases, there is a reexamination of the political, social, and economic conditions facing the community and how the members of the community have been affected (Maguire 1987).

Conclusion

We started this introductory chapter with a premise about choice. Researchers make choices throughout the process, and the first one—which methodology fits the questions and constructs they are trying to learn more about—is a key element to intentional research design. The key point in our analysis is that choosing to undertake PAR is a question of fit. Is PAR the right fit for the questions, place, people, and time? PAR's lengthy legacy illuminates a research paradigm that pushes against others. Its researchers aim to improve thoughts, organizations, actions, and lives of others. In doing so, they make deliberate choices, some related to their own goals and others leveraging their ability to subject those goals to the will of the group. PAR researchers, like others engaged in the work of human improvement (e.g., teachers, nurses, social workers), cannot do their work without the active and intelligent engagement of those they seek to support. No matter how refined the expertise of PAR researchers is, it will be inadequate because it requires communal others. As Cohen (2011) explicated, "Expertise is precious but chronically insufficient" (p. 190). Cohen said that the expertise "improvers" bring to bear is inadequate because the work of improving others' lives is mired in the unpredictability of working with other humans. There are always competing interest, ideas, and intentions, yet the conflicts and the tensions can give rise to acceptable solutions and rich cultural improvements. Hope, courage, persistence—these are the necessary supplements, according to

Cohen, for expertise to flourish. These are not the typical attributes discussed in a research analysis or in a methodological argument. For PAR, an omission of these points would ignore the core of PAR. Nevertheless, as we have argued in this chapter, targeting these points alone is incomplete.

Although researchers often have keen perspectives and insights, we check ourselves and find flaws in our own ideas before taking them to others, and we accept there will be meaningful critiques. Occasionally we might bring others deeply into our thinking so they can tear it apart from the inside. Bringing people into our thinking and delving into theirs is messy, hard work. PAR researchers are required to bring the fragmentation together and simultaneously let it unfold. Doing so requires suppleness and constraint; an ability to fashion but not interfere; to provoke but not conflict; to sketch and frame and not measure and favor.

In McTaggart's (1991) attempt to define the principles of PAR in cross-cultural contexts, he suggested that successful PAR can improve the lives of those involved in the process and highlighted the critical importance of sharing examples of meaningful and productive work. Our own theoretical perspectives have changed in light of the chapters in this volume. Our efforts to draw this collection together echoes the work of those we mentioned who proposed that knowledge generation need not adhere to the boundaries established by positivism. Although critics of this volume may argue that researchers often overlook the complexity involved in carrying this knowledge generation off successfully, we suggest that there are manageable ways to incorporate both interpretive and critical approaches to the practice of knowledge generation. From this perspective, PAR is a meaningful methodology for approaching the research process.

Refining definitions of PAR have been our attempt to stimulate the thinking of those aspiring to utilize PAR as a rigorous methodology in South Asia. Our analysis implies that researchers can use this chapter to reflect and wrestle with the challenges they may encounter engaging within communities, particularly honing in on the critical need for executing PAR methodology through defining plans and taking actions. The thinking tools proposed in this chapter are aimed to help PAR researchers consider the actions necessary to solve contextual problems and leverage opportunities for social justice. We leave you with the words of Freire (1970), which continue to inspire our PAR advocacy and critique. Others may find, as they consider their role in the process, that this is the gift of working alongside communities to foster meaningful transformation:

Teachers and students (leadership and people), co-intent on reality, are both Subjects, not only in the task of unveiling that reality, and thereby coming to know it critically, but in the task of re-creating that knowledge. As they attain this knowledge of reality through common reflection and action, they discover themselves as its permanent re-creators. In this way, the presence of the oppressed in the struggle for their liberation will be what it should be: not pseudo-participation, but committed involvement. (p. 56)

NOTES

1. Sigmund Freud and several of his colleagues were wrong in several child sex abuse cases, where they maintained that the victim narratives were fantasy (see, e.g., Karle 1992; Masson 1989, 1992; Rowe 1989; Sanderson 1990; Webster 1995 in Chambers 1997). The basis for these assumptions were Freud's held assertions and analysis that children are sexually attracted to their parents and therefore that the accounts were manifestations of their imagination.
2. Smith rejects the term "post-colonial" as it infers that colonialism is complete. From her perspective, that the legacy and implications of colonialism, though, continue and therefore colonialism continues.

REFERENCES

Adelman, C. (1993). Kurt Lewin and the origins of action research. *Educational Action Research, 1*(1), 7–24.

Argyris, C., & Schön, D. A. (1989). Participatory action research and action science compared: A commentary. *The American Behavioral Scientist, 32*(5), 612–623.

Argyris, C., & Schön, D. (1991). Participatory action research and action science compared. In W. F. Whyte (Ed.), *Participatory action research* (pp. 85–96). Newbury Park, NJ: SAGE.

Ariyadasa, E., & McIntyre-Mills, J. (2015). Quality of life of Sri Lankan children: Participatory action research to address the governance issues of voluntary children's homes. *Systemic Practice and Action Research, 28*(5), 453–478.

Arratia, M., & de la Maza, I. (1997). Grounding a long-term ideal: Working with the Aymara for community development. In S. E. Smith, D. G. Willams, & N. A. Johnson (Eds.), *Nurtured by knowledge: Learning to do participatory action research* (pp. 111–137). New York: Apex Press.

Aziz, A., Shams, M., & Khan, K. S. (2011). Participatory action research as the approach for women's empowerment. *Action Research, 9*(3), 303–323.

Bakhtin, M. M., & Holquist, M. (1981). *The dialogic imagination: Four essays* (Vol. 1). Austin: University of Texas press.

Ball, D. L. (2000). Working on the inside: Using one's own practice as a site for studying teaching and learning. In A. E. Kelly & R. Lesh (Eds.), *Handbook of research design in mathematics and science education* (pp. 365–402). Mahwah, NJ: Lawrence Erlbaum.

Baskerville, R. L. (1999). Investigating information systems with action research. *Communications of the Association for Information Systems, 2*, 2–32.

Braun, M., & Saroar, M. (2012). *Participatory action research on climate risk management, Bangladesh*. Penang: WorldFish, Studies & Reviews.

Brydon-Miller, M. (1993). Breaking down barriers: Accessibility self-advocacy in the disabled community. In P. Park, M. Brydon-Miller, B. Hall, & T. Jackson (Eds.), *Voices of change: Participatory research in the United States and Canada* (pp. 125–143). WEst Port, CT: Bergin and Garvey.

Brydon-Miller, M. (1997). Participatory action research: Psychology and social change. *Journal of Social Issues, 53*(4), 657–666.

Brydon-Miller, M., Kral, M., Maguire, P., Noffke, S., & Sabhlok, A. (2011). Jazz and the Banyan Tree. In N. K. Denzin & Y. S. Lincoln (Eds.), *Handbook of qualitative research* (2nd ed., pp. 387–400). Thousand Oaks, CA: SAGE.

Center for the Study of Teaching and Policy, Wilson, S. M., Floden, R. E., & Ferrini-Mundy, J. (2001). Teacher preparation research: Current knowledge, gaps, and recommendations: A Research Report prepared for the US Department of Education and the Office for Educational Research and Improvement, February 2001. Center for the Study of Teaching and Policy.

Chambers, R. (1997). *Whose reality counts? Putting the first last*. London: Intermediate Technology.

Cobb, P., Confrey, J., Lehrer, R., & Schauble, L. (2003). Design experiments in educational research. *Educational Researcher, 32*(1), 9–13.

Cohen, D. K. (2011). *Teaching and its predicaments*. Cambridge, MA: Harvard University Press.

Collier, J. (1945). United States Indian Administration as a laboratory of ethnic relations. *Social Research, 12*(3), 265–303.

Corbett, A. M., Francis, K., & Chapman, Y. (2007). Feminist-informed participatory action research: A methodology of choice for examining critical nursing issues. *International Journal of Nursing Practice, 13*(2), 81–88.

Corey, S. M. (1954). Action research in education. *The Journal of Educational Research, 47*(5), 375–380.

Creswell, J. W. (2012). *Qualitative inquiry and research design: Choosing among five approaches* (3rd ed.). Los Angeles: Sage Publications.

Debbink, G., & Ornelas, A. (1997). Cows for campesinos. In S. E. Smith, D. G. Willms, & N. A. Johnson (Eds.), *Nurtured by knowledge* (pp. 13–33). New York: Apex.

The Design-Based Research Collective. (2003). Design-based research: An emerging paradigm for educational inquiry. *Educational Researcher, 32*(1), 5–8.

Dewey, J. (1916). *Democracy and education: An introduction to the philosophy of education*. New York: Macmillan.
Dewey, J. (1938). *Education as experience*. New York: Collier.
Edelson, D. C. (2002). Design research: What we learn when we engage in design. *The Journal of the Learning Sciences, 11*(1), 105–121.
Erickson, F. (1986). Qualitative methods on research on teaching. In M. Wittrock (Ed.), *Handbook of research on teaching* (3rd ed., pp. 119–161). New York, NY: Macmillan.
Erickson, F. (2006). Definition and analysis of data from videotape: Some Research procedures and their rationales. In J. Green, G. Camilli, P. Elmore, A. Skukauskaite, & E. Grace (Eds.), *Handbook of complementary methods in education research* (pp. 177–192). Washington, DC: American Educational Research Association.
Fals Borda, O. (1977, April). For praxis: The problem of how to investigate reality in order to transform it. In *African Regional Workshop on Participatory Research*.
Fals Borda, O. (1999). *The origins and challenges of participatory action research*. David Kinsey dialogue series, Lecture No. 1. Amherst, MA: University of Massachusetts, Center for International Education.
Fals-Borda, O. (2001). Participatory (action) research in social theory. In P. Reason & H. Bradbury (Eds.), *Handbook of action research* (pp. 27–37). Thousand Oaks, CA: SAGE.
Fals-Borda, O., & Rahman, M. A. (Eds.). (1991). *Action and knowledge: Breaking the monopoly with participatory action research*. New York: Apex Press.
Feyerabend, P. (1975). *Against method: Outline of an anarchistic theory of knowledge*. London: New Left Books.
Freire, P. (1970). *Pedagogy of the oppressed*. New York: The Continuum Publishing Company.
Freire, P. (Ed.). (1997). *Mentoring the mentor: A critical dialogue with Paulo Freire* (Vol. 60). New York: Peter Lang Publications Incorporated.
Gadamer, H. (1960). *Truth and method*. London: Sheed & Ward.
Gibbon, M. (2002). Doing a doctorate using a participatory action research framework in the context of community health. *Qualitative Health Research, 12*(4), 546–558.
Hall, B. L. (1981). Participatory research, popular knowledge and power: A personal reflection. *Convergence, 14*(3), 6–17.
Hall, S. (1997). The centrality of culture: Notes on the cultural revolutions of our time. In K. Thomson (Ed.), *Media and cultural regulation*. London: SAGE.
Heaton, R. M. (1994). *Creating and studying a practice of teaching elementary mathematics for understanding*. Unpublished doctoral dissertation, Michigan State University, East Lansing.
Herrick, H. E. (1953). Review of the book *Action research, fundamental research and educational practice*, by S. M. Corey. *Educational Leadership*, 198–201.

Hinchey, P. H. (2008). *Action research primer*. New York: Peter Lang.
Islam, M., & Nag, N. C. (2010). *Economic integration in South Asia: Issues and pathways*. Delhi: Pearson.
Iyengar, R., Witenstein, M. A., & Byker, E. J. (2014). Comparative perspectives on teacher education in South Asia. *Annual Review of Comparative and International Education*, 99–106.
Kellner, D. (2007). The Frankfurt school. In T. Edwards (Ed.), *Cultural theory: Classical and contemporary positions* (pp. 49–68). Los Angeles: SAGE.
Kemmis, S. (1980). *Action research in retrospect and prospect*. Paper presented to the annual meeting of the Australian Association for Research in Education. Sydney, Australia.
Kim, Y. (2010). The pilot study in qualitative inquiry identifying issues and learning lessons for culturally competent research. *Qualitative Social Work, 10*(2), 190–206.
Lampert, M. (2001). *Teaching problems and the problems of teaching*. New Haven: Yale University Press.
Lee, C. D. (2007). *Culture, literacy, & learning: Taking bloom in the midst of the whirlwind*. Teachers College Press.
Lewin, K. (1946). Action research and minority problems. *Journal of Social Issues, 2*(4), 34–46.
Lortie, D. C. (1975). *Schoolteacher: A sociological study*. Chicago: University of Chicago Press.
Maguire, P. (1987). *Doing participatory research: A feminist approach*. Amherst, MA: Center for International Education, School of Education, University of Massachusetts.
Marrow, A. J. (1969). *The practical theorist the life and work of Kurt Lewin*. New York: Basic Books.
Maxwell, J. A. (2013). *Qualitative research design: An interactive approach* (3rd ed.). Thousand Oaks, CA: Sage Publications.
McNiff, J., & Whitehead, J. (2011). *All you need to know about action research*. Thousand Oaks: SAGE.
McTaggart, R. (1991). Principles for participatory action research. *Adult Education Quarterly, 41*(3), 168–187.
Miles, M. B., & Huberman, A. M. (1994). *Qualitative data analysis: An expanded sourcebook* (2nd ed.). Thousand Oaks, CA: Sage Publications.
Minkler, M. (2000). Using participatory action research to build healthy communities. *Public Health Reports, 115*(2–3), 191.
Nilsen, A. G. (2012). Adivasis in and against the state: Subaltern politics and state power in contemporary India. *Critical Asian Studies, 44*(2), 251–282.
Noffke, S. E. (1997). Professional, personal, and political dimensions of action research. *Review of Research in Education, 22*, 305–343.

Ottosson, S. (2003). Participation action research: A key to improved knowledge of management. *Technovation, 23*(2), 87–94.

Patton, M. Q. (1990). *Qualitative evaluation and research methods.* Thousands Oaks, CA: Sage Publications, Inc.

Patton, M. Q. (2005). *Qualitative research.* New York: John Wiley & Sons, Ltd.

Rammelt, C. F. (2013). Participatory action research in marginalised communities: Safe drinking water in rural Bangladesh. *Systemic Practice and Action Research, 27*(3), 195–210.

Said, E. W. (1979). *Orientalism.* New York: Vintage Books.

Setty, R. (2013). *Being explicit about modeling: A first person study in India.* Doctoral dissertation, University Of Michigan.

Setty, R. (2016). *Intellectualising teachers' education: A study of practice-based teacher education in teaching-learning resources for School Education.* Thousand Oaks, CA: Sage Publications.

Shor, I., & Freire, P. (1987). *A pedagogy for liberation: Dialogues on transforming education.* Westport, CT: Bergin and Garvey Publishers.

Silverman, D. (Ed.). (2016). *Qualitative research.* London: Sage.

Spivak, G. (1989). Who claims alterity? *Remaking History, 4,* 269–292.

Szal, R. J. (1979). Popular participation, employment and the fulfilment of basic needs. *International Labour Review, 118*(1), 27–38.

Tobias, S. (1982). When do instructional methods make a difference? *Educational Researcher, 11*(4), 4–9.

Tuhiwai Smith, L. (1999). *Decolonizing methodologies research and indigenous people.* London: Zed Books.

Yin, R. K. (2009). *Case study research: Design and methods, essential guide to qualitative methods in organizational research* (5th ed.). Thousand Oaks, CA: SAGE.

CHAPTER 2

Utilizing "a Version of PAR" to Explore Children's Voices on Inclusion: The Case of Two Primary Schools in Bangladesh

Tahiya Mahbub

Launching In

Academic research is always conducted within certain contexts bound to a given time and space. Through the works of scholars across the fields of sociology, anthropology, and education, the impact, significance, and relativity of research contexts have proved to be crucial time and time again. No two contexts are the same; hence no two research projects are identical either. Context in research is defined by many boundaries (Maxey 1999). Two of those often are national/cultural and physical boundaries. The context of a research project is defined by the physical reality of where a certain study is taking place—for example, at a school, community center, or child's home (Punch 2002; Maxey 1999). Similarly, it is defined by the culture within which the study occurs—for example, a country's norms, practices, and traditions. Depending on the context in which research is conducted, the results or findings will vary, as will the relationships and ethical dimensions of investigators and participants (Riessman 2005).

T. Mahbub (✉)
Montreal, QC, Canada
e-mail: tahiya.mahbub@mail.mcgill.ca

My experience as a diasporic researcher affiliated with a research-intensive university of the Global North returning to my native country of Bangladesh to conduct research in the Global South[1] posed subjective challenges in regards to how I engaged with research participants in their given context (Mukherjee and Mahbub 2015).

As a native of Bangladesh who has lived abroad for many years, my transnational spatial location and "double consciousness"—to use the term employed by W.E.B. Du Bois (2007)—as a native and an alien acculturated within a Western academic environment posed unique subjective challenges when I worked within my national and cultural space (Mukherjee and Mahbub 2015). This chapter is about that experience.

OBJECTIVES

Hence, I present my experiences of working at two Building Resources Across Communities (BRAC)[2] primary inclusive schools in Bangladesh using a version of participatory action research (PAR) as my research methodology. The chapter is nested within the larger questions and concerns of PAR that have to do with how this research strategy changes as it traverses national and geographical boundaries. It also asks if PAR, when conducted in the field, is determined more by context or theory or rather through a careful and measured balance of both. Further, my goal is to illustrate how a version of PAR, as I like to call my research process, can be useful to illustrate and highlight the benefits and limitations of this hugely popular and growing methodology. The choice to deploy PAR as the framework for the research design stemmed from my methodological affiliations and ideological positioning, which are clarified in more detail later in the chapter.

More specifically, through a collaborative and reflexive PAR methodology, I utilized observations, Photovoice, written scripts, *adda*[3] sessions, and a questionnaire to explore children's perspectives on issues at school that they liked and disliked as related to inclusive education. The utilization of a range of methods was vital to answering my main research question:

> *What do children in nominally inclusive primary schools operated by the NGO Building Resources Across Communities (more commonly known as BRAC) express when asked about their likes and dislikes at school?*

I had two subquestions in addition to this one. The first was related to finding central motifs from children's perspectives and the second was about distilling their voices through the educational philosophy of Bengali theorist and educational scholar Rabindranath Tagore.

The motivations behind my research questions were manifold. First, I wanted to work with children, who are one of the least ethnographically researched groups in Bangladesh and generally the Global South. Second, I wanted to illustrate the possible theoretical, philosophical, and hermeneutical links between Tagore's humanistic framework of education and that of inclusive education and what it could mean for today's Bangladesh—a country messily traversing tradition versus novelty, especially in fields of social change including education. I wanted to do this in order to base the discussion of inclusive education in Bangladesh more on the indigenous Bengali milieu, to make a slight push away from all the Northern-based literature that dominates glocal educational concepts in Bangladesh currently.

However, my goal in this chapter is not to discuss my entire study. Rather I aim to present the intricacies of my methodological journey, with a focus on field methods, showing how I mapped the research arena through tools of PAR and reflexivity. It is, hence, a contribution toward this book's overall aim to divulge, dissect, and discuss the challenges and processes of conducting PAR in Southern country contexts, methods that differ significantly from doing PAR in Northern contexts. Further, a focus on *only the field process* is just as important as an overall discussion of the study, as PAR fieldwork with young people is rarely conducted and written about from the context of Bangladesh. As a result, I do not discuss final results and findings as they resulted from my doctoral study in this chapter.

Rather, I start the chapter with a short discussion on PAR and then unpack notions of reflexivity as it worked as a theme throughout my research process. After that, I focus on how both PAR and reflexivity impacted my research design, methods, and tools of data collection utilized at the two BRAC schools. Other definite methodological considerations were made throughout the entire methodological process, such as analysis, trustworthiness, and ethical parameters; however, those are beyond the scope of this chapter also. The chapter ends with a discussion on the dynamics of "voice"[4] and how that can be negotiated through tools of PAR and reflexivity while conducting research with young people.

I specifically chose to focus on the issue of voice as participation is an integral component of PAR, and participation (or not) can be understood only through a discussion of voice (or, simply put, what participants state and do not state), and the multiple considerations surrounding how to "hear" them, a process shrouded in complexity.

PAR

As explained by Baum et al. (2006), "At the heart of [the research approach PAR, participatory action research] is collective, self reflective inquiry that researchers and participants undertake so that they can understand and improve upon the practices in which they participate and the situations in which they find themselves" (p. 854). According to scholars, PAR is a research approach with the specific intent to create social change. More importantly, it is about the degree of participation achieved in any particular research project. Later I discuss in more detail which "degree" of participation I utilized.

PAR is not an approach that can be imposed as an intent, as no one can know in advance how a particular research process will become fully participatory; rather it is a process that must be generated (Greenwood et al. 1993). The intent plants the seed, which starts the process but continues to build through the progression of any research endeavor. Thus it is an emergent process. This process can evolve in several characteristics—collaboration, incorporation of local knowledge, and linking "scientific" research understandings to social action—and it depends on the particular research context and case how that unfolds.

PAR as a research methodology draws on the epistemology or worldview of advocacy and participation. Other worldviews can also be nestled within the methodology of PAR. In my case, I was additionally influenced by constructivism and phenomenology. Hence, I used only some elements from the advocacy aspect of PAR, and I make no claim to have conducted "complete PAR." I worked closely with participants but used their input in only certain aspects of the study. For example, the degree of participation in PAR differs from study to study, but the integral aspect at the heart of the process is the value placed on participation. In my study, this was done mostly through children having autonomy in deciding how they wanted to engage with the proposed methods. They were open to suggest changes and had full flexibility in offering propositions that better worked to access their ideas within each method. However, they did not participate in establishing the study's methods themselves.

The decision to involve children in the manner I did was done intentionally as I believe that meaning is not discovered but rather constructed and that phenomena come into meaning only when consciousness engages with that particular singularity (Crotty 1998). I also believe that in order to co-create the constructed meanings, we must engage the *self* and the *participants* in the research process. I agree that "nothing can be accomplished without subjectivity, so its elimination is not the solution. Rather how the subject is present is what matters, and objectivity itself is an achievement of subjectivity" (Giorgi 1994, p. 205). Understanding this results from "a dialectic between the researcher's pre-understandings and the research process, between the self-interpreted constructions of the researcher and those of the participant" (Finlay 2002, p. 534). Through my methodological journey, therefore, I explore and transparently present my enmeshment as an integral part of this research endeavor. Hence, my role as the researcher, through the overall process and often contesting with the ideas of PAR itself, was a bit more involved than that of the participants.

In this sense, as the researcher-participant who was also a guest teacher at times at the schools, I conducted only a version of PAR. There are certainly other versions of PAR as the spectrum of research on PAR is vast. For me, however, the part of PAR wherein the self-reflective and collective process that researchers and participants often find themselves involved in was of utmost importance. Hence, I leaned towards reflexivity.

Reflexivity

The practice of reflexivity is a process that allows for "detachment, internal dialogue, and constant scrutiny of the process through which the researcher constructs and questions his/her interpretations of field experiences" (Ahsan 2009, p. 398). In other words, reflexivity involves researchers being honest about contemplating their own feelings, assumptions, biases, and experiences and allowing themselves the space needed to navigate those in relation to the research process. Reflexivity occurs during and after a certain process in the field, as researchers cannot enter a field and be completely objective, leaving biases, identities, and personal understandings of the world behind. During the research process, these issues play into how researchers engage with participants. Afterward, reflexivity on the research process occurs as researchers go through the process again in their own minds and in writing, addressing how their "selves" in the moment of and soon after the fieldwork affected the research process. Reflexivity happens during and after the event, in essence because as researchers interact in the field, they are aware of what they bring onto the field, and later they address those biases in their write-ups. Ahsan (2009) stated that reflexivity is not only useful but a methodological necessity when conducting research in the Global South; she used reflexivity as a methodological tool in her study of children's rights and child participation in Tangail, Bangladesh.

In my work, based also in Bangladesh, I use reflexivity as a form of methodological scrutiny, mostly as a form of discussion between what happened in the field and what I did in my position as the researcher in order to question, resolve, or challenge what occurred. Therefore, my stance has always been one of a critique, and my work has been informed mostly by the critical standpoint that reflexivity provides.

Research Design: Qualitative Inquiry

Keeping PAR and reflexive intentions as a priority, I designed my research study as a qualitative inquiry. Within it, practices of visual, written, and spoken methods informed data collection while phenomenological tools informed data analysis. I chose such approaches because I had to make methodological decisions that suited me as a researcher and also best suited the study of young children. It should be mentioned that all of these methods were conducted keeping the PAR methodology in mind, wherein the ongoing interaction between participants and researcher formed and informed the field process.

Why this design?

Very briefly, by choosing to use qualitative methods, I gave myself the flexibility to make creative choices regarding methods and, at the same time, to allow my research project to become a therapeutic process (Denzin and Lincoln 2005). As I worked on this project, to which I have dedicated almost six years of my life, I have become more aware and connected to my complex identity as a Bangladeshi woman doing research in Bangladesh. My stream of "double consciousness" (Du Bois 2007), developed through my long tenure in Northern educational institutions—first in Bangladesh and later on at universities in the United States, United Kingdom, and Canada—provided me a unique yet challenging position in terms of my research topic, questions, and participants. Therefore, as an individual, I always felt as if my identity were divided into several parts, which made it difficult or impossible to have one unified sense of self in my project. This stream of double consciousness, for example, allowed me to relate to my study at one level because I too grew up in Bangladesh and faced some of the challenges that children there face. However, at the same time, my education and acculturation within Western academic environments revealed a certain linguistic, cultural power gap from my participants. For example, I struggled to speak entirely in Bengali in the field, often unconsciously utilizing English words during my daily banter with participants. I instantly caught myself and translated the word used into Bengali. However, as a reflexive thinker, I must question how that may have had an impact on my position and relationship with my participants. It may have caused a moment of discomfort or even utter incomprehension, which may have affected participants' thoughts.

A further more direct reason I chose a qualitative approach is that it is highly suited to working with children. Children prefer flexible, interactive, and engaging methods, which qualitative research allows (Punch 2002). In addition, children as individuals and as a social group are often powerless and vulnerable in relation to adults (McDowell 2001). Adult researchers—with their physical presence, institutional positioning, social standing, and life experiences—possess a great deal of power in contrast to their child participants (Valentine 1999). Qualitative methodologies allow researchers to at least partially bridge this gap, because in qualitative work, researchers have the flexibility to be emergent rather than predetermined, participant driven rather than researcher driven, and open and accommodating rather than imposing. Creswell (2007) explained that power can be deemphasized by collaborating directly with participants, by having them suggest methods of data collection or help with the research questions. In the case of children, it allows for multiple realities and voices to be represented in a complex, thick, in-depth description.

How did I navigate chosen research design?

Within the design of the qualitative inquiry, I depended on a mix of visual, spoken, and written methods to collect data and used phenomenology to analyze my findings. These approaches all share certain elements in common with qualitative research but at the same time expand it to fit evident, more specific research criteria. For instance, I used visuals especially because they allow vulnerable, often disempowered individuals to express the ineffable in a creative way. I used phenomenology because it allows researchers to distill multiple perspectives from any given situation. Both of these points can be better explained through examples.

Regarding visuals, one day during a picture-taking session at school, one pupil took a photo of a picture (from his textbook) of bumblebees flying out of a tree. This photo seemed unrelated to the issue of the school's "like" or "dislike" aspects, but in conversation, I discovered that the most important aspect of that photo for the child was the idea of "flight." He took that photo because in it bees were shown as being able to fly. He told me how his reason for coming to school was to learn what could enable him to "fly" far, far away and become a police officer one day. These ideas of freedom and flight would have been very difficult to unearth through another method, especially in a context and situation where neither flight nor freedom were topics of discussion. One could argue that I could unearth this information through an interview. However, I contend that taking the photograph unleashed a creative part of the child's mind that a mere conversation could not have. Through conversation, I would not have learned about how he visualizes not only his learning but also his future goals. If I asked him about his goals, perhaps he would never have been able to draw the relationship with the flight of a bee. Further, the application of visuals within PAR specifically enabled me to access information through the children via direct participatory-creative methods, which were translated into action as this boy spoke to me. In other words, this child's answer came up the way it did because he felt comfortable in participating and speaking openly. He knew he had the autonomy to state whatever he wanted to regarding his photo rather than aiming to discuss some aspect of direct application of the photograph as if it were related only to education. The phenomenon of trying to please the researcher with the "right" answer is often an obstacle of fieldwork in the Global South, where participants view researchers as having more power than they have (Mukherjee 2015). PAR, however, allows space to work around that.

Regarding phenomenology, one of my methodological steps involved groups of children creating albums of their photographs. In reflecting back on the activity, I discovered that the perspectives of the group leaders varied significantly from those of the shyer, more reserved group members. Although the group leaders commented on the fun, communal, and inclusive aspects of the project, some of the introverted children mentioned how the task made them feel unnoticed, especially when the group leader preferred to list his or her picture and name first in the album. Through phenomenological considerations, I discovered that each of these alternative interpretations of the same incident is valid in its own right; it is up to the phenomenologist to recognize these differences and acknowledge the tangled messiness of multiplicity pervading social research. As explained by Denscombe (2003), "phenomenology rejects the notion that there is one universal reality and accepts, instead, that things can be seen in different ways by different people at different times in different circumstances, and each alternative version needs to be recognized as valid in its one right" (p. 100). Phenomenology is hence especially useful and related to the PAR approach. All voices have equal power in the research design, process, and outcomes.

Important Considerations in the Field

Once I decided on my research design and approach, I embarked on my field study of doing research at two BRAC primary schools, "U" and "M," with a total of 66 young pupils. I chose the two schools based on two important criteria: the value of the data and the population makeup.

The value of the data, or the possibility of gaining rich, detailed information, was determined by two factors: children's ability to complete the research activities I had planned and the attitudes of participants and gatekeepers toward my project. What really stood out and helped me purposefully choose these two schools had to do with my second criterion for data value: people's attitudes. During the sampling process, I got a general idea of the attitudes of various teachers, program officers, and children toward my research. I found that at both of these schools, all the people who played different but vital roles were generally open, approachable, and excited about my project. However, obtaining buy-in from host institutions in South Asia while guarding against validity problems is always complex.

As I wanted to explore specifically the opinions of children in inclusive environs, another very important criterion was the issue of mixed populations at the chosen schools. The focus of inclusivity in settings is a characteristic of PAR in South Asia that researchers should pay closer attention to. Although it is more difficult to meet, regardless, it is an important aspect. For me, this issue was more difficult to meet, since there were no children belonging to ethnic minorities at both schools. Nevertheless, the student populations at the two schools were mixed in several other ways, as shown in Table 2.1.

Table 2.1 Students at Schools "U" and "M"

Aspect	School "U" Grade 3	School "M" Grade 2
School location	Urban	Semiurban
Age	8–14	7–12
Gender	12 boys	10 boys
	24 girls	20 girls
Ability factor of	1 physical impairment: female	2 visual impairments: 1 male, 1 female
Religion	36 Muslims	3 Hindus
		27 Muslims

STEPS INVOLVED IN COLLECTING DATA FROM THE FIELD

After I chose the schools, I was ready to spend time with the children in each one to conduct the planned research methods. In the succeeding sections, I unpack the details of how I conducted each method. The methods are presented in a linear fashion in this chapter, but, as with most research journeys, the path was not always linear. Rather, it was at times recursive and simultaneous.

Unstructured Observations

I entered the field as a participant observer. The classic definition of participant observation is:

> The method in which the observer participates in the daily life of the people under study, either openly in the role of the researcher or covertly in some disguised role, observing things that happen, listening to what is said, and questioning people, over some length of time. (Becker and Geer 1957, cited in Denscombe 2010, p. 206)

That was specifically my goal: to enter each school and establish close relationships with the children and teacher(s), allowing them to recognize my role as a researcher (Robson 1993; Denscombe 2003). Establishing close relationships was necessary for this inquiry as it dealt primarily with children, with whom building rapport became essential (Lewis and Lindsay 2000). When I observed, I used unstructured methods in the field with no preconceived notions as to the discrete behaviors I might observe.

I picked up what was important and determined how to focus on those aspects as "the field" unfolded in front of me. I observed for a total of 28 hours covering seven full class sessions at School "U" and 16 hours covering four full class sessions at School "M." An important point to mention here is that even if my goal was to capture the essence of the organically flowing classroom as an outsider, the extent to which this was possible must be questioned. For example, at times the students and teachers behaved in prescribed ways. At School "U," the teacher disciplined her students often. At both schools children were admonished quickly for bad behavior. This indicated to me that the school staff, although involved and excited in the project, may have felt a sense of discomfort at times owing to my presence.

Photovoice

Increasingly, qualitative researchers have embraced visual methods, especially photography, as a means to create, represent, and disseminate knowledge (Schell et al. 2009). There are various photographic methodologies, and in my research I used Photovoice, a form of visual inquiry that emphasizes the role of participants, which are usually people with little money, power, or status, to take and use photographic images to engender collaborative reflection on local phenomena. When working with children, the methodology of Photovoice must undergo slight shifts, however. Often social constructivists working with children utilize Photovoice to emphasize the role of participants in taking and using photographic images. However, it is not always clear whether those types of research can directly result in facilitating social change at grassroots and policy levels. In my research, I approached Photo-voice in this manner, wherein the participation of children in actually taking photos were most emphasized.

At the schools, as a facilitator, I conducted a Photovoice project within one week at each school. During this task, my goal was twofold. The first goal was to discover what pupils considered important aspects in enjoying their school life and feeling included in their environment (Cook and Hess 2007). The second was to discover what pupils considered unimportant in enjoying their school life and what made them feel excluded from their environment. As this was an inquiry into inclusive education, I did not exclude any pupil from participating in the Photovoice project (unless he or she chose to be excluded). However, soon into the project, I realized that, overall, a majority the children were not comfortable taking photos of things they disliked. In order to gather knowledge on children's dislikes, I therefore had to adjust my methodological plan and adopt free-associative writing methods, which are described later in this chapter.

The photo sessions consisted of several steps. Using digital mobile phone cameras it involved asking children to take practice photos, taking the actual photos, and disseminating and discussing the the photos. The whole process was monitored closely by the teacher and me. Further into the project, some "experts" emerged among the groups of children, and pupils helped one another to take the photos. Child expertise was encouraged, keeping in mind the PAR framework.

At each school, although similar steps were followed to conduct this activity, the Photovoice experiences were different, and I faced some challenges along the way. One challenge that impacted my work extensively came out of School "U."

In the small, approximately 336-square-foot room of School "U,"[5] it was not possible for the children not to impact one another's work. Therefore, as each group took photos on the same day, I noticed some stark similarities between the photographs. Thus, the relative independence in each child's thought process during the Photovoice project at School "U" is questionable. Whether a photo truly depicted a child's personal choice is not clear. For example, when one participant, from Group *Surjo Mukhi* (Sunflower), took the first picture of his favorite item at school—a lesson he liked called "*Mou Macchhi*" (Bumble Bee)—almost all members of his group felt compelled to take similar photos of lessons they liked. Hence, during the photographing process, even when requested to focus on items outside the lesson books, the children in this group chose not to do so. To overcome this obstacle, during the reflections, together we focused on thrashing out the reasons, meanings, or application of the photos to their school's experience. I asked the children if their photos meant something in relation to their school experience. As the children wrote in their reflections and explained later on, often they did. The children mentioned how the lessons they photographed inspired and impacted their behavior both in and out of school.

One criticism that could be made here is the question of why I decided to stay with the Photovoice method if it faced critical obstacles in the field. Although I agree that qualitative research is about rigor, knowledge production, internal validity, and consistency, to me the strains of PAR that I drew from emphasized the importance of engagement, processes, and participant involvement. The fact that children did not feel comfortable taking dislike photos did not negate their enthusiasm and excitement about using cameras for the photos they did want to take about their school, as photography was a novel experience for all of them. Further, creating space within the research process wherein children's choices and voices could have value and direction in the research was a paramount epistemological issue for me. Last, I could access the information on dislikes in other measures relative to the expression of a form of communication (albeit what is communicated has the potential of slight alteration), and reflexivity has been used to create transparency through that process. These are the reasons why I still utilized photos regardless of the obstacles I faced.

Questionnaire

I also used a questionnaire in the field. I considered the questionnaire a good methodological addition for getting specific answers for my research questions because, as Denscombe (2003) noted, it is "fitting in a range of options offered by the researcher" (p. 159). I based the questionnaire on three points: (1) a pre-phenomenological analysis of the photographs of children's likes; (2) a reflection on the themes considered necessary in inclusive schools as outlined in the *Index for Inclusion: Developing Learning and Participation in Schools* (Booth et al. 2000); and (3) my previous experience of having worked with BRAC students. The questionnaire, therefore, directly asked the children to reflect more coherently and specifically on thematic issues relevant to inclusive education, such as their peer relations, classroom organization, and their teacher's behaviors. A total of 50 questionnaire questions were administered over two school days. At School "U," 34 students completed the questionnaire; at School "M," 27 students did.

I administered the questionnaires in larger group settings inside each school. The classroom teacher at each school, who was familiar with the children's reading and writing level, facilitated the session. In looking at the questions beforehand, the teacher informed me that they would not be difficult for her pupils. Then we got started. I did ask the children to put their names on their respective sheets just so I could return it to them for our second session the following day. It is essential to consider that the children included their names on the questionnaire and the impact that may have had on the results. Other issues that may have impacted the results include my presence, the teacher's presence, the school as the venue, the wording of the questions, the children's tendencies to show conformity regarding answers, peer discussions, and the overall classroom setting.

Informal Focus Groups: Addas

I followed up the questionnaire session with informal focus groups, or *addas*. Hennessy and Heary (2005) explained that focus groups have several advantages over other methods, especially when working with children. These advantages include: creating a safe peer environment and replicating the type of small-group settings that children are familiar with in the classroom; redressing the power imbalance between adults and children that exists in one-to-one interviews; providing an encouraging environment for the children; and jogging their memory as they hear the contributions of others (Hill et al. 1996; Mauthner 1997). For the specific context of Bangladesh, focus groups were especially effective because they resonate with one of the most widely practiced trends of information exchange in Bengal—the *adda* (pronounced "uddah"). *Addas* can be defined as long, informal conversations held between friends—popular among people of all classes, ages, and places, including schools and colleges (Chakrabarty 1999). Framed as an *adda*, or friendly banter, and not as a simple question and answer information session, my goal was to allow group conversations to flow in a more fun, relevant, and interactive manner. Further, it worked to contextualize and make more relevant a foreign methodology while at the same time balancing out the power relationships between the participants and me, the researcher.

Two large *adda* sessions were carried out at each school. At School "U," 34 of the 36 students were present on the day of the first *adda* and 33 out of 36 on the second. At School "M," 28 out of 30 participated on the first day and 29 out of 30 on the second. In each school, two days and approximately two to three hours were dedicated to each *adda* session. During the sessions held at the respective schools, I addressed each questionnaire question in more detail. I reminded the students to also think back on their photographs during the sessions.

During the *addas*, in order to get the children to converse about their school, I had to keep the conversational space safe. With the teacher's help, I had to minimize any incipient arguments. I also had to keep the group on task, working to eliminate power imbalances and personal biases, and had to bring the conversations to a close properly. I also made sure that I allowed enough silent time and space for children to take the time they needed to respond; when they could not answer a specific topic or question, I encouraged them to make spontaneous contributions.

Each of the *adda* sessions was voice recorded. Some of the recordings had great amounts of background noise, which made the sometimes short, curt monosyllabic words of the younger children difficult to understand. I had to go back and question those children again on several occasions. Therefore, throughout the *addas* and even afterward as I was working with children, I had to probe and ask for clarification several times in order to elicit detailed and relevant answers. Further, the children's responses often went off in tangents that had nothing to do with the topic of discussion. Therefore, throughout the process, I had to reflect and patiently weigh the given responses while also being aware of group dynamics, tensions, and sensitive moments in the activity.

Communicating Through Writing

As I conducted my research, it began to become more and more clear, during the photo sessions and the *addas*, that children wanted to have a more private and individual method of communicating. Therefore, I had to incorporate writing into the research procedures. According to Freeman and Mathison (2009), for the purpose of research with children, writing should not be defined in narrow terms. They explained that communicating through writing in research can entail responding to prompts in conventional paragraph or essay form; expressive forms of journaling, sketches, cartoons, free associative writing, and poetry; and responses to questions while sitting side by side. In the schools, the children produced different variations of pieces of writing.[6] In School "U," where I spent more time and the children were older, a greater number of pieces were produced. Moreover, the children depended more on writing in that school. In Table 2.2, I have summarized the written documents produced at each school.

Table 2.2 Written documents

School "U"	*School "M"*
A. Explanation of photos with reasons why	A. Explanation of photos with reasons why
B. Detailed list of dislikes at school with reasons why	B. Summarized list of dislikes at school
C. My best friend and why	C. My best friend and why
D. If we had "X" at school, it would have been good, and reasons why	D. –
E. Poems and/or paragraphs about school, and benefits of coming to school	E. –

The free associative processes A through E gave the children time to stop and think about their responses individually before answering. This was an effective mechanism, as it was not always possible to ensure the children's privacy from the two adults, the teacher and me, and from the rest of the children. Further, shy students were not comfortable speaking up. Writing allowed them to participate and contribute more comfortably and effectively. In addition, since it was given as "classwork" on a tangible sheet of paper that the children could write on, it was an effective way to get their attention and keep it there. For example, when it came to writing poems and paragraphs about school (which a single student nonchalantly suggested in conversation), the children displayed exceptional openness and creativity. Again, involving students in the research method had to do with my epistemological inclination toward PAR.

Memos

As explained by Arora (2012), memoing is a practice that helps researchers clarify thoughts about the research. Originally used in grounded theory approaches, memos can help document researchers' journeys by creating a space where researchers can reflect on their reactions after a certain methodological endeavor, expose personal thoughts and feelings, consider with their biases, and reflect on prior or current experience (Birks et al. 2008).

While I was in the field, I kept a reflective journal. This was not a method I conducted "with" participants but rather as a practice of reflexivity throughout my research process and during the writing phase. In this journal, I recorded reflective memos regularly. As I wrote the memos, usually after each methodological endeavor or classroom observation, they became a rich source of information, especially if I needed to double check and cross-reference information on emerging themes, refresh my memory on how I felt about certain situations, understand my reactions to quotes and words participants had used, or question certain incidents and what they meant for my research. Self-reflexive memoing for me is connected to PAR, especially in the Global South, where the meanings of PAR are in transition. Memoing is a useful way to assess how PAR methods actually play out in the Southern context through researchers, who are often the bearers of "Northern" tools and knowledge. If the intention of PAR is to empower participants on the field, keeping self-reflexive memos in real time can allow researchers to check back on whether, through each research process and endeavor, participants were empowered and, if not, how the process faltered. Here researchers are the medium, as they always are, but now researchers are fully aware of the self as the medium in the research process and know how that self impacted that specific PAR process in the given research context.

BRIDGING THE DISCUSSION

After I conducted the observations, Photovoice sessions, the questionnaire, *addas*, free-associative writing, and memos in the field, I was left with a huge amount of data, including written words, recorded conversations, visuals, and questionnaire results. Specifically, in the major data collections, I had 65 photos, 61 completed questionnaires, and a total of 360 pages of typed data. As previously mentioned, considerations of trustworthiness and ethics were paramount when I collected these data, but a discussion on those issues is beyond the scope of this chapter. I also do not discuss the details of the intricate processes of phenomenological data analysis. Rather, in the next section, I scrutinize and reflect on an important field issue that occurred during the data collection process and has more clearly in line with PAR and reflexivity. This is the issue of "voice." This discussion is very important because my data in essence are supposed to be representations of participants' voices. My data are supposed to be a result of childrens' answers to my queries. Yet is this issue of voice as straightforward as it seemed to be in this study, or are some struggles and questions embedded within it?

THE METHODOLOGICAL STRUGGLE OF "VOICE" AND ITS RELATIONSHIP TO PAR AND REFLEXIVITY

As a researcher working in a Southern context with children, it is important for me to reflect on and clarify the point of the "representation of voice" in my research. This is especially important because the issue of voice is intrinsically linked to epistemologies of PAR (Ahsan 2009) and reflexivity, as an important consideration on the degree of power and autonomy in any given research context. Hence, for me, voice was a methodological struggle in the field. This struggle was just as important as other research field considerations, such as methods or sampling, and at times it was even more important because, while working with children, I constantly had to be wary of what James (2007, p. 262) called the three interlocking dangers in childhood research:

1. Matters of authenticity or how children need to be "given a hand" and only then can their voices "be heard."
2. The risk of lumping children together into a single homogenous group that has "one, undifferentiated voice" and no diversity or multivocality among the children.
3. Not questioning the nature of children's participation in the study as well as the differences of power that impact how the research is conducted.

While conducting an inquiry with children, the relationship between the researcher and the participant is of utmost importance. According to the seminal work by James (2007), childhood researchers need to critically reflect on their role in the process of representing children's voices in their work. James suggested that the way to do this is be to "[revisit] … in whatever cultural context, and in relation to any child, [the] relationship [that] defines who [children] are, how we as adult researchers understand them, and how they understand their own experiences" (p. 270). In other words, researchers need not only to represent children's voices but also to explore the "authenticity" of that voice by further scrutinizing the realities of the exchange that occurred between researcher and participant allowing for the "emergence of the voice" in the first place. Moreover, in childhood studies, we must be able to deconstruct the very notion of "voice" and be aware of how much autonomy, rationality, and intention the child's speaking voice actually has (Komulainen 2007). Voice, according to Komulainen (2007), is actually social and co-constructed rather than individual, fixed, straightforward, linear, or clear. Voice definitely is shaped by a multitude of factors, such as our use of language and assumptions about children, the institutional contexts in which we operate, and the overall ideological and discursive climates that prevail (Spyrou 2011; Komulainen 2007). Last, but importantly, as explained by Spyrou (2011) and by Jackson and Mazzei (2008), it is almost impossible to grasp voice and represent its essence due to the problem of "authenticity." The problem rests largely on our wrongly held assumption that it is possible to capture the authentic essence through words people speak. The best we can do as researchers is to reflect on the power relations and contextual realities that led to the words in question to be spoken and to present them transparently. The issue of the representation of voice in my study can best be illustrated through three examples from the field. Each example draws on a different aspect of the process. The first is one of gaining access, the second is related to the use of a certain method, and the third is an example in which power relations were switched. All three examples highlight the organic and constant manner in which the issue of voice permeated this study and how, at certain times, it was not possible for me to separate it from my methodological process.

Children's Voices Getting Lost in Negotiating Access

The first salient episode that impacted the representation of voice was the process of negotiating access. In order to access both the schools and the pupils within the schools, I had to negotiate and renegotiate my terms of access with the adult gatekeepers, including officials at BRAC's head office, several program officers overseeing each school, and classroom teachers. In total, at the two schools, I had to negotiate access with six gatekeepers from BRAC's side (not including the parents) in order to approach the children. The parents also had to be consulted as I was working with children below the age of 18. The process of gaining access through various hierarchies of adult gatekeepers impacted the "authenticity" of the children's "voice." As mentioned by Ahsan (2009), in her own work, this same process of negotiating access to children's voices through multiple adult gatekeepers made the young people vulnerable not only to feeling disempowered in their choice to be a part of the project but also greatly filtered how they voice themselves, or what information they impart to the researcher in the project. This struggle to identify the authentic voice, and whether that is even possible, can be illustrated by reflexively discussing some examples.

The adult gatekeepers, especially the classroom teacher and the program officers, usually were present during most of my research exercises. Their relationship and views of the children in the classroom impacted the children's words, and this occurred in slightly different ways in my first visit to both schools "U" and "M." Twice after the children were introduced and we spoke briefly to get acquainted with each other, the program officers who knew about my project launched into a speech. These speeches, by different men, consisted of the topic of how I had arrived from "a faraway land, Canada," "all the way" to listen to what they, the children, have to say about school. On both occasions the men mentioned how special this ought to make the children feel. At School "U," the program officer said, for example, "Do everything you can to help *Apa* [Apa means "older sister" or "respected sister" in Bengali] out. Answer her when she asks a question." I remember stepping in to say that no one was required to answer anything; however, he went on to explain in front of the class that, "after all," they were Grade 3 children who must often be reminded what their purpose will be in this project and that if they did not answer me, why would I work with them? Then he turned to the pupils and said, "Won't you all speak to Apa?" At that point, all children nodded that they would. In the field, I could not prevent such "intrusions," as they were all conducted out of goodwill on part of the people who granted me access in the first place. They felt they had the right to exercise their positions, which often entailed helping me along the way and mediating between me and the children. Hence, while gathering my data, I had to be aware of how much authenticity, autonomy, rationality, and intention the child's speaking voice actually had (Komulainen 2007). How much of any of those four aspects can a child actually have when he or she feels compelled to speak on a topic? In a culture such as Bangladesh's, where obedience is highly valued and children's positions in a community are often based on their degree of obedience to their elders, how much authenticity or autonomy does the looming ideology of obedience allow? If instructed to participate by the program officer, does a child really have autonomous power to decide not to be a part of my project? In other words, Ahsan's (2009) point is that negotiating access to children's voice through multiple adult gatekeepers makes young people vulnerable in significant ways that impact the very outcome of the project's findings; I faced this reality throughout my fieldwork. Therefore, I had to continuously question how I could gain access the children's authentic voice and whether my research methodology needed to be tweaked along the way. This is where tools of PAR were most useful. I tried to read children's stated and unstated words, intentions, and language in order to incorporate some of what they wanted. Beazley et al. (2009) well explained the situation:

> We have found through experience that the best action-oriented research results from a process in which all researchers (including children) have a stake in all aspects of the research, from identifying the topic to writing the report and disseminating the results. Yet, when children are included as researchers or even as research assistants, the question arises "Where should the adult researcher position him/herself in the process of children-focused, rights-based research?" Positionality is [an essential issue] ... there is always a role for adults in research with children—even if children are involved in all aspects. [Others] challenge the idea of adopting the role of "atypical" or "incompetent" adult. (p. 375)

Hence, working with children within the PAR framework in the Global South is complex and messy. There is no one formula that researchers can use; rather, they must adapt and hone in on each specific context in a continuous struggle and opportunity as they embark on this journey.

Quiet Voices Getting Lost in the Crowd

When I entered the field, I assumed that the design of my informal focus groups—*addas*—would work effectively to capture pupils' voices in an informal and playful manner. Although the methodology was largely successful in providing a communal way for pupils to come forward, as it encouraged spontaneity and "group-force" (Sawyer 2006), there were some disadvantages: (1) how authentic can individual voices be when "group-force" is present, and (2) can shy students feel comfortable enough in groups? For example, one very outspoken pupil, whom I will call Roni, age 10, was often seen "leading" the conversation in his *adda* group, and, although his voice was represented in the group, what he said impacted his friends and made some of the girls feel uncomfortable. When Roni first said that he looked forward to come to school because it gave him an opportunity to interact with his friends and also sing and dance, somehow this became the reason of the majority of the students in that group. For some other students, once Roni contributed, they could not do the same because they stated that they did not have such a "good story" for coming to school and were "scared of talking" since they had nothing interesting to add. For such students, I had to switch to writing.

Oppositional Model of Voice: Choosing Cameras

Another example of my struggle with the representation of voice occurred during my decision regarding the use of certain cameras. However, this occasion was distinctly different from the previous one and allowed me to question the oppositional model of the power of voice (Gallagher 2008) in which power is seen as a commodity held by the dominant adult group and not by the subordinate children. This conceptualization masks the complex and multiple ways power is exercised as well as its impact on voice in the research field. Thus, it is possible, at times, for children to have greater control over the research process when they appropriate their autonomous and authentic voice for their own interests (Ahsan 2009), regardless of the researcher–participant dynamic. Also, like Ahsan, since I was in the field as a native young female attempting to take on the role of a friendly adult employing participatory and artistic research techniques, I sometimes was in a position in which the children ended up exerting control over me. This was most apparent when the use of cameras came into question.

I entered the field with disposable cameras with which the children could snap pictures, which would later be developed and shared in the classroom. However, after entering the first school, "U," and trying to use those cameras, one of the older students, whom I will call Robi, age 13, asked, "Apa, your phone doesn't have a camera?" I replied that it did, and he said, "Can I use your phone camera? I have a camera in my dad's phone I have used it before."

At first I was hesitant to allow the children to use my phone and my iPod; however, they were not sufficiently motivated to participate actively when using disposable cameras. They did not overtly state their disdain for the disposable cameras but rather displayed it, looking at me in confusion when I insisted that they be used. Perhaps they did not like the yellow paper covering on the cameras, or the fact that they could not see the picture(s) they took instantly. Furthermore, they found it somewhat flimsy and hard to use.

Much like what happened to Ahsan (2009), I experienced a moment where the young people's power and voice overpowered my own. They appropriated the situation to fit their own preferences, and as we reverted to using my phone and iPod cameras, I saw how I started to gain a sense of camaraderie and rapport with them. Further, these cameras allowed the children to have much more control over the photography activity, wherein they had more of an instant say as to whether they wanted a certain picture to represent their likes in the classroom. If they disliked a certain photo, they could take another one right away. In short, the decision to use the phone or iPod camera was made by the children (almost covertly) but still demonstrates that within the organic dynamics of certain research processes and contexts, the tables can be turned on the exercise of voice.

Concluding Remarks

In this chapter, I outlined in detail my research with children at two BRAC primary schools by utilizing an aspect of PAR and the tools of reflexivity. I addressed issues such as context, worldviews, and methods of data collection in the struggle to locate children's authentic voice in research. It is clear that, regardless of the rigor of the method used, finding authentic voice is an elusive and complicated endeavor. As I explained earlier, I did not unpack my findings or extend deeply into my analytical framework utilizing Tagore's humanistic approach to research.

Through my reflexive journey on each research issue and decision, my goal has always been to remain transparent and engaging in order to illustrate the organic and multifaceted relationship that research requires of both "doer" and "knower." It is never an easy path to tread and the process is often messy, filled with ups and downs, limitations, and struggles. Nevertheless, the goal for me as a researcher was always to take problems in stride and move forward to unearth children's perspectives on their inclusive experiences at their respective schools. This is an important endeavor because working through reflexivity with children in Southern contexts, framed within PAR, is rare. Hence, this study contributes to the body of work that some scholars are exploring. Further, it depicts the messy and often compartmentalized but at the same time flowing aspects of research in which complex terrain is simultaneously bound and broken. Especially in cases of PAR, where power, participation, and voice intermingle in new and novel ways, breaking through ceilings of what used to define research, today there is fertile ground for understanding who plays the major role in defining research outcomes and impacting what we explore, find, analyze, and then share with the world.

Notes

1. As defined by the Center for the Global South of the American University (2016), the Global South can refers to the nations of Africa, Central and Latin America, and most of Asia:countries that currently face great political, social, and economic challenges and generally are "poorer" in the sense of their gross domestic products. Further, most of the countries of the Global South share a colonial past and are not in dominant positions in international developments but rather have less developed or severely limited resources. Hence, the populations of these nations bear the larger share of the brunt of poverty, environmental degradation, human and civil rights abuses, ethnic and regional conflicts, mass displacements of refugees, hunger, and disease (Singal 2004).
2. BRAC is the largest nongovernmental organization in the world and currently is active in diverse fields, such as education, health, women empowerment, and sustainable development. Its main aim is to alleviate poverty in the Global South.

3. "Friendly banter or conversations" in Bengali.
4. Bengali word for easy flowing but informative conversations between friends.
5. The room of School "M" was not substantially bigger. However, the problem of groupthink did not impact the sessions at this school as the students made a list of their liked items individually first and then photographed those items. I initiated this small change due to the obstacles I had faced at School "U."
6. The order in which the "written documents" were carried out is needs to be considered. They are presented at a certain juncture in the thesis, but in the actual research process, they were conducted as and when gaps came up. Fieldwork is rarely a linear process. For example, soon after I identified the children's preference not to take photos of their dislikes, I asked them to write about it before moving on to other activities. Even after the *adda* sessions, children wrote about who their best friends were and why. At each school, the order in which the written "assignments" appeared also differed.

REFERENCES

Ahsan, M. (2009). The potential and challenges of rights-based research with children and young people: Experiences from Bangladesh. *Children's Geographies*, 7(4), 393. doi:10.1080/14733280903234451.

American University: Center for Global South. (2016, June 20). *Homepage*. Retrieved from http://www1.american.edu/academic.depts/acainst/cgs/about.html

Arora, R. P. (2012). *Discovering the postmodern nomad: An artful inquiry into the career stories of emerging adults transitioning under the Caribbean sun*. Unpublished doctoral dissertation. McGill University Faculty of Education, Montreal, Quebec.

Baum, F., MacDougall, C., & Smith, D. (2006). Participatory action research. *Journal of Epidemiology and Community Health*, 60(10), 854–857. doi:10.1136/jech.2004.028662.

Beazley, H., Bessell, S., Ennew, J., & Waterson, R. (2009). The right to be properly researched: Research with children in a messy, real world. *Children's Geographies*, 7(4), 365–378. doi:10.1080/14733280903234428.

Birks, M., Chapman, Y., & Francis, K. (2008). Memoing in qualitative research: Probing data and processes. *Journal of Research in Nursing*, 13(1), 68–75. doi:10.1177/1744987107081254.

Booth, T., Ainscow, M., Black-Hawkins, K., Vaughan, M., & Shaw, I. (2000). *Index for inclusion: Developing learning and participation in schools*. Bristol, UK: Centre for Studies on Inclusive Education.

Butler-Kisber, L. (2010). *Qualitative inquiry: Thematic, narrative and arts-informed perspectives.* Thousand Oaks, CA: SAGE.
Chakrabarty, D. (1999). Adda, Calcutta: Dwelling in modernity. *Public Culture, 11*(1), 109–145. doi:10.1215/08992363-11-1-109.
Cook, T., & Hess, E. (2007). What the camera sees and from whose perspective: Fun methodologies for engaging children in enlightening adults. *Childhood, 14*(1), 29–45. doi:10.1177/0907568207068562.
Creswell, J. W. (2007). *Qualitative inquiry and research design: Choosing among five approaches.* Thousand Oaks, CA: SAGE.
Crotty, M. J. (1998). *The foundations of social research: Meaning and perspective in the research process.* London: Sage.
Denscombe, M. (2003). *The good research guide for small-scale social research projects* (2nd ed.). Maidenhead, UK: Open University Press.
Denscombe, M. (2010). *The good research guide for small-scale social research projects* (4th ed.). Maidenhead, England: Open University Press.
Denzin, N. K., & Lincoln, Y. S. (Eds.). (2005). *The SAGE handbook of qualitative research* (3rd ed.). Thousand Oaks, CA: SAGE.
Du Bois, W. E. B. (2007). *Dusk of dawn: An essay toward an autobiography of a race concept: The Oxford W.E.B. Du Bois Reader* (Vol. 8). Oxford: Oxford University Press.
Finlay, L. (2002). Negotiating the swamp: The opportunity and challenge of reflexivity in research practice. *Qualitative Research, 2* (2), 209–230. doi:10.1177/146879410200200205.
Freeman, M., & Mathison, S. (2009). *Researching children's experiences.* New York: Guilford.
Gallagher, M. (2008). 'Power is not an evil': Rethinking power in participatory methods. *Children's Geographies, 6*(2), 137–150. doi:10.1080/14733280801963045.
Giorgi, A. (1994). A phenomenological perspective on certain qualitative research methods. *Journal of Phenomenological Psychology, 25*(2), 190–220. doi:10.1163/156916294x00034.
Greenwood, D. J., Whyte, W. F., & Harkavy, I. (1993). Participatory action research as a process and as a goal. *Human Relations, 46*(2), 175–192.
Hennessy, E., & Heary, C. (2005). Exploring children's views through focus groups. In S. Greene & D. Hogan (Eds.), *Researching children's experiences methods and approaches* (pp. 236–252). London: SAGE.
Hill, M., Laybourn, A., & Borland, M. (1996). Engaging with primary-aged children about their emotions and well-being: Methodological considerations. *Children & Society, 10* (2), 129–144. doi:10.1111/j.1099-0860.1996.tb00463.x.
James, A. (2007). Giving voice to children's voices: Practices and problems, pitfalls and potentials. *American Anthropologist, 109* (2), 261–272. doi:10.1525/aa.2007.109.2.261.

Komulainen, S. (2007). The ambiguity of the child's 'voice' in social research. *Childhood, 14*(1), 11–28. doi:10.1177/0907568207068561.
Lewis, A., & Lindsay, G. (2000). *Researching children's perspectives.* Buckingham, UK: Open University Press.
Mauthner, M. (1997). Methodological aspects of collecting data from children: Lessons from three research projects. *Children & Society, 11* (1), 16–28. doi:10.1111/j.1099-0860.1997.tb00003.x.
Maxey, I. (1999). Beyond boundaries? Activism, academia, reflexivity and research. *Area, 31* (3), 199–208.
Mazzei, L. (2008). An impossibly full voice. In L. A. Mazzei & A. Y. Jackson (Eds.), *Voice in qualitative inquiry: Challenging conventional, interpretive, and critical conceptions in qualitative research* (pp. 45–62). New York: Routledge.
McDowell, L. (2001). 'It's that Linda again': Ethical, practical and political issues involved in longitudinal research with young men. *Ethics, Place and Environment, 4* (2), 87–100. doi:10.1080/13668790120061460.
Mukherjee, M. (2015). *Inclusive education and school reform in postcolonial India.* Unpublished doctoral dissertation, University of Melbourne Graduate School of Education, Melbourne, Australia.
Mukherjee, M., & Mahbub, T. (2015). *"Double consciousness" of transnational researchers in the Global South: Ethical dilemmas of space and intercultural dialogue.* Paper presented at the 2015 American Educational Research Association Conference, Chicago, IL, April 26–20.
Punch, S. (2002). Research with children: The same or different from research with adults? *Childhood, 9* (3), 321–341. doi:10.1177/0907568202009003005.
Riessman, C. K. (2005). Exporting ethics: A narrative about narrative research in South India. *Health: An Interdisciplinary Journal for the Social Study of Health, Illness and Medicine, 9* (4), 1363–4593. doi:10.1177/1363459305056414.
Robson, C. (1993). *Real world research: A resource for social scientists and Practitioner-researchers* (1st ed.). Oxford: Blackwell.
Sawyer, R. K. (2006). Educating for innovation. *Thinking Skills and Creativity, 1*(1), 41–48. doi:10.1016/j.tsc.2005.08.001.
Schell, K., Ferguson, A., Hamoline, R., Shea, J., & Thomas-Maclean, R. (2009). Photovoice as a teaching tool: Learning by doing with visual methods. *International Journal of Teaching and Learning in Higher Education, 21*(3), 340–352.
Spyrou, S. (2011). The limits of children's voices: From authenticity to critical, reflexive representation. *Childhood, 18*(2), 151–165. doi:10.1177/0907568210387834.
Valentine, G. (1999). Being seen and heard? The ethical complexities of working with children and young people at home and at school. *Ethics, Place and Environment, 2* (2), 141–155.

CHAPTER 3

The ASER "Translating Policy into Practice" Toolkit: From Participatory Action Research to Evidence-Based Action

Suman Bhattacharjea and Erik Jon Byker

It is the beginning of a warm autumn morning in rural Faridabad, just south of New Delhi in the Indian state of Haryana. The bellowing of cows can be heard as they munch on vegetation next to fields of *jowar* (sorghum) and *bajra* (millet). Children are making their way to school for another day of studies. At a bus stop on the main road to Faridabad, teacher candidates exit a bus and walk down a dusty path to the District Institute of Education Training (DIET), where they are studying to become primary school teachers in Haryana's government-run public schools.[1]

Today the teacher candidates at the Faridabad DIET are making field visits to nearby elementary schools. They are accompanied by staff from Pratham, India's largest nongovernmental organization focused on education, and from its research and evaluation unit known as ASER Centre.

S. Bhattacharjea (✉)
ASER Centre, New Delhi, India
e-mail: sbhattacharjea@gmail.com

E.J. Byker
University of North Carolina at Charlotte, Charlotte, NC, USA
e-mail: ebyker@gmail.com

© The Author(s) 2017
H. Kidwai et al. (eds.), *Participatory Action Research and Educational Development*, South Asian Education Policy, Research, and Practice,
DOI 10.1007/978-3-319-48905-6_4

They had spent the previous day learning about India's Right of Children to Free and Compulsory Education Act (RTE), which was passed in 2009, and understanding how to use a survey tool to collect basic data on whether the schools they would be visiting were in compliance with the provisions of the act. With pencils and survey formats in hand, groups of six to seven teacher candidates squeeze into auto-rickshaws and are carted off to government-run schools within about a six-mile radius of the DIET.

When the teacher candidates arrive at the school, they first meet with the school's principal or head teacher. They share the purpose of their visit and explain how they will use the survey to collect information about the school. They ask the head teacher questions about the school's daily schedule and teacher and student strengths. Then they walk through the school observing and recording students' and teachers' attendance for that day, the school's facilities and infrastructure (e.g., checking whether there are working toilets for both the girls and boys; blackboards in each classroom; etc.). In all, the teacher candidates spend more than two hours in the school.

The field visit culminates with a bumpy auto-rickshaw trip back to the DIET. Upon their return, the teacher candidates debrief and reflect on their experience in the eight or ten schools they have visited between them. They start with a question about what they observed while at the school. Teacher candidates are eager to share. One explains how she noticed the murals painted on the school walls, such as the one that spelled out TEACHER in capital letters. Each letter stood for a teaching trait:

T – Trained
E – Enlightened
A – Alert
C – Creative
H – Honest
E – Energetic
R – Responsible

Another teacher candidate shares how she noticed the STUDENT acronym mural spelled out as:

S – Sincerity
T – Tolerance
U – Unity
D – Dedication
E – Earnestness

N – Neatness
T – Thoughtfulness

The teacher candidates discussed how the words in the acronyms captured the ideals of being a teacher and a student. However, the realities of the schools were somewhat different. The teacher candidates began looking through the data they had collected using the survey tool. They commented that two teachers had been absent from one field visit school and that a school's computer lab was locked and the key seemed to be missing. One teacher candidate commented that using the survey tool was eye-opening and enlightening. Another shared, "Before doing these field visits, I never had a chance to think about a school in these ways."

This chapter began with a descriptive narrative of how teacher candidates use a survey tool to identify and analyze the types of resources available in government-run public schools and to compare their findings to policy objectives. During other sessions, teacher candidates use different tools to collect data on other aspects of the primary schools in their vicinity. These tools include a rapid assessment of children's foundational learning skills, a questionnaire examining the role of parents and the School Management Committee in the school, and a simple classroom observation tool to capture some aspects of teacher–children interactions in the classroom. These tools, and the teaching-learning processes in which their use is embedded, are designed to help teacher candidates view their future places of employment through a number of different lenses and to reflect on how best to fill the gaps that they identify. Together, these sessions are known as Translating Policy into Practice (TPP) workshops.

As the comment of the teacher candidate quoted earlier reflects, schools are seldom viewed through these different lenses. Evidence from the ground is rarely used to inform either macro-level policy decisions or local-level thinking about what teachers need to know and do. In the DIETs and elsewhere, teacher candidates are taught about the curriculum they will be required to transact with children but not how to tailor their actions to the context in which they will be doing so.

The instruments used in the TPP workshops have a common genesis. Each tool has either been used in the national assessment of children's foundational learning abilities known as the ASER, or is an adaption of one of these tools, or else is designed with the same principles in mind. The tools are simple to understand and quick to administer, requiring no prior knowledge or expertise; the data they generate are easy to analyze and communicate; and the findings are straightforward to translate into concrete action on the ground. Like the ASER survey itself, which is described later in this chapter, these tools are designed to facilitate the engagement of ordinary people in evidence-based discussions of important issues in the school education sector. We refer to this collection of tools and processes as the ASER TPP toolkit.

Like any toolkit, the contents of the ASER TPP toolkit can be combined in different ways to suit a range of purposes and contexts. The toolkit can be used by teacher candidates, education policy makers, and everyday citizens. The contents of the toolkit go beyond just survey instruments; they are tools for social action. This chapter examines how the ASER TPP toolkit is an instrument for participatory action research (PAR). To do so, we describe and report on a case study of the uses and perceptions on the ASER toolkit by 62 teacher candidates. The case study includes a mix of qualitative and quantitative research methods.

The chapter is organized into four sections. First, we provide contextual details related to the sociohistorical development of the ASER TPP toolkit. The details include an overview of its origin and evolution within the Pratham network and the ways in which its constituent parts have been used to facilitate the engagement of different stakeholders with issues related to educational quality. Second, we map the chapter's purpose on to the conceptual framework for the possibilities of PAR in the field of education and schooling. Third, we describe and examine in detail a case study of the ways in which teacher candidates from a government teacher training college were introduced to and used the ASER TPP toolkit to enrich their understanding of—and potentially their contribution toward resolving—issues of educational quality in India. Finally, we wrap up the chapter with a discussion of the relationships between PAR and evidence-based action through the ASER TPP toolkit.

BACKGROUND AND CONTEXT FOR THE ASER TPP TOOLKIT

The ASER TPP toolkit has its origins in the ASER survey, an annual, large-scale survey of children's basic learning outcomes in rural India.[2] Conducted every year since 2005, the survey reaches more than 600,000 children across the country each year. At the heart of the ASER survey is a tool for rapid one-on-one assessment of a child's ability to read simple text and do basic arithmetic. Today widely known as the ASER learning assessment tool, this instrument was developed by Pratham, a nongovernmental organization working in the education sector in India for the last 20 years. Pratham currently works in 21 states of India and is committed to high-quality, low-cost, scalable, and replicable interventions to improve children's learning. The mission of Pratham is *every child in school and learning well*. In this context, the learning assessment tool was developed to empower staff with a simple instrument for assessing each child's foundational reading ability; on the basis of the assessment, Pratham staff could make decisions regarding how best to organize and teach their classes. The ASER Centre website (2014) explained: "The tool consisted of a single sheet of paper with four levels of text: letters; simple, common words; a short paragraph consisting of four easy sentences; and a longer text containing slightly more complex vocabulary" (para. 2). Pratham teams found the tool easy to understand and use, both to evaluate what children knew how to do and to establish clear learning goals for each child and for the class as a whole. Children were grouped by their level of reading proficiency and taught using methods and materials appropriate to their ability level. Individual children moved to the next group as their proficiency increased. The tool also provided a framework, metrics, and vocabulary for a common assessment of children's basic reading ability across the Pratham network.

Later, the tool evolved into the ASER learning assessment instrument, which is used as part of the national ASER survey that Pratham facilitates every year. The objective behind the ASER survey was to document the learning levels of elementary-age children on scale via the involvement of thousands of ordinary citizens across the country. The national findings from the first ASER surveys were not surprising to Pratham; they matched the observations Pratham made from its interventions with children over the years. Although by the early 2000s, most of India's children were indeed in school, they were years behind where the curriculum expected them to be with respect to learning. ASER was designed as a household survey of children's basic learning outcomes in rural India which would produce estimates that were representative at district and state levels. In addition to learning assessment data, key household and school-level indicators were collected and refined over time.

The instruments used in the ASER survey can be thought of as citizen-action instruments that enable citizens to collect data on villages, schools, households, and children. Since 2005, the ASER survey tools have been utilized by hundreds of thousands of India's young people, many of them college and university students, who volunteer to go to villages and households and collect data on children's literacy and mathematics levels (ASER 2015; Byker 2014a; Kingdon and French 2010). These volunteers are known as citizen-led basic learning assessors (Byker and Banerjee 2016, p. 5).

The ASER assessment tool remains at the core of the ASER data collection. It is effective because it allows for rapid data collection in the field by the volunteers and encourages interest and discussion on a subject of importance but about which parents and communities often have little information. Teams of volunteers, usually in pairs, conduct the survey in a village over a weekend. The schedule on Saturday, which is usually the first day and typically a school day for many of India's children, starts with a meeting with a visit to the *sarpanch*, or village leader. The objective of this meeting is to share the purpose of the survey and obtain permission to conduct the survey in the village. The meeting is also a useful time to gather basic information about the village's facilities and services, including the schools located there. The volunteer pair then visits the village's largest government-run primary school to collect basic information on school infrastructure and enrollment. After the school visit, the volunteer pair walks around the village and draw a map of the village's geography. On the map, they sketch the boundary roads around the village and draw in significant landmarks, such as temples and health centers, all the while talking to curious passersby about what they are doing and why. They mark the village's center, which is often distinguished by a temple, and then divide the village into four quadrants. The quadrant system is purposeful as it organizes how the volunteer pair will go about the household survey later in the day.

Towards the end of that day and on the second day, usually a Sunday, the volunteer pair randomly selects five households from each quadrant by following a method known as the every fifth household rule. They survey a total of 20 households in the village. During the household survey, the volunteer pair records information about the household's residents and economic status. They then record details of every child living in the household who is between three and sixteen years of age, including the names and educational levels of their parents. They then use the ASER assessment tool to test the basic reading and arithmetic ability of each child in the age group five to sixteen. Depending on the number of children, it takes the volunteer pair 15 to 20 minutes to conduct the survey in each household. Both the tool itself and the process by which it is administered are designed to spark interest, provoke conversation, and facilitate the participation of ordinary people in discussions about educational quality.

The design of the ASER learning assessment tool lends itself to its use for different purposes and in different contexts. For example, in addition to being at the core of India's only annual initiative to measure children's learning outcomes on scale, teachers and teacher candidates can use it to quickly assess their students' basic skill levels in literacy and math and tailor more individualized forms of instruction and remediation accordingly. Citizens can use the ASER assessment tool and data to advocate for the implementation of curricula and pedagogies that help children become proficient in reading and math. Educators and education policy makers can use data from both the ASER school survey and the learning assessment to examine the distance between a policy's stated objectives and the reality on the ground. The ASER tools are versatile, intuitive, and assessor friendly. The inclusion of only a few key indicators and the simple design reduces the usual gaps among data collection, analysis, and action.

One key lesson learned over the initial years of implementing the ASER survey was that simply generating evidence was not enough to improve outcomes. As India lacks a "culture of measurement" (Byker and Banerjee 2016, p. 6), evidence is rarely used to identify problems and design solutions. Therefore, in 2008, after three years of facilitating the ASER survey, ASER Centre was formed as an autonomous assessment, survey, evaluation, and research unit within the Pratham network. Headquartered in New Delhi, ASER Centre has the vision of creating a robust measurement culture where the results of the measurement inform and propel citizens toward action (ASER 2014). In this way, ASER seeks to bridge the gap between theory and practice (Byker and Banerjee 2016). ASER's work revolves around the theory of change that measurement enables understanding; understanding enables communication; and communication facilitates change. Guided by this theory, ASER Centre focuses on generating, analyzing, and communicating evidence related to key social sector outcomes, primarily in the field of education. ASER Centre also guides and facilitates other organizations and institutions to similarly create a culture of measurement.

The ASER survey tools and processes have inspired other countries around the world—including Kenya, Mali, Mexico, Nigeria, Pakistan, Senegal, Tanzania, and Uganda—to implement similar types of annual household-based assessments of basic learning. This approach is now known internationally as the citizen-led assessment model. Countries implementing citizen-led assessment have recently established the People's Action for Learning network. The ASER survey has morphed into a model that has comparative and international utility (Byker and Banerjee 2016).

Within ASER Centre, the principles guiding the design of the learning assessment have been used to expand, adapt, and develop new instruments intended to capture key information about other actors or processes within the education system. A subset of these tools—the TPP toolkit—was developed specifically around key policies in the education sector. All tools in this steadily expanding toolkit are designed to be simple and quick to administer, intuitive to understand, and directly linkable to action on the ground. In parallel, processes that were effective at communicating the utility of this approach were developed and piloted in the form of capacity-building courses and workshops conducted both internally and with a range of partner organizations, from government institutions to college students to staff of other nongovernmental organizations. Over time, effective ways to build understanding of how to collect, understand, and use evidence were identified and refined.[3]

Conceptual Framework

We contend that the ASER TPP toolkit comprises a set of instruments and processes that facilitates citizen-led participatory action research (PAR). These tools are straightforward measurements that provide contextual evidence on different aspects of primary schooling. The evidence is easy to understand and encourages toolkit users to identify concrete actions that need to be taken in order to meet policy objectives, whether these relate to improving school organization and facilities or to improving children's learning. For teacher candidates in particular, the ASER learning assessment tool can potentially transform their vision of the teacher's role from being just a cog in the education system to being an agent of change. A teacher's agency begins with understanding that what she does in the classroom directly impacts opportunities for children to grow and learn. As Suman Bhattacharjea and her colleagues (2011) put it: "If we begin with the assumption that all children can learn, then mechanisms for assessment should be designed to focus attention on the question of what schools can do differently to help children learn better" (p. 86). Helping children learn better is at the heart of PAR in the field of education. Sean Kemmis and his colleagues (2004) explained that PAR is the examination of actual practices and lived experiences in order to effect change.

PAR is a conceptual framework, a methodology, and a social endeavor that provides evidence for the improvement of social practices (Koshy 2009; McTaggart 1991). First, PAR provides a conceptual framework to support data collection in the field of education and development (McTaggart 1991). In addition, scholars assert that PAR encompasses a robust, grassroots methodology for connecting people to policy, especially as it relates to initiatives aimed at the development of underprivileged and marginalized communities (Cooke and Kothari 2001; Hickey and Mohan 2004; Small 1995). We incorporate a number of PAR components as a conceptual lens for our study. Among these components is the possibility of using PAR to guide citizens to investigate challenges—such as teacher absences or resource scarcity in schools—that emerge from their own community context. Building capacity for social change is another PAR component that is fundamental to our chapter. We show how teacher candidates are trained with the policy and pedagogical knowledge critical to carrying out the PAR process (McTaggart 1991; Small 1995). The ASER TPP toolkit provides clear-cut ways to measure the impact of interventions and the implications of policies. We specifically draw on the PAR framework as a lens to examine how teacher candidates use the ASER TPP toolkit to become more aware of national policies that impact education and schooling. Our study examines three research questions framed around the premises of PAR:

1. How are India's DIET teacher candidates being prepared to use the ASER TPP toolkit in India's government-run public schools?
2. What are perceptions among the DIET teacher candidates about their training and field experiences with these tools?
3. To what degree, if any, did the PAR-related experiences with the ASER TPP toolkit affect how the DIET teacher candidates perceive their future teaching practice in India's government-run public schools?

Method

We use the case study method (Yin 2008) to examine the three research questions. Robert Yin (2008) explained that the case study method is a research design for empirical inquiry that allows for the investigation of complex phenomena in authentic contexts. Case study research design allows researchers to examine *how* and *why* questions. A *how* question is useful for identifying how social actors use tools to negotiate and meet their objectives; the *why* question addresses the larger context that situates the actors. To investigate how and why questions, our case study research design uses qualitative and quantitative methods to describe and investigate the study's sample population.

The Setting

The study took place at a two-day TPP workshop at a DIET in the state of Haryana. As the government's teacher training institutions, DIETs exist in almost every district of India. Over the years, increasing numbers of them have partnered with ASER Centre to conduct the annual ASER survey. For example, teacher candidates from 243 DIETs participated in ASER during the 2014 data collection (ASER 2015), surveying 40% of all districts surveyed that year. The ASER survey process involves a short engagement of perhaps a week's duration; during 2015–2016, however, almost 100 DIETs from different states opted to engage in a deeper, year-long partnership with Pratham.

The target population at the Haryana DIET consisted of teacher candidates who were participating in this longer program aiming to improve the ability of teacher candidates to assess student learning levels and organize and teach classes using Pratham's teaching at the right level methodology (Bhattacharjea et al. 2011).[4] As part of this program, in some DIETs students also participate in a series of two-day modules that examine the distance between educational policies and ground realities, known as TPP modules.

The Sample

The study's sample was drawn from teacher candidates who attended the first TPP workshop at a DIET in rural Faridabad, Haryana. The participants' ages ranged from 18 to 20 years. Almost 86% of the participants were female and 14% were male. The majority of the participants lived within about a nine-mile radius of the DIET. In sum, the study's participants included 62 teacher candidates at the DIET.

Data Collection

We collected qualitative and quantitative data. One benefit of using case study research design is that it allows for the inclusion of mixed methods (Creswell 2014; Yin 2008). There were three qualitative data sources: field notes from on-site observations, focus group interviews, and collected artifacts. The field note observations were recorded using time stamp notations and an observation protocol to help guide the note taking. The protocol included taking notes about the TPP training's pedagogies, schedule, and the interactions among the TPP trainers and the study's participants. The focus group interviews were conducted in a semistructured interview approach. The focus group interview question protocol incorporated questions about the participants' word associations with their DIET training as well as their perceptions about the time in the field collecting data. Artifacts like the school surveys that the teacher candidates completed during their training comprised a third source of qualitative data.

There were two sources of quantitative data. One source was a questionnaire that the teacher candidates completed about their DIET training. The questionnaire had basic demographic-related questions that could be examined using descriptive statistics. The questionnaire also included questions about the participants' perception about their role as future teachers in India. Quantitative data were also derived from an evaluation survey that all the teacher candidates completed at the end of their TPP training session. Both qualitative and quantitative data derived from other TPP workshops were examined, when available, and used to supplement the conclusions emerging from the case study.

Data Analysis

We analyzed the qualitative data using Miles and Huberman's (1994) three-step interpretive approach. First, we read the data and then coded these data as part of data reduction. We identified frequencies in the data and further analyzed these frequencies to establish patterns. Second, the data were displayed in visual ways—with charts and figures—to compare, contrast, and probe for additional categories across the artifacts and field observations. Third, conclusions were drawn as the categories were organized into themes. Additionally, we used the constant-comparative method (Glaser and Strauss 1967) to compare findings.

The quantitative analysis was primarily at a descriptive level. Case study method relies on multiple data sources and thus is known as triangulated research design (Yin 2008). The descriptive statistics provided another way analyze the study's findings through a triangulation of at least three data sources. Descriptive statistics provide "snapshots" of the participants' perceptions of the TPP training. Our quantitative analysis also reports on the participants' demographics. Using descriptive data, we were able to triangulate and contextualize findings about the TPP process. However, the quantitative data are not meant to imply causation or the universality of findings in the larger teacher candidate population.

FINDINGS

There were a number of findings related to the study's research questions. We organize these findings by addressing the chapter's three research questions in order. First, we explain how the participants were prepared to use the ASER TPP toolkit. Second, we share the participants' perceptions of this preparation. Third, we examine the potential effects of the participants' PAR related experiences with the ASER TPP toolkit with respect to their future teaching practice in schools.

Finding 1: Preparation

In all, the study's participants took part in a series of four TPP training workshops, each of two days' duration. Each module is designed around a particular policy or set of policies in the education sector. The four workshop modules are: (1) The Right to Education Act (RTE), (2) School Management Committees and Parental Involvement in School Education, (3) Learning Assessment, and (4) Inside Classrooms. The first workshop module of the TPP program provides the participants with background knowledge about an important policy document—the RTE. The TPP program facilitators discuss RTE and identify the key stakeholder roles and responsibilities within RTE. Since this is a legal document, the teacher candidates are given a packet of RTE flash cards that define the RTE vocabulary and explain key provisions of the legislation. For example, one flash card contains the definitions of RTE-related terminology, such as "elementary," "free," and "compulsory." The TPP facilitators give the teacher candidates a summary of RTE, which the teacher candidates read and are quizzed on. Later, the teacher candidates work in groups to prepare short presentations about key provisions in RTE. On day 2, during their field visit, the teacher candidates see for themselves whether these provisions are being implemented in nearby schools. As described earlier in this chapter, on returning from their field visit, they analyze the data they have collected and reflect on its implications.

The second TPP module is about school management committees and the role of parents in the school. The module's objective is to provide a greater awareness of the importance of parental participation in schools and throughout a child's education. During the field visit, the teacher candidates meet and collect data from school management committee members and parents.

The third TPP module is about assessment. In this module, the teacher candidates learn about different kinds of learning assessments. In the field, they use the ASER learning assessment tools to measure the learning levels of children in basic reading and arithmetic. The teacher candidates use the Do It Yourself ASER Survey tool to create a school report card.

The fourth TPP module examines key policies with respect to teaching and learning, specifically the National Curriculum Framework (NCF). The module identifies key behaviors and practices that are espoused by the NCF as essential elements of constructivist pedagogy independent of the subject matter being taught. For example, NCF refers to the importance of creating a secure, friendly, safe environment in the classroom where children feel respected and able to voice their thoughts and opinions freely (NCERT 2005). Similarly, it reinforces the need to use a variety of teaching strategies that allow children to construct their own knowledge rather than sticking to the traditional "chalk and talk" method in the classroom. Using an observation tool designed on the ASER principles of simplicity and ease of use, the teacher trainee participants observe classrooms and later discuss whether the principles of the NCF are being implemented on the ground. In sum, the TPP modules aim to equip teacher candidates to use a set of tools that are adapted from or designed on the same principles as the ASER survey to measure how policy objectives, in documents like RTE and NCF, are actualized in government-run elementary schools. The overall purpose of the TPP modules is to prepare teacher candidates to use their participatory research in the field to identify the gaps between policy and practice and then think about what can be done to close them.

Finding 2: Perceptions

The second research question inquires about the teacher candidates' perceptions of the TPP training. On their workshop evaluation forms, the participants shared favorable responses to the training. Table 3.1 shows a breakdown of how the participants rated the training in several categories, including the materials and fieldwork experiences.

Table 3.1 Teacher candidates' ratings of TPP module 1

	Poor	Fair	Good	Very good	Excellent
Workshop materials	0	0.14	0.39	0.37	0.10
Reading materials	0	0	0.39	0.42	0.19
Group activities/tasks	0	0.10	0.32	0.39	0.19
Field work	0	0.06	0.36	0.29	0.29
Design of the workshop	0	0.11	0.32	0.42	0.15
Group participation	0	0.02	0.18	0.39	0.41

As Table 3.1 shows, in the observed workshop, 80% of teacher candidates ranked the TPP training's group participation to be very good or excellent. Close to 60% of the participants found the fieldwork component to be very good or excellent. An analysis of feedback from about 1500 students collected from 29 TPP workshops held in 16 DIETs across the country confirms that students rate group activities and participation and the field visits very highly (average rating of close to 80%).

These favorable perceptions of the TPP training were also reflected in the participants' open-ended responses on the evaluation. In particular, the participants perceived that the TPP training was a useful and practical overview of RTE. The evaluation included the following open-ended question: "Did you learn anything new? If yes, what?" Here is a sampling of how the participants responded to that question:

- Yes, I learned fully about RTE and why and for who RTE is used for.
- Yes, I learned about how RTE protects a child's education.
- I learned a lot about RTE and about the school I visited.
- I learned about RTE and never knew about it and learned so much about RTE.
- I had the opportunity to learn so much about ASER and work they do.
- Yes, I learned many things in this activity like flash cards, charts, ASER, and RTE.
- Learned about the RTE Act—very useful.

In the focus group interviews, the teacher candidates shared similar perceptions and discussed how the exercise of using the survey tools to collect data helped them to better understand the need for policies like RTE. One participant explained how "visiting the school and doing the field research helped me to know the children's learning levels but also to see the lack of resources in the school." Another participant shared how "the TPP training and the field experience at the school were important. I learned about the poor condition of the school and how I can work to change it when I am a teacher." The participants perceived that they were better prepared as future teachers from having participating in the TPP training and field research school visits.

Finding 3: Effects

It is beyond the scope of this chapter to track the extent to which teacher candidates' favorable responses to the TPP workshops will translate into ground-level actions once they become teachers. However, one noticeable effect of the TPP training, which was measured by responses on the evaluation tool, was that the participants reported increased knowledge and skills after going through the workshop. On their exit evaluation, the participants were asked to: "Rate your level of knowledge and skills about this module before and after the training on the scale of zero to five, where zero indicates no knowledge or skills and five indicates a high degree of knowledge and skills." In the case study workshop, two participants did not answer this question. For the participants who did answer, 2.48 was the mean score of their self-rated knowledge and skills before the TPP training. This increased to a significantly higher 4.68 mean rating after participating in the training. Self-ratings from 1500 participants across 29 TPP workshops in 16 different DIETs show increases of similar magnitudes.

Not only did the participants feel that they increased their knowledge and skills, they also gained a deeper awareness of the ASER TPP toolkit and the ASER survey process. In the open-ended response question of the evaluation survey, many participants mentioned the field visits and tools in their response to the overall impression of the workshop. Here are some of the participants' responses:

- I love going to the school and was very impressed about interacting with the children and the opportunity to learn at the school.
- I was impressed with the whole process of ASER.

- Impressed with ASER and would be interested in participating more in ASER activities.
- I was very impressed with this activity and learned a lot about RTE, which I didn't know about; I also learned about ASER.
- I would really like to conduct the whole ASER survey.
- I was impressed with the exercise and did field visits and learned more about what goes on in the schools.
- I was very impressed with all we learned in the field visit. We got to go gather the data face-to-face and in an *asli* [or authentic] way.

The participants' open-ended responses resonated with what they shared during the focus group interviews. During the interviews, participants appreciated the relevance of the field research to their future teaching practice. Many agreed that learning how to use the ASER TPP toolkit was authentic to the practice of being a teacher. One participant explained, "Being in the school was a good reminder of why I want to be a teacher. I want to make a change to make a child's life better." Participants also shared about the powerful impact of participating in data collection at the elementary schools. Another participant explained the impact like this: "I want to make the government-run public schools better for the children I teach. Using the ASER tools helped me to see what the children know and how to help them improve." These quotes along with the participants' data demonstrate the uses for the ASER TPP toolkit as well as the impact of participating in research that was guided by the toolkit.

Discussion

Researchers point out that there is an enormous disconnect between educational policy and the ground-level practice of teachers (Bhattacharjea et al. 2011; Byker 2015). For example, Bhattacharjea and her colleagues (2011) described how teachers often know the "right answer" with regard to the importance of child-friendly classrooms for children's learning but completely fail to create these environments in their own day-to-day practice. They go on to recommend that "translating policy into practice is the key to transformation, and to do this, the realities of current practice must inform policy" (p. 46). The ASER TPP toolkit is an instrument for PAR that future teachers can utilize in empowering ways. McTaggart (1991) explained that PAR is a way for groups of people, such as teacher candidates, to "conduct substantive research on the practices which affect their lives in their own context" (p. 169). We argue that the ASER TPP toolkit is a mechanism for PAR-related data collection. In this discussion section, we revisit the PAR conceptual framework in order to build our argument through the unpacking of the study's findings. First, we analyze the adaptability of the ASER TPP toolkit for conducting participatory research. Second, we examine how the ASER TPP toolkit contextualizes PAR-related findings within an evidence-based action framework. Third, we discuss the notions of what it means to be participatory actors—and agents of change—as future schoolteachers in India.

Adaptability

One feature of PAR is a communitarian participation in research (McTaggart 1991). The ASER TPP toolkit is an adaptable instrument for such a collective research method. Sophisticated instruments for measurement are useful only to the extent that there are experts available to interpret the results. Yet this is antithetical to the PAR approach, which is grounded in the understanding that everyday people have "responsible agency in the production of knowledge for the improvement of their community's practice" (McTaggart 1991, p. 171). Given the scale of the "learning problem"—UNESCO's (2014) Global Monitoring Report has estimated that one-third of all primary school–age children worldwide are not learning the basics, whether they have been to school or not—the use of simple metrics and methods that facilitate the engagement of a range of community stakeholders in identifying the problem can potentially become a part of the solution. Simplicity and ease of use are fundamental characteristics of all instruments in the ASER TPP toolkit, characteristics that enable these tools, processes, and results to be useful for a wide variety of community actors and contexts. This chapter has described how the ASER learning assessment tool has been used by hundreds of thousands of young volunteers to collect data on children's foundational learning abilities. The ASER survey process has had significant impact not only on individual surveyors but also on education policy in India, which now clearly acknowledges the need to ensure basic learning outcomes for all children. The same tool has been used extensively by Pratham staff and by government school teachers, in states where Pratham works collaboratively with state governments, to guide classroom organization and teaching. The TPP toolkit has been used with teacher candidates, with students from other disciplines and faculties, and with government education officials in several states. The TPP toolkit is quite adaptable for a variety of audiences and is an instrument that facilitates citizen-led knowledge production *about* and *for* the communities where the citizens are situated.

Contextualization

Scholars have pointed to the importance of contextualizing teacher training into the practices of localized school settings (Byker 2014b; Iyengar et al. 2014; Kumar 2004). The notion here is that teaching is primarily bound within the local. Most schools have a specific geographic location that reflects the history, culture, language, and customs of the community. Of course, many schools do include awareness and an appreciation for the global in their curricula. Indeed, the development of global citizenship and global competencies is becoming an increasingly important facet of education (Byker 2016). Yet teaching and learning are still quite localized activities. One of the aims of PAR is to empower community members to make a difference in their community through informed decision making based on data they collect and analyze about their community. Burgess (2006) described such empowerment as a "collective dynamic process where community members become co-learners, co-researchers, and co-activists of a common concern" (p. 429). The ASER TPP toolkit equips teacher candidates, for example, to be community members for PAR's collective dynamic process. The toolkit starts with context. Using the toolkit's village mapping instrument or the school observation sheet, teacher candidates collect contextual data about the schools in their communities. These data can include items like the community infrastructure, number of playgrounds, types and availability of computer technology, student attendance, and teacher absences. These data provide context for identifying problems in schools and working toward solutions as community members. According to the PAR framework, contextualization supports the informed action of community members as they have real ownership in the decision-making process that impacts their community (McTaggart 1991). The ASER TPP toolkit aids teacher candidates in collecting these contextual data as they start to, as one teacher candidate put it, "think about a school" in different ways. PAR connects a school's context within the larger community.

Participatory Actors

Context begets action; that is the hope anyway. PAR hinges on community members being informed and taking action. Within the formal education system, children's learning takes place primarily inside the classroom. Primary school teachers are thus in a position to ensure that regardless of who children are or where they come from, they gain at least the basic language and arithmetic skills that will enable them to progress through the school system. In India, as in many countries, classrooms are textbook-driven, and the assumption is that all children in a given classroom have the knowledge and abilities that the curriculum expects them to have. This chapter has shown that the TPP toolkit provides powerful learning experiences for future teachers, in terms of both questioning common assumptions and thinking about possible solutions. If the problem of poor learning outcomes is to be solved on scale, then providing teachers and teacher candidates with tools to think about how to accomplish these goals in the real world of schools with insufficient teachers and students with a wide range of learning levels is a critical task. At its core, the ASER TPP toolkit is about assessment. The toolkit is empowering because of how it provides everyday citizens, such as teacher candidates, ways to assess in order to take informed action.

Preparing teachers to assess is a key aspect of learning how to teach effectively in order for all children to learn. Such preparation is as one teacher candidate put it: *asli*. In Hindi, the word *asli* means "authentic and genuine experience." The ASER TPP toolkit helps to guide authentic experiences of data collection. Authentic participation is a primary tenet of PAR. As McTaggart (1991) explained: "PAR is research through which people reflect and work towards the improvement of their own practices" (p. 175). Reflection is a feature that PAR helps facilitate. Likewise, reflection is a participatory practice fostered by the ASER TPP toolkit, which aids teacher and teacher candidates in examining data and in self-examining their capabilities to meet the learning needs in a school. The point of PAR is to assist in the development of participatory actors in a community where everyday citizens participate and collaborate in all research phases to make a difference in their communities (McTaggart 1991). The teacher candidates in this chapter are examples of such citizens who use the ASER TPP toolkit to conduct substantive research on the policies, schools, and practices that they will fully embody one day. The hope is that such PAR reminds teacher candidates about the importance of teaching and moves them to act on behalf of children in order to make changes to make, as one of our study's participant so powerfully stated, a child's life better.

Conclusion

In much of South Asia, teacher education is largely a top-down, hierarchical model. The inclusion of PAR in teacher education is an alternative approach that hinges on authentic experiences to guide teacher candidates' development. The chapter's study demonstrates how PAR can be utilized in concert with the ASER TPP toolkit. We contend that utilizing PAR with the ASER TPP toolkit is empowering for teacher candidates as they participate in researching their communities to see how policies are enacted. Such participation can transform teacher candidates as they make a commitment to making a difference in their community. More research is needed about the long-term impact of a PAR approach to teacher education and the longitudinal effects that it has on teacher practices and children's learning in schools. Additionally, there are very few studies that we know of where teacher candidates or teachers, for that matter, use a PAR framework to make institutional changes in their schools. Change takes time and effort; this is especially true for institutional transformation. Sometimes it is challenging even to know how to get started. The ASER TPP toolkit provides simple and adaptable ways to begin PAR and, thereby, empower teachers and teacher candidates to actively participate in making informed changes on behalf of the children they teach.

Notes

1. DIETs were established in the late 1980s as a third, district-level tier of institutions responsible for training and support to the burgeoning number of primary schools and teachers across the country. A key function of the DIETs is to provide preservice and in-service training to teachers and teacher candidates in the primary education sector.
2. See http://www.asercentre.org/Survey/Basic/Pack/Sampling/History/p/54.html for more details on the ASER survey.
3. More information about ASER Centre capacity-building activities is available at http://www.asercentre.org/Keywords/p/265.html
4. Over the last 15 years, several iterations of the Teaching at the Right Level model have been subject to rigorous evaluations by the Abdul Latif Jameel Poverty Action Lab.

References

Annual Status of Education Report 2013 (ASER). (2014). New Delhi: Pratham Resource Center.
Annual Status of Education Report 2014 (ASER). (2015). New Delhi: Pratham Resource Center.
ASER Centre. (2014). History of ASER—1996–2005: Foundations. Retrieved from http://www.asercentre.org/p/158.html
Bhattacharjea, S., Wadhwa, W., & Banerji, R. (2011). *Inside primary schools: A study of teaching and learning in rural India.* New Delhi: ASER Centre.
Burgess, J. (2006). Participatory action research. *Action Research, 4*(4), 419–437.
Byker, E. J. (2014a). ICT in India's elementary schools: The vision and realities. *International Education Journal, 13*(2), 27–40.
Byker, E. J. (2014b). ICT oriented toward nyaya: Community computing in India's slums. *International Journal of Education and Development using ICT, 10*(2), 19–28.
Byker, E. J. (2015). Teaching for 'global telephony': A case study of a community school for India's 21st century. *Policy Futures in Education, 13*(2), 234–246.
Byker, E. J. (2016). Developing global citizenship consciousness: Case studies of critical cosmopolitan theory. *Journal of Research in Curriculum & Instruction, 20*(3), 264–275.
Byker, E. J., & Banerjee, A. (2016). Evidence for action: Translating field research into a large scale assessment. *Journal of Current Issues in Comparative Education, 18*(1), 1–13.
Cooke, B., & Kothari, U. (2001). The case for participation as tyranny. In B. Cooke & U. Kotari (Eds.), *Participation: The new tyranny?* (pp. 1–15). New York: Zed Books.
Creswell, J. W. (2014). *Research design: Qualitative, quantitative, and mixed methods approaches* (4th ed.). Thousand Oaks, CA: SAGE Press.
French, R., & Kingdon, G. (2010). *The relative effectiveness of private and government schools in Rural India: Evidence from ASER data.* London: Institute of Education.
Glaser, B., & Strauss, A. (1967). *The discovery of grounded theory: Strategies for Qualitative Research.* Chicago: Aldine Publishing Co.
Hickey, S., & Mohan, G. (2004). Towards participation as transformation: Critical themes and challenges. In S. Hickey & G. Mohan (Eds.), *Participation: From tyranny to transformation? Exploring new approaches to participation in development* (pp. 3–24). New York: Zed Books.
Iyengar, R., Witenstein, M. A., & Byker, E. J. (2014). Comparative perspectives on teacher education in South Asia. In A. W. Wiseman & E. Anderson (Eds.), *Annual Review of Comparative and International Education 2014* (pp. 99–106). doi:10.1108/S1479-3679_2014_0000025010.

Kemmis, S., McTaggart, R., & Retallick, J. (2004). *The action research planner: Doing critical participatory action research.* Singapore: Springer Publishing.

Koshy, V. (2009). *Action research for improving educational practice: A step-by-step guide.* Thousand Oaks, CA: SAGE Publishing.

Kumar, K. (2004). *Perspectives on learning in elementary schools.* Plenary address. National Conference on Leadership in India's Elementary Schools. Retrieved from http://www.azimpremjifoundation.org/downloads/Plenary%20Address.pdf

McTaggart, R. (1991). Principles for participatory action research. *Adult Education Quarterly, 41*(3), 168–187.

Miles, M. B., & Huberman, A. M. (1994). *Qualitative data analysis: An expanded sourcebook.* Thousand Oaks: Sage Publications.

National Council of Educational Research and Training [NCERT]. (2005). *National curriculum for elementary and secondary education: The 2005 framework.* New Delhi: NCERT.

Small, S. (1995). Action-oriented research: Models and methods. *Journal of Marriage and the Family, 57*(4), 941–952.

UNESCO. (2014). *Teaching and learning: Achieving quality for all. EFA Global Monitoring Report 2013/14.* Paris: UNESCO.

Yin, R. (2008). *Case study research: Design and methods* (4th ed.). Thousand Oaks, CA: SAGE Publishing.

CHAPTER 4

Northern Province Education System in Sri Lanka: Participatory Review, Recommendation, Implementation, and Monitoring

Meera Pathmarajah and Nagalingam Ethirveerasingam

Participation in education remained high in Sri Lanka's Northern Province during the civil war, which lasted from 1983 to 2009. Amid ongoing bombing and shelling, teachers, principals, and administrators continuously worked to keep schools running. Many erected temporary huts for students to attend school and take exams even under the stressful conditions of living in internally displaced persons camps. However, despite the critical role they played as first responders, both throughout the war and following the 2004 tsunami, education personnel and local communities were virtually excluded from participating in long-term relief and rehabilitation plans (Uyangoda 2013). A concerning pattern emerged in the aftermath of emergencies whereby the involvement of communities

---

M. Pathmarajah (✉)
University of San Francisco, San Francisco, CA, USA
e-mail: mpathmar@gmail.com

N. Ethirveerasingam
Northern Province Ministry of Education—Sri Lanka, Cerritos, CA, USA
e-mail: ethir@yahoo.com

© The Author(s) 2017
H. Kidwai et al. (eds.), *Participatory Action Research and Educational Development*, South Asian Education Policy, Research, and Practice,
DOI 10.1007/978-3-319-48905-6_5

reduced as the role of the government and external donors increased (Harris 2006; Uyangoda 2013). Postwar development efforts brought new possibilities for local participation. In 2013, the long-awaited Northern Provincial government was finally formed amid ongoing tensions between the Sri Lankan government and the Tamil-speaking minority population. Despite its many limitations, the provincial system enabled the predominantly Tamil population in the North to begin addressing some of the massive problems brought about by decades of war, discrimination, and oppressive policies (Freire and Macedo 2001). For the education system, this was significant, considering that education had always been centrally administered and that after the war ended in 2009, the President of Sri Lanka appointed a General as Governor. In the absence of an elected Provincial Council, retired General Chadrasiri was in charge of all government sectors, including education.

When the Northern Provincial Council was elected in October 2013, the education minister, Thambyrajah Gurukularajah, a former teacher and administrator of the North himself, recognized the need to solicit broad participation in assessing the needs of the Northern Provincial education system. He initiated a participatory Northern Education System Review (NESR) and invited one of this chapter's authors, Nagalingam Ethirveerasingam, to facilitate the entire process as a volunteer. The review was undertaken in the spirit of what Batliwala and Sheela (1997) have noted about participatory research—that it is not a contained, specific activity but rather a strategy in which every action is infused with "the need to join people in learning about their environment and locating solutions to problems" (p. 264). Over 400 stakeholders from all walks of life, from auto-rickshaw drivers to doctors and education professors, contributed their observations and recommendations to the NESR.

In this chapter, we present a case study of the NESR as an example of participatory action research (PAR) for educational development and policy making. Although a large literature exists on the experiences of foreign aid projects in conflict and postconflict societies, there is little documentation of national educational rehabilitation programs in postwar contexts (Burde 2005). Our purpose in detailing the methods involved in conducting the NESR is twofold. First, we emphasize the importance of including implementation as a critical aspect of PAR. We highlight the need to conceptualize "implementation" as part of the research agenda from the start so that research findings do not simply gather dust but are actually applied, in this case, through the implementation of policy recommendations. Toward this end, we propose the term "PARI," for "participatory action research and implementation." Second, we reflect on the challenges of implementation in the face of bureaucratic obstacles, limited human resources, and colonial legacies that limit processes of empowerment which participation is intended to enable. Our findings help address ethical concerns that arise when follow-up action fails to follow participatory research where expectations for change have been raised (Holland et al. 1998).

Beginning with a brief background on educational policymaking, school types, and the impact of war in northern Sri Lanka, this chapter then describes the PARI methods that were used to guide the NESR. The next section examines three of the recommendations to illustrate how implementation responsibilities were developed as part of the overall review process. This is followed by a discussion of challenges encountered in the implementation of recommendations. To conclude, we reflect on the significance of the participatory processes that guided the NESR.

Background

Educational Policy Making in Sri Lanka

Even before Sri Lanka's independence from Britain in 1948, C.W.W. Kannangara, the first Minister of Education, ushered in free education, mother tongue education (in Sinhalese and Tamil), and the concept of central schools. These policies were supported with high levels of social spending, resulting in wide expansion of the education system. By 1991, Sri Lanka had already reached an 89% primary school net enrollment ratio and a 90% literacy rate among individuals 15 years and older (Little 2003). By the late 1990s, gender parity in literacy rates was also high (98%) among youth between 15 and 24 years old (UNICEF 2013).

Successive education ministers expressed support for the Kannangara theme of equal opportunity, but in practice, they issued policies that favored the Sinhala-Buddhist majority and eliminated English as the link language. For instance, the 1956 Sinhala Only Act made Sinhala the official language of the country. In 1971, the Standardization of Education Act introduced a discriminatory quota system that restricted university admission for the minority Tamil-speaking population. These policies increasingly disaffected youth in the North and East, eventually resulting in their use of violence as a means to bring about change.

Education policy in Sri Lanka has been largely ad hoc (Little 2011). The president is personally advised by the National Education Commission and often intervenes in educational policy making. Furthermore, education policy has primarily responded to economic policies since 1977, when the United National Party returned to power and introduced liberalization and deregulation measures. As a result, the number of foreign qualification suppliers in Sri Lanka increased dramatically (Little and Evans 2005). Private education and private "tutories" (tuition centers) mushroomed, while state control over the granting of academic and vocational qualifications weakened. These changes significantly distorted Sri Lanka's "free" public education system (Arunatilake and Jayawardena 2010; Cole 2015).

Low government expenditures on education, coupled with politicized, centralized policy making, have left provinces bereft of policy ownership (Little 2011; Little and Evans 2005). Between 2006 and 2015, the government of Sri Lanka consistently allocated only around 2% of the gross domestic product on education. In 2016, the percentage increased to 6%, although a large share is designated for educational infrastructure (Wedagedara et al. 2015). Moreover, the practice of historical fund allocation contributes to sustained disparities across provinces. Most school budgets are prepared with limited stakeholder involvement and according to finance commission guidelines rather than quality input allocation (Arunatilake and de Silva 2004). Generally, the Ministry of Education (MOE) and the National Institute of Education tend to focus on policy implementation rather than policy formulation. It is commendable that the National Education Commission has included many of the key recommendations of the NESR report in its 2017 Education Policy. For example, Vocational and Technical education will be included; compulsory education for all until year 13 (19 years) will replace the current up to year 12 (16 years) requirement; national examinations, curricula, teacher education and teaching methods are to be revised; a new education administration system will be introduced.

In 1987, the provincial council system intended to decentralize certain powers of educational administration from the national level to the provinces. As shown in Fig. 4.1, this system added new administrative layers reporting up to the Provincial MOE from schools, including divisional education offices, zonal education offices, and the Provincial Department of Education. However, there are significant limitations to provincial decentralization (Srinivasan 2015).

In addition to inadequate funding, lower levels of the bureaucracy lack adequately qualified administrative and human resources to monitor project supervision and implementation. For instance, the Northern Province Education Department has a planning unit, but it focuses primarily on the next year's activities and quarterly and monthly activities of the current year, except for building-related activities. It is not adequately staffed to

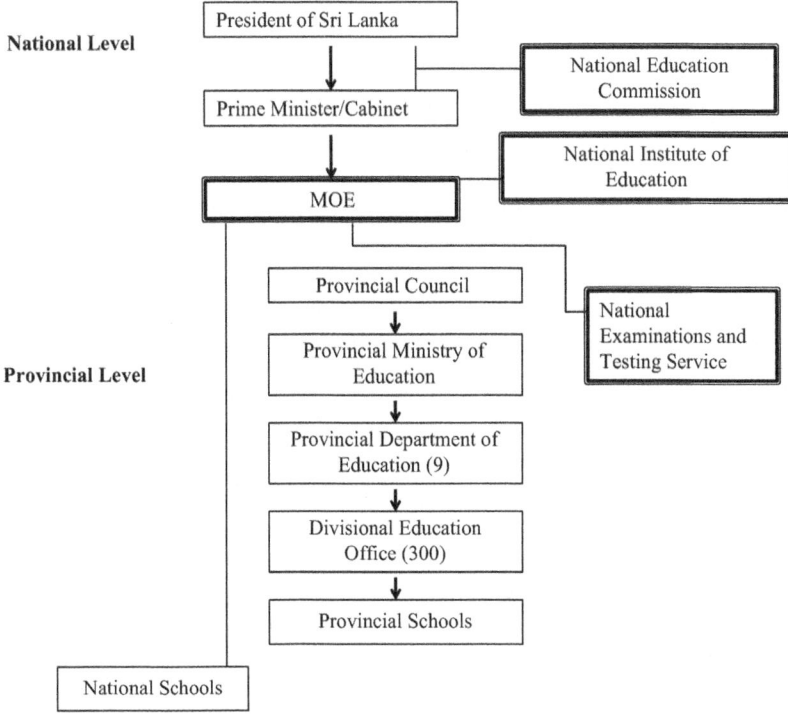

Fig. 4.1 Sri Lanka Ministry of Education administrative structure

make five-year plans in any significant, implementable way. From 2015 to 2017 there were only two staff. The Planning Unit's work is done by those holding other positions within the department. They have no formal training in educational planning or educational finance.

Overview of School Types

Despite Sri Lanka's noteworthy achievements in educational access, opportunities beyond primary school remain unequal. The education system is comprised of 13 grades, with children beginning grade 1 at five years old. Grade 1 and Grade 13 in Sri Lanka are kindergarten and Grade 12, respectively, in the Western education system.

In all nine provinces, there are four types of schools: 1AB, 1C, II, and III. Type 1AB schools are the most resourced. They offer grades up to General Certificate of Education (GCE), Advanced Level (AL), in four main streams—Arts, Science-Mathematics, Commerce and Technology. Type 1C schools also offer classes up to Grade 13 but offer only Arts and/or Commerce streams. The pattern of a large proportion of schools being Type II and Type III is reflected throughout the country. Type II schools primarily offer Grades 1 to 11, and they prepare students for the GCE Ordinary Level. Type III schools have only Grade 1 to 5 primary schools (with the exception of some schools that may have an additional one or two grades due to their remote locations).

The administration of schools is designated to either the national or provincial MOE or a school board, in the case of assisted schools.[1] There are 352 national schools, which fall within the purview of the national MOE, though the provincial department of education oversees their day-to-day activities. This divided responsibility/authority relationship with a lot of gray areas leads to administrative issues. National schools fall into the general 1AB category. Provincial schools are the full responsibility of the provincial MOE, although the Sri Lanka MOE approves the allocations of teaching and administrative positions.

Students across all school types spend significant amounts of time attending "private tutories" to prepare for high-stakes national exams. Private tutories are after-school learning centers that typically are held in sheds similar to those one would see in urban slums. (See Photos 4.1 and 4.2 of typical tutories.) Parents pay for their children in Grades 1 to 13 to attend lectures in spaces that accommodate from 50 to 200 students, cramped on crudely constructed benches. The teachers are either retired or serving teachers. A popular teacher would earn three times the salary that the government pays a teacher.

Students attend tutories after or before school, and on Saturdays and Sundays. On average, a student in Grade 5, 10, 11, 12, and 13 will attend 15 to 20 hours of classes in tuition centers per week. Grade 13 students, with the consent of the schools, attend tuition centers during school hours from January to July before the August examinations. It is popularly believed that students who do not attend tuition centers do not pass the national examinations.

The War's Impact on Education in the Northern Province

The Northern Province was granted a provincial council only in 2013 due to the long-standing ethnic conflict between Sri Lanka's majority Sinhalese military forces and the Liberation Tigers of Tamil Eelam. Over 200,000 people lost their lives and more than 1 million people were displaced due to the conflict (Mittal 2015). Even after the war, life for

Photo 4.1 Jaffa Central College (a national school), established in 1816 by Methodists

many Tamils in the North remained precarious, owing to large-scale military involvement in civilian affairs (ICG 2012), land grabs, unresolved processes of resettlement (Saparamadu and Lall 2014), unemployment, the agony of searching for disappeared relatives, gender-based violence (Gowrinathan and Cronin-Furman 2015) and the aggressive implementation of development and state-building projects (ICG 2011).

For much of the conflict, violence and a general embargo arrested educational development and student and teacher performance in the Northern Province. The embargo included building materials, school laboratory chemicals, equipment, and materials, including restrictions on fuel to the North. A large number of schools were destroyed or damaged, with nearly half of the 983 total schools in the Northern Province rated "Very Uncongenial" in a 2007 "Congeniality Index" developed by the MOE to determine the condition of school facilities (Ethirveerasingam 2014).

There is considerable variation in school access across and within provinces. Table 4.1 shows the uneven distribution of school types across the 12 zones

Photo 4.2 A popular tutory in Jaffna

that comprise the Northern Province. In total, a majority of schools in the North fall under the category of Type II (33%) and Type III (46%) schools. Only 11% of schools are Type 1C, and 10% are Type 1AB. A majority of students who complete primary school in a Type III school will be channeled into schools that offer instruction up to only Grade 11 (Type II schools).

Multiple displacements in the North and East, which included the displacement of schools, students, teachers, and parents, stunted teaching and learning. For instance, the inability of staff to pursue higher educational qualifications and take promotion examinations resulted in many teaching and administrative staff holding positions for which they were not prepared. Such administrative staff were given appointments as "Performing" Principal or "Performing" Assistant Director/Deputy Director to fill the vacant positions. Furthermore, the brain drain resulting from the war created an acute shortage of math, science, and English teachers. Immigration and emigration and customs checkpoints and no-man's lands between the two warring communities prevented teacher training workshops from being held.

The war ended violently in May 2009. The United Nations estimates that more than 40,000 civilian Tamil people were killed and many more were maimed. Approximately 300,000 people from three districts, including

Table 4.1 Number of schools and enrolment by type of school by zone—2015

No.	Zone	1AB Student	1AB School	1C Student	1C School	Type II Student	Type II School	Type III Student	Type III School	Total Student	Total School
1	Jaffna	22771	17	5311	11	9794	41	7142	35	45018	104
2	Island	2382	4	1617	7	3246	20	2057	33	9302	64
3	Valikamara	13710	13	7493	14	8191	39	6899	69	36293	135
4	Thenmara	5345	6	1797	5	3072	20	2532	28	12746	59
5	Vadamara	8711	11	3481	8	6273	29	3874	33	22339	81
6	Kilinochchi	9737	11	5892	13	10329	39	5994	41	31952	104
7	Mullaitivu	4657	5	4045	7	7713	27	3401	23	19816	62
8	Thunukkai	2765	7	703	2	2572	16	2342	36	8382	61
9	Madhu	525	2	2565	10	2019	14	1172	25	6281	51
10	Mannar	9503	10	6889	16	4606	25	2890	37	23885	88
11	Vavuniya North	1936	4	1264	7	2570	20	1902	54	7672	85
12	Vavuniya South	10868	8	7757	13	7514	32	2860	43	28999	96
	Total	92910	98	48814	113	67899	322	43065	457	252685	990

Source: Northern Provincial Department of Education (2015). Education Management Information System

students, teachers, and education administrators, were displaced for three to six months. They languished in poorly equipped camps, deprived of adequate nutrition, sanitation and health care, while also suffering from the trauma of witnessing family members injured and killed during the chaotic last phase of war (ICG 2010; Somasundaram 2007). Their freedom of movement outside the camps was restricted. The education administrators and teachers were released after 3 to 4 months. Most of the civilians were released in December 2010, in batches, to return to their place of residence or holding areas near their homes. Most of their homes were destroyed, damaged or occupied by the armed forces. Many educators returned but were not able to start their schools for many reasons including lack of enough students or teachers who had not returned. Schools in army occupied areas were closed until end of December 2015. Many remained without accommodation, livelihood, and counseling for five or more years. All aspects of the education system were affected. It was disabled and continued on survival mode as it had for the previous twenty-plus years.

Principles of Participatory Action Research

Action research methods have been practiced since the early 20th century by a variety of disciplines and philosophical traditions. Two principles of PAR include a commitment to group-based decision making and a commitment to improvement. PAR methods are premised on (1) involving the people living and working in the setting of interest to actively contribute to the research and (2) orienting the research toward enabling change for and by the participants themselves (Kemmis et al. 2014).

Kurt Lewin is often credited with pioneering PAR. In the 1940s, Kurt Lewin and coworker Alec Barvelas discovered the practical gains in workplace efficiency and social relationships made by democratic rather than autocratic processes (Adelman 1997). They found that allowing workers to discuss their problems and make group decisions resulted in consistently higher levels of group morale and productivity. In Lewin's experimental research, he showed that group participation is vital not just for identifying problems but also for monitoring follow-up action. By regularly reviewing progress on decisions, particular strategies can be completed and new issues can be identified.

Participatory Action Research and Implementation

Participatory research became increasingly popular among development practitioners in the 1970s. Amid growing critiques of top-down policy and program approaches, participatory research methods were introduced to help improve planning and implementation processes (Bowd, Ozerdem & Kassa 2010). Including local communities in designing programs had a number of benefits. Local knowledge would better inform the program design, program ownership would increase the likelihood of program participation, and the process would help build capacity among participants.

Although participatory approaches have become widespread in development rhetoric, their practice is diverse in quality, application, and inclusiveness. In some cases, PAR has been reduced to a set of prescriptive techniques that is more researcher-driven than community-driven (Cooke 2003). Yet there are plenty of examples where participatory research has successfully benefited local communities.

Micro-level participatory approaches are much more common than macro-level models. Robins (2008), for instance, narrated an ethnographic study that took place over six months in postconflict Nepal. He spent two months jointly designing the study with leaders and members of two associations of missing persons. The involvement of the associations led not only to their ownership of the research goals and methodologies but to providing counseling and support to victims' families. The stories they participated in collecting were used as advocacy tools for victims' families (Robins 2008). In this case, participants contributed throughout the process of designing and implementing the action research.

Scaling such participatory processes to a macro level is particularly challenging and rare. Kerala's 1996 "People's Campaign for Decentralized Planning" offered an insightful example of participatory planning for national development (Chaudhuri 2003). Following India's 1993 constitutional amendment that enabled devolution of certain planning responsibilities to local governments, Kerala sought to increase local participation in development policy making and budgeting. Biannual *grama sabhas* (local-level assemblies) were introduced to solicit input into planning and budgeting processes. In its first year, a massive training exercise took place in which about 600 state-level resource persons, 12,000 district-level trainees, 15,000 elected representatives, 25,000 officials, and 75,000 volunteers participated in trainings on using grama sabhas to identify local development problems, generate priorities, and form sector proposals (Chaudhuri 2003). Participation rates in the planning grama sabhas were high (over 10% of the rural electorate) with great participation of historically excluded individuals across two years of the study.

In both of these examples, the act of participation involves identifying or conceptualizing an action and then carrying it out. There is an emphasis on the participatory aspect of the process, but it is unclear whether the time frame of participation is finite or ongoing. In the case of participatory action for policy development, we highlight the importance of participatory implementation in addition to PAR. This necessitates the creation of mechanisms for implementing and monitoring policies in a participatory way. Collaborative reflection should underpin the ongoing implementation, review, and contextualization of policies. It is expected that this will improve accountability and ownership of policy decisions, particularly in contexts where bureaucratic delays and political interference tend to obstruct implementation processes. In order to bring into focus an emphasis on participatory policy implementation, we propose the phrase "participatory action research and implementation."

Participatory Action Research and Implementation Methods for the Northern Education System Review

Whereas most participatory methods have been carried out in community settings, the NESR was anchored within the Northern Provincial MOE. The NESR sought to incorporate participants within and across the entire primary and secondary education system, inviting all interested individuals to submit their opinions, from government staff to ordinary citizens. In this section, we provide some contextual information about the review process followed by a description of the participatory methods undertaken to conduct the NESR.

For a region that had endured decades of violent conflict, militarization, and control, owning the processes of problem identification, solution making, and implementation was a novel opportunity. The draconian Prevention of Terrorism Act as well as 40 years of emergency rule in Sri Lanka vested significant powers in state police and the military, contributing to a sharp rise in arrests and detentions, a culture of impunity, and overt censorship, both by the media and by everyday citizens. Somasundaram (2007) asserted that "the chronic climate of terror, insecurity and uncertainty was a prominent cause of the collective trauma" (p. 12) experienced by Tamils in northern Sri Lanka. His description of life in the North reflects the exhaustion produced by decades of war:

> People have learned to simply attend to their immediate needs and survive to the next day. Any involvement or participation carried considerable risk, particularly at the frequent changes in those in power. The repeated displacements, [and] disruption of livelihood have made people dependent on handouts and relief rations. Similar to Seligman's *"learned helplessness,"* this dependence

hampers rehabilitation and development efforts. People have lost their self-reliance, earlier a hallmark of Tamil society. They have lost their motivation for advancement, progress or betterment. There is a general sense of resignation to fate. People no longer feel motivated to work, or better their lots. (p. 15)

Seen in this context, the NESR methods not only catalyzed educational development but also gave voice to hundreds of students, teachers, parents, and administrators who had long been suppressed by the controlling tendency of the nation-state (Thiranagama 2011). The act of engaging in dialogue about the future of education in northern Sri Lanka helped participants feel that they were beginning to take back control over their lives and communities.

At the same time, conducting participatory research in postconflict environments presented particular challenges. As in many other contexts, "postwar" in Sri Lanka does not equate to "postconflict". Hence unresolved individual, social, and political disputes are all likely to affect the research process. Indeed, as we discuss later, some NESR policy recommendations became politically challenging to implement.

Studies on postconflict participatory research identify challenges relating to participant access, emotional issues due to the sensitivity of data and how to effectively collect rich data. However, the NESR was unique in that the principal researcher-practitioner, Ethirveerasingam (the coauthor of this chapter), was able to leverage his background in order to facilitate certain aspects of the review. For 20 years, Ethirveerasingam has lived in the North as a volunteer educator and sports activist. Ethirveerasingam is a graduate of Jaffna Central College and is known in Sri Lanka as an Olympian in 1952 and 1956 and for winning the first Asian Games gold medal in 1958. Thus, his influential status as a former athlete, academic, and government advisor positioned him well for leading the NESR and helped minimize issues of access to respondents and politicians.[2]

The task of uniting and motivating any heterogeneous group of individuals to collaborate requires extensive trust building and dialogue. One can only imagine how much more challenging this might be in a postwar context. While maintaining sensitivity to various power differentials, Ethirveerasingam drew from his personal roots as a Jaffna Tamil as well as his professional background to facilitate the review process. His work of guiding groups to debate issues and identify solutions was further facilitated by the historically high value that Tamils in northern Sri Lanka have placed on education. Colonial and missionary education reached

Jaffna as early as the 16th century, and Tamil intellectuals had long ago popularized the instrumental role that schools play in habituating students and constructing a public sphere (Ambalavanar 2006). More recently, value for education also became strongly associated with the desire to gain private sector employment, which has greatly outpaced public sector jobs in the era after economic liberalization (Little and Evans 2005). Thus, participants' strong commitment to addressing educational inequalities helped build a sense of motivation, solidarity, and focus from the start of the process.

The involvement of the Tamil diaspora, numbering over 1 million people across more than 30 countries, was also of considerable significance, although they comprised only a small number of participants. The Sri Lankan diaspora has remained a major stakeholder in northern provincial development (Vimalarajah and Cheran 2010). There is much to gain from Tamil diaspora members, particularly those who have developed powerful levels of social, human, and economic capital and are motivated to contribute their knowledge and experience to develop their ancestral land. At the same time, involving diaspora members necessitates careful management of power differentials. As Fals Borda (1995) cautioned: "Do not monopolize your knowledge nor impose arrogantly your techniques but respect and combine your skills with the knowledge of the researched or grassroots communities, taking them as full partners and co-researchers." It was in this spirit that correspondence with members of the diaspora took place as part of the NESR.

Formation of Study Coordinators

The review process commenced with the first meeting of senior staff of the Northern Provincial MOE and Department of Education, held on October 22, 2013, under the chairmanship of the Northern Province minister of education. At this meeting, six coordinators were selected to form six subcommittees with 10 members each. The subcommittees were given the option of inviting additional persons. Their mandate was to identify and analyze the issues in the Northern Province Education System and propose recommendations. The members formed the steering committee of the NESR. A secretariat was also formed to assist the facilitator, Dr. Ethirveerasingam, and the steering committee.

Each of the six coordinators and their subcommittees took on the responsibility of investigating one of these areas:

1. Teaching, learning, and teacher education
2. Student–teacher discipline and counseling
3. Teachers' and administrators' issues
4. Finance, staff requirements, expenditure and teacher salaries
5. Education administrative structure and alternatives
6. e-Planning database, research, and development

At the first meeting, steering committee members came to an agreement that the review would focus on participatory processes that considered the child as the center of the education system. They also agreed to consider only those recommendations that enhanced children's physical and emotional growth, learning, and performance in their social and cultural context. These guiding principles helped inform processes for soliciting opinions and recommendations from those who were and are stakeholders in the education system. Individuals who were part of the system in the past, whether currently in the North or living elsewhere, were invited to participate.

Focus Group Discussions

Separate daylong meetings were planned and held with stakeholders in the Northern Province. They were Tamil-speaking parents, teachers, students, and zonal directors selected from the 12 zonal directorates. The same took place with Sinhala-speaking parents, teachers, and students, selected by the principals and zonal directors from South Vavuniya and Manal Aru (Weli Oya). The students were also given an opportunity to submit concerns about their education anonymously.

Inviting Submissions Through Multiple Mediums

An advertisement was placed in various public newspapers inviting submissions, observations, and/or recommendations, anonymously or otherwise, on the areas identified above via regular post or email or by submitting an online form.[3] All submissions were addressed to the facilitator, who reviewed and considered each submission, whether it arrived before or after the deadline expired. An additional advertisement to this effect was also placed in all the Tamil and Sinhala newspapers.[4]

Oral submissions at the workshop from those who had not responded to the advertisement were discouraged. Their written submissions were reviewed first by the facilitator and then by the respective groups for consideration. All submissions that had a return address were acknowledged. Personal issues and complaints were noted and referred to the relevant office. Some of the individuals who had detailed firsthand knowledge of the problems and submitted viable solutions were invited to participate in the relevant group discussions.

In addition, the minister, facilitator, and a select committee invited three groups of students, teachers, and parents separately to listen to their problems and ideas for solutions. The groups were invited from Jaffna Education Zone, Vavunia North Education Zone, and two Sinhala medium schools in Vavuniaya South and Manal Aru (Weli Oya) from Mullaitivu Education Zone. Much was learned from the fruitful and enthusiastic group discussions that ensued from these forums.

The issues raised by the submissions and interviews from the public and stakeholders were reviewed by the facilitator, acknowledged, and submitted to the six coordinators through the Steering Committee Secretariat. The submissions are all currently on file at the MOE. After reading through all of the submissions, the facilitator categorized them into the following areas:

- On students
- On teachers
- On use of computers and teaching materials
- On curricula and examinations
- On principals
- On schools and school environment
- On school community environment
- On parents and home environment
- On ministry and education administration

Documentation and Presentation of Findings

A first draft report was written, reviewing each of the six areas identified earlier in a separate chapter. Each chapter presented the consensus on the current situation, identified special areas of concern, and recommended solutions for implementation immediately (six months), in the short term (one year), and midterm (three years).

The first draft was discussed by a larger membership of the Steering Committee in late January 2014. On the advice of that committee, the focus groups were then expanded to 11. Each group presented its findings and recommendations twice. These were improved upon each time. The groups presented their cumulative observations and recommendations at the consultation workshop on April 23 and 24, 2014.

Symposium

A symposium was held in April 2014 to consider the draft report and the recommendations of the 11 groups. The national minister of education, directors responsible for various departments at the national Ministry of Education and directors of the National Institute of Education were invited and participated in the three-day symposium. Those invited from universities in Sri Lanka and the United States, who were not able to attend, submitted their inputs by email. Emeritus Professor Angela Little from the University of London, Institute of Education gave her input in a meeting in Colombo. Additional participants included the Steering Committee, school principals, tertiary institution and university staff, representatives from the community at large, and those who contributed by mail and email.

In total, over 300 people attended the symposium, engaged in dialogue in the 11 groups, and approved the final recommendations. The recommendations were then revised, and a final draft was approved by the Steering Committee before it was printed and released on July 17, 2014 at a ceremony and on the EMIS website (www.edudept.np.gov.lk).

Recommendation Implementation and Monitoring Panel

The review process generated 245 recommendations aimed at improving teaching, learning, and the education system. Out of those, 130 of them could be administered or implemented by the zonal directors, staff, and schools without cost or approval from other authorities. Many of the recommendations stated the need for more efficiency in educational administration. This chapter's appendix contains 10 of the recommendations being implemented by the Northern Province secretary of education and the provincial director of education and give a glimpse of the issues facing teaching and learning in schools, especially schools that are in the rural area of the Northern Province. Seventeen recommendations needed directives and instruction from the Northern Province secretary of education and the Northern Province director of education. Only the recommendation for appointing new positions in the system needed the approval of the National MOE.

Recognizing that the system was overloaded and in order to ensure follow-up action, the Steering Committee and the symposium recommended the establishment of an independent Recommendation Implementation and Monitoring Panel (RIMP). A board consisting of some members of the Steering Committee and members from the community was established with an executive committee reporting to the board. The minister chaired the board and the secretary for education and the director of education were members.

The establishment of the RIMP board and the following recommendations required approval from the Northern Province board of ministers and the governor:

- New zonal administration in the Thunukkai Zone as a pilot project
- Establishing an Institute of Tamil Medium Education
- Establishing a substitute teacher system

RIMP was allocated space and staffed to form a secretariat. It is to function until the end of 2018 and should complete implementing all recommendations. RIMP formed five subcommittees consisting of 10 to 15 members:

1. Psychosocial well-being
2. Education management information system (EMIS)
3. Research and publication
4. New zonal administrative system
5. Institute of Tamil Medium Education

Two more subcommittees are to be established for preschool education and special education. It is the responsibility of the subcommittees to make decisions and implement the recommendations under the guidance of the RIMP executive committee.

To provide an idea of the type of analysis and recommendations generated by the participatory review process, in the next sections, we describe three of the areas reviewed by the Steering Committee.

I. Teaching, Learning, and Examinations (National)

There are three national examinations that all students have to take:

1. The Grade 5 (Age 10) Scholarship examination is used to award admission to leading schools and to provide scholarships. It was originally intended to grant scholarships and admission to leading schools for students in need.
2. The Grade 11 (Age 16) General Certificate of Education, Ordinary Level (GCE O/L) determines admission to Grade 12 when a

required number of passes and credit passes are obtained in given subjects. Approximately 50% of students who take the GCE O/L go on to Grade 12. Others are pushed out of the school system.
3. The Grade 13 (Age 18) General Certificate of Education, Advanced Level (GCE A/L) determines admission to universities, in one of the four streams that are offered, and to colleges of education. Admission is based on both merit and district quotas. Quotas are set based on the degree of disadvantage among districts. Z scores are used as cut-off points for admissions. Approximately 60% qualify for admissions. Out of that, a lesser number of students are admitted to universities depending on space availability. The remaining 40% can enter vocational or technical institutes at the tertiary level based on their performance on the A/L examination.

GCE O/L and A/L examinations generally test knowledge and comprehension. Very few or no questions test for application, analysis, synthesis, and evaluation abilities. Teaching is mostly in the classroom, and chalk and talk is the method preferred by teachers. There is hardly any interaction between students and teachers, even when computers and internet access is available. Teachers ask rhetorical questions that a few students answer in chorus. No questions are initiated by students and teachers do not encourage students to ask questions. There are no practical examinations, and teachers spend very little time doing anything practical, although some demonstrate some practice in science classes.

Provinces set the term and end-of-year examinations for all grades other than Grade 5, Grade 11 GCE O/L, and Grade 13 GCE A/L. Tests by the provinces duplicate past national examinations. National examinations are composed in Sinhala or English and then translated into Tamil. Often the translation in Tamil is longer than the other two languages. In multiple-choice questions, questions and answer choices are so long they are often difficult to understand. The teaching methods are dictated by the national examinations questions, where rote learning and reproduction is rewarded.

For many lessons during the year and especially during the last two months of the year, all teachers in all subjects focus on teaching to answer questions from past exams. The education department produces question papers and distributes them so that teachers will drill the students to get a high pass rate. The parents and the system demand this practice. Such is the learning and teaching process not only in the North but in schools across the country.

A province has no powers to alter national examinations, although it can recommend the need for change. University education faculty have made recommendations, but no appreciable changes have taken place.

RIMP, with the assistance of a nonprofit organization called SERVE eLearning Institute (www.servelearn.org), distributed DVDs on mathematics and science lessons for Grades 10 and 11 (last two years of the GCE O/L) to 150 schools and trained teachers to use them with computers for teaching and learning. The e-lessons have illustrations, diagrams, animation, and interactive questions. The lessons were tested, and the learning improved twofold based on trials in schools and students' GCE O/L results. Teacher trainers were trained to train teachers in 500 more schools. Schools with computer laboratories let students learn on their own assisted by the teacher. Those that have one computer and a multimedia projector use the DVD and teach students using the e-lessons. There are e-lessons for all grades in Sinhala and English produced by the MOE and the National Institute of education, but only a few lessons in some grades have been produced in Tamil.

Due to the failure to train Tamil staff in curriculum and teaching aids development, the NESR review recommended the establishment of an Institute of Tamil Medium Education. The Northern Province board of ministers and the governor approved the proposal. The national MOE and the National Institute of Education also supported the recommendations. The Institute of Tamil Medium Education is in the process of being established.

II. Psychosocial Well-Being of Students and Teachers: Student–Teacher Discipline, Classroom Management and Counseling

Rote teaching learning methods and examination pressure from the system, parents, principals, and teachers leads to boredom and stress among students. Compounded with the trauma of war, this leads to student misbehavior in classrooms. Teachers routinely practice corporal punishment. In the 1940s and 1950s, when coauthor Ethirveerasingam was in school in Jaffna, there was no corporal punishment in schools, although in extreme circumstances, the principal and vice principal were authorized to use a cane on a student's palm. Such caning was a rare occurrence. Although corporal punishment did exist in schools before the 1940s, it became prevalent in most schools by the 1970s. Research on this subject is taboo, as most of the schools and teachers, both male and female, practice it.

An informal survey of 40 students in Grade 10 and 11 by the coauthor revealed that canings take place twice or three times per day. Mainly a stick is used for caning, but often male teachers use their hands to beat male students and a stick to hit female students. The reverse is true for female teachers. The two months before the GCE O/L examinations, October and November, are times when corporal punishment occurs most often. Students and teachers are under stress to finish the syllabus, and memorization techniques are used for "drilling knowledge" into students.

In the face-to-face meetings that were conducted with parents, teachers, and students, the minister put the question of corporal punishment to all three groups. The teachers did not admit or deny that they use corporal punishment to manage classroom misbehavior. The parents wanted the teachers to hit their children if they misbehaved. None of the groups of students responded to the questions nor did they write about it when given a chance to identify problems in learning. One student did respond by saying that he did not want to talk negatively about his school.

Repeated instructions to stop corporal punishment have been sent to teachers since 1927. The last most important circular on making corporal punishment in schools illegal was sent in 2005 and again in 2012. Principals and teachers ignored it. The same circular was sent to principals and teachers by the Northern Provincial Ministry in August 2015, and the principals and teachers signed on to it. Plans to monitor corporal punishment in schools are under way.

Based on physicians' presentations to teachers and administrators, there has been a rise of drugs and alcohol consumption by students since the end of the war. Pregnancy among school children and teenagers has also increased after the war, as compared to before or during the war. Teachers have been advised to include education on reproductive health and the implications of teenage pregnancy for girls, the child, and their parents. Abortions and giving birth outside the home has led to increased deaths among children and teenage unmarried mothers since the end of the war.

The Psychosocial Well-being Committee, composed of psychologists, psychiatrists, parents, teachers with counseling experience, and administrators, commissioned the SERVE eLearning Institute to produce a DVD on classroom management. It was reviewed by members of the Psychosocial Well-being Committee. Six thousand DVDs were produced and distributed to principals and teachers. The committee has started workshops for psychologists and qualified counselors to train trainers to train the 15,000 teachers in the system on counseling and classroom management. In addition, each of the schools will have drop-in centers called *mahilaham* (a place to relax and enjoy activities) for students and staff. Fourteen *mahilagams* have already been established. The centers will be used for recreation as well as for counseling and guidance by trained counselors. Every school with 300 or more students is to have a counselor. So far, 78 counselors have been appointed.

III. New Zonal Administration—Thunukkai Zone

Decision-making is centralized in the national MOE. In 2013, with the election and forming of the Northern Provincial Council, more decision-making was devolved to the Province. Unfortunately, the provincial MOE and the provincial department of education still control the recruitment and deployment of teachers and principals. Disparities in educational achievement across schools will be difficult to address unless zonal administrations take on this function.

Most of the teachers in the Northern Province are from the Jaffna District, where western formal education dates back 200 years. Students at universities and colleges of education are mostly from schools in Jaffna, which has almost half the population of the Northern Province. Since teachers, principals, and administrators are primarily from the Jaffna District, they do not like to be posted to other districts. However, to fill the teaching positions, the system depends on mandatory transfers to rural schools. Most teachers find ways, mostly through nepotism, to return to schools in their district. This leads to many classes in rural schools without teachers or with teachers who are not qualified in mathematics, science, and English. For this reason, rural schools achieve only half, and in many cases one quarter, of the pass rates of the many leading schools in the Jaffna District.

The New Zonal Administration is being piloted in the Thunukkai Zone. It will have a zonal board of education that will take over decision making by the Northern MOE, except for curricula, examinations, pensions, and the like. The zonal board of education (ZBE) will do all recruitment and termination of teachers and principals. Thunukkai is the only education zone in Sri Lanka that is trying the New Zonal Administration.

An awareness program was conducted by Dr. N. Ethirveerasingam, Additional Provincial Director Mr. K. Premakanthan, Zonal Director Mr. S. Krishnakumar and staff to the principals of schools in the Thunukkai Zone on the bylaws of the ZBE. Parents and community leaders in the Thunukkai Zone also participated in the same program. They then elected representatives, 10 of whom were elected for the ZBE. Elections were held during a ZBE meeting. Meetings were held to brief principals about selecting 44 student representatives from each of the different school types, half girls and half boys. An awareness program and the bylaws workshop was held for the students. Many questions were posed and discussions held. Students were encouraged to answer their own questions. All unanimously expressed that it was the first time someone asked their opinion and asked them to answer their own questions.

The 44 student representatives also elected three girls and three boys as members of the ZBE. The minister, the secretary, and the provincial director appointed 10 members to make up the 26-member ZBE. All 26 members were briefed on their responsibilities and authority. Also, one hour of their meetings was open to the public living in the Thunukkai Zone to present issues in writing or in person.

Participatory Action Research and Implementation: Reflections, Challenges, and Limitations

As mentioned at the opening of this chapter, the exclusion of communities and educational personnel from long-term development processes became normalized over decades of war, political conflict, and extensive involvement of foreign aid agencies in northern Sri Lanka. Thus, the invitation to contribute toward improving the NP education system through the NESR was an unexpected, empowering process for all who participated. This section discusses some reflections, challenges, and limitations of PARI methods undertaken for the NESR.

Strengths

The PARI process that characterized the NESR was a momentous undertaking for a number of reasons. First, it created a democratic, collaborative opportunity for people in northern Sri Lanka to express their feelings, views, and ideas in a postwar context marked by uncertainty and vulnerability due to the long years of multiple displacement and living in camps while community and family social norms and structures broke down. People were told what to do and were herded. For many people, PARI enabled a greater sense of confidence and purpose simply because someone had asked them their opinion for the first time. In many ways, it changed the participants just as much as it changed aspects of the education system (Fals Borda 1995; Kemmis and McTaggart 2005). Second, participation was open to all stakeholders of the education system, irrespective of their location geographically or hierarchically. Many participants and Steering Committee members enthusiastically contributed countless volunteer hours, enabling a tremendous amount of work to be accomplished for a very low budget (around $27,000). Third, taking action through the RIMP brought the research process full circle and helped ensure follow up in an overburdened system.

The significance of the participatory NESR process can be further understood when considering the exclusionary approach typical of many past government and donor initiatives. The 1000 Secondary Schools Development Program, for example, is the main national educational development program planned for 2012 to 2016. The program will equip 1000 schools with science, language, mathematics, and information and communication technology laboratories. However, while the technological upgrade of schools is commendable, the selective inclusion of only about one-third of the over 2775 secondary schools (Type 1AB and 1C) in the country is sure to increase disparity across schools. Enhanced facilities to conduct practical experiments will be available only for some school students preparing for national exams. In the Northern Province, only 90 out of 196 1AB and 1C schools (46%) will be provided with the new technology facilities.

The insensitivity of agencies such as the Asian Development Bank further demonstrates the biased development projects that people in northern Sri Lanka have repeatedly witnessed. On June 4, 2014, the Sri Lankan newspaper, *Daily Financial Times,* reported that the bank translated the Khan Academy and MathCloud e-learning programs into Sinhala under a $725,000 grant. Twenty schools would pilot the program for six months to assess its impact on student performance. It is astounding that after a 30-year war, the Asian Development Bank would choose to fund a project that so blatantly discriminates against the Tamil-speaking communities, especially as it is widely agreed that language was one of the root causes of the war. To translate the learning material into Sinhala only, without at the same time providing Tamil translations, disenfranchises the Tamil-speaking people on the island. International donors should be more cognizant of the effects of their policies and programs and ensure that they do not create or exacerbate conflict. The Asian Development Bank should develop its own conflict filter, especially for education projects.

Challenges and Limitations of the Participatory Implementation Process

Participatory processes require a sustained commitment to dialogue, decision making, and follow-up implementation. These values and behaviors do not often present themselves spontaneously in individuals. More often, they are learned over time, through experience, and with the support of an enabling environment.

Participatory decision-making for implementation in countries that have been under colonial administration for many years—350 years in the case of Sri Lanka, which was also earlier a feudal system of government—is a rather foreign practice. In addition to such a history, the Northern Province was also subject to authoritarian rule by the government and the rebels over the past 30 years. Such a legacy did not prepare the education administrators, teachers, principals, and the general public to accept, take responsibility for, and dedicate themselves to implement new approaches in education and governance.

The key recommendations that required staff and recurrent budgets needed approval from the Northern Province board of ministers and the governor. Both approved the implementation of the key recommendations in August 2015. However, there were difficulties in implementation due to bureacratic delays in obtaining funds. Implementation with participation from the various units of the Northern Province Education Department began again only in December 2015. Furthermore, although the e-learning materials were produced, there were severe delays in planning and implementing teacher training sessions.

There were also systemic challenges relating to the capacity of Education Department staff. Those charged with making decisions to organize and direct the implementation were often unwilling to take up the challenge. The dedication needed to work cooperatively and efficiently to adopt innovative solutions seemed inadequate. Also, the system uses what is termed "performing" to post persons to positions for which they are not officially qualified. Such staff members were teachers and came with the salary of the teacher cadre. They had little or no experience in educational planning, finance, or curriculum development. Meanwhile, the teacher cadre in the school where they came from stayed vacant.

Finally, individuals who opposed the project hampered the new Zonal Board of Education, which was to function as a pilot project in Thunukkai Zone in the Mullaitivu District. The multiple seminars for zonal staff, parents, teachers, students, and principals on the responsibilities and the bylaws of the Zonal Board were well received. Elections were held to elect representatives of students, parents, community members, and the Northern MOE. All of this was done with the approval of the 30-member board of the RIMP. Concrete plans were even made to inaugurate the New Zonal Board of Education for the Thunukkai Zone by the governor of the

Northern Province. However, a small group of individuals did not want the zonal board inaugurated. They raised the issue with their members of the provincial council and parliament, who in turn brought the issue to the chief minister. He instructed the Northern Province minister of education to postpone the inauguration. After the inauguration was suspended at the end of May 2016, at last on December 8, 2016, the Governor of the Northern Province inaugurated the Zonal Board of Education.

The NESR explicitly sought to include as many stakeholders of the education system as possible, but there were limitations. One limitation was that international education specialists and educators from other provinces in Sri Lanka could not be invited due to reasons beyond the facilitator's control. Another limitation was in attracting an equal number of males and females to participate in the review process. School principals were tasked with selecting students for face-to-face meetings. Although due consideration was made for both Sinhala and Tamil speakers, a larger number of males than females participated in the review. This reflected the existing gender imbalance in teaching and educational administration.[5]

Despite these limitations, the NESR mobilized a diverse range of participants, all of whom have a stake in seeing that the recommendations are properly monitored and implemented. RIMP was organically formed as part of the overall NESR process. The Steering Committee members and many stakeholders recommended the creation of RIMP when they foresaw the risk of inefficiency and nonimplementation, which is endemic in the northern provincial education system. Toward this end, a secretariat was formed to carry out the functions of RIMP. As discussed in the three example recommendations we described, RIMP will be responsible for monitoring a wide range of follow-up action, from conducting teacher trainings to establishing drop-in counseling centers to pilot testing a new zonal administration.

Conclusion

This chapter documented the participatory action research and implementation process that sought to transform the northern provincial education system. PARI allows for a holistic process, enabling a constantly fluctuating focus on both research and implementation. It is particularly effective in educational policy development contexts, where bottom-up approaches tend to be more the exception than the norm.

The National Education Commission has invited RIMP for a meeting to explore the possibility of replicating the NESR in other provinces. It will also consider incorporating within its policy framework the principles of some of the NESR recommendations that are common to all provinces, especially those that have a high rural population. The chairman of tertiary education and vocational technical education will also be meeting with RIMP members to plan for implementation of the NESR recommendations related to vocational and technical education. It is possible that students who are not continuing to tertiary education can stay in school for another two years after upper secondary grades until they are 18 and learn job skills rather than be pushed out of the school system at 16 years. In Northern Sri Lanka and island-wide, participatory implementation of the NESR recommendations is slow and difficult. However, promising signs are present. RIMP was invited for a meeting with the National Education Commission (NEC) to explore the possibility of replicating the NESR in other provinces. Furthermore, according to personal communications with the Chairman of the NEC, many of the policies in the National Education Commission's 2017–2018 report, which was handed to the President of Sri Lanka on January 26th, 2017, have incorporated recommendations found in the NESR report. Indeed, implementation of the NESR recommendations is very slow, but taking place.

Appendix

Ten recommendations being implemented by the NP secretary of education and the Northern Province director of education:

1. Grade 1 and 6 enrollment to be limited to 30 + 2 starting January 2015. Total number of students in Grades 6 to Grades 13 schools is limited to 1500.
2. Schools with enrollment less than 200 and with student–teacher ratio less than 20:1 should be amalgamated with schools with students less than 100.
3. Corporal Punishment is banned in all schools in the North. The Principals should give a Weekly email report to the Secretary, PDE with a copy to Chairman of RIMP of the teachers who used corporal punishment in their classroom and in the school premises and the reasons the teacher gave and the reasons the student gave. The Principal should maintain a Corporal Punishment Record Book.
4. Every school should assign private space and establish a Counseling, academic and employment guidance for schools with enrollment of 300 or more is approved.

5. Grade 13 attendance register should be signed by all students and teachers in all 1AB schools. Attendance shall be monitored till June 30 of each year and the percentage of attendance of students required to sit for the examination will be calculated from January to June. July can be Independent Study in or out of school.
6. The 90 schools with 40 computers, a Mathematics and Language laboratories, to be open to use by schools in the Zones after-school hours including Saturdays for teaching science, Mathematics, English and IT. This is a condition in the 1000 school implementation process.
7. All students should take-part in outdoor physical education activity three days a week during the last period of the school day. One day per week can be reserved in the classes or Halls indoors for Yoga.
8. Schools that have excess teachers in any of the subjects over and above the Cadres required for teaching those subjects should be released from their duties from that school and posted to the PDE Office and referred to the Secretary.
9. Teachers in any school will be paid with the funds from that school allocation only. One school allocation for a teaching position should not be used to pay for another teacher posted to another school in excess or otherwise.
10. No classrooms should be without a teacher. Until those positions are filled, qualified Substitute Teachers should be appointed temporarily on a daily basis.

Source: Ethirveerasingam, N. (2014). Northern education system review. Jaffna, Sri Lanka: Northern Province Ministry of Education.

Notes

1. In 1961, the government of Mrs. Bandaranaike nationalized all schools. Some Catholic and Anglican mission schools chose not to be part of the government school system. All capital and recurrent expenditures, including salaries, were denied to such schools. When the government of Dudley Senanayake was elected in 1964, it partially restored assistance to schools that opted to operate their schools with private funds. The government paid salaries, textbooks, supplies, and uniforms. They were then called assisted schools, although they were governed by their own school board and recruited their own teachers.

2. Ethirveerasingam also drew from his previous experience in a participatory study for education reform and policy making in Sierra Leone in 1970–1971. At the time, he was a senior lecturer in the Faculty of Education at Niala University College, University of Sierra Leone. The study collected problems, issues, and ideas through interviews with schools, teachers, principals, parents, and community leaders at a total of six colleges. The Sierra Leone Ministry of Education directly implemented the recommendations, yet there was no independent participatory implementation or monitoring of the recommendations.
3. http://tinyurl.com/npereview.
4. Francis Cody (2009) has written about the dramatic growth of a newspaper reading culture among South Indian Tamils. Similar findings are likely applicable to Sri Lankan Tamils who have a shared literary heritage with Indian Tamils.
5. Feminization of the teaching workforce has existed in Sri Lanka since independence. A UNESCO (2011) study on women and the teaching profession showed that around 70% of teachers in public schools both across Sri Lanka and in three districts of the North (Jaffna, Killinochchi, and Mannar) were female. At the same time, only 23% of schools in Jaffna and 29% of schools in Mannar had female principals. Data were not available on female school principals in Killinochchi. Overall, gender representation among participants was biased toward males.

References

Adelman, C. (1997). Action research: The problem of participation. In R. McTaggart (Ed.), *Participatory action research*. New York: State University of New York.

Ambalavanar, D. N. (2006). *Arumuga Navalar and the construction of a Caiva public in colonial Jaffna*. Doctor of Philosophy, Harvard University, Cambridge, MA.

Arunatilake, N., & de Silva, R. (2004). *Overview of education budgeting and resource allocation processes in Sri Lanka*. Sri Lanka: Institute of Policy Studies.

Arunatilake, N., & Jayawardena, P. (2010). Formula funding and decentralized management of schools—Has it improved resource allocation in schools in Sri Lanka? *International Journal of Educational Development*, 30(1), 44–53. doi:10.1016/j.ijedudev.2009.05.007.

Batliwala, S. P., & Sheela. (1997). A census as participatory research. In R. McTaggart (Ed.), *Participatory action research: International contexts and consequences* (pp. 263–277). Albany, NY: State University of New York Press.

Bowd, R., Ozerdem, A., & Kassa, D. G. (2010). Participatory research methodologies: Development and post-disaster/conflict reconstruction. In A. Ozerdem & R. Bowd (Eds.), *Surrey*. England: Ashgate.

Burde, D. (2005). *Education in crisis situations: Mapping the field*. New York: USAID.

Cody, F. (2013). *The light of knowledge: Literacy activism and the politics of writing in South India*. Ithaca, NY: Cornell University Press.
Cole, R. (2015). *Free education, equity, and private educational spending in Sri Lanka*. Doctor of Philosophy Dissertation, New York University, New York.
Chaudhuri, S., & Heller, P. (2003). *The plasticity of participation: Evidence from a participatory governance experiment*. Working Paper, Institute for Social and Economic Research and Policy Colubmia University.
Cooke, B. (2003). A new continuity with colonial administration: Participation in development management. *Third World Quarterly, 24*(1), 47–61.
Ethirveerasingam, N. (2014). *Northern education system review*. Jaffna: Northern Province Ministry of Education.
Fals Borda, O. (1995). *Research for social justice: Some North-South convergences*. Paper presented at the Southern Sociological Society Meeting, Atlanta.
Freire, P., & Macedo, D. (2001). *Pedagogy of the oppressed*. Continuum.
Gowrinathan, N., & Cronin-Furman, K. (2015). *The forever victims? Tamil women in post-war Sri Lanka*. New York: The City College of New York.
Harris, S. (2006). Disasters and dilemmas: Aid agency recruitment and HRD in post-tsunami Sri Lanka. *Human Resource Development International, 9*(2), 291–298.
Holland, J., Blackburn, J., & Chambers, R. (1998). *Whose voice?: Participatory research and policy change*. Intermediate Technology Publications.
ICG. (2010). War crimes in Sri Lanka. *Asia Report*. International Crisis Group.
ICG. (2011). Reconciliation in Sri Lanka: Harder than ever. *Asia Report*. International Crisis Group.
ICG. (2012). Sri Lanka's North II: Rebuilding under the military. *Asia Report*. International Crisis Group.
Kelleher, F. (2011). *Women and the teaching profession: Exploring the feminisation debate*. London: Commonwealth Secretariat and UNESCO.
Kemmis, S., & McTaggart, R. (2005). Participatory action research: Communicative action and the public sphere. In N. K. Denzin & Y. S. Lincoln (Eds.), *The Sage handbook of qualitative research* (pp. 559–603). Thousand Oaks, CA: Sage Publications.
Kemmis, S., McTaggart, R., & Nixon, R. (2014). *The action research planner: Doing critical participatory action research*. doi:10.1007/978-981-4560-67-2.
Little, A. W. (2003). Education for all: Policy and planning lessons from Sri Lanka. *DFID: Educational Papers*. UK: DFID.
Little, A. W. (2011). Education policy reform in Sri Lanka: The double-edged sword of political will. *Journal of Education Policy, 26*(4), 499–512. doi:10.1080/02680939.2011.555005.
Little, A. W., & Evans, J. (2005). The growth of foreign qualification suppliers in Sri Lanka: *de facto* decentralisation? *Compare, 35*(2), 181–191.
Mittal, A. (2015). *The long shadow of war: The struggle for justice in postwar Sri Lanka*. Oakland, CA: The Oakland Institute.

Robins, S. (2008). *A participatory approach to ethnographic research with victims of gross human rights violations: Studying families of the disappeared in post-conflict Nepal.* Paper presented at the Workshop on field research and ethics in post-conflict environments, CUNY.

Saparamadu, C., & Lall, A. (2014). *Resettlement of conflict-induced IDPs in Northern Sri Lanka: Political economy of state policy and practice.* Sri Lanka: Centre for poverty analysis.

Somasundaram, D. (2007). Collective trauma in northern Sri Lanka: A qualitative psychosocial-ecological study. [journal article]. *International Journal of Mental Health Systems, 1*(1), 1–27. doi:10.1186/1752-4458-1-5.

Srinivasan, M. (2015, March 12). Time to replace 13th Amendment with a more dynamic system. *The Hindu.* Retrieved from http://www.thehindu.com/news/international/south-asia/time-to-replace-13th-amendment-with-a-more-dynamic-system/article6983176.ece

Thiranagama, S. (2011). *In my mother's house: Civil war in Sri Lanka.* Philadelphia: University of Pennsylvania Press.

UNICEF. (2013). Sri Lanka Statistics. Retrieved January 28, 2016, from http://www.unicef.org/infobycountry/sri_lanka_statistics.html

Uyangoda, D. (2013). Education in emergencies in Sri Lanka (2001–2010): Lessons learned. Retrieved from doi:http://www.ineesite.org/en/resources/education-in-emergencies-in-sri-lanka-lessons-learned

Vimalarajah, L., & Cheran, R. (2010). *Empowering diasporas: The dynamics of post-war transnational tamil politics.* Berlin: Bergh of Peace Support.

Wedagedara, A., Lakmali, H., & Kadirgamar, N. (2015). Increasing the education budget & the merging of education & business. *Colombo Telegraph.* Retrieved from https://http://www.colombotelegraph.com/index.php/increasing-the-education-budget-the-merging-of-education-business/

CHAPTER 5

Unpacking Participation: The Case of Child-Centered Pedagogy in India

Neha Miglani, Jayasree Subramanian, and Vishnuteerth Agnihotri

INTRODUCTION

This chapter presents a large-scale, mixed-method evaluation of a program employing participatory and child-centered education reform in India.[1] Participatory education has been strongly associated with approaches that

---

Authors are thankful to UNICEF, the Ministry of Human Resource Development and the state governments for commissioning the study on which this chapter is based.

N. Miglani (✉)
Rossier School of Education, University of Southern California,
Los Angeles, CA, USA
e-mail: nmiglani@usc.edu

J. Subramanian
Homi Bhabha Centre for Science Education, Tata Institute of Fundamental Research, Mumbai, Maharashtra, India
e-mail: jsree.t.s@gmail.com

V. Agnihotri
Independent Researcher, Bengaluru, Karnataka, India
e-mail: vishnu.agnihotri@gmail.com

claim to involve learners in shaping curricular goals or classroom processes. However, participatory approaches have also received increasing criticism regarding how they adhere to their theoretical aims. This evaluation attempts to critique and show possibilities of student and teacher participation in classrooms from seven states. As part of the larger Indian public education context, this chapter aims to contribute to the debates on relevance and sustainability of large-scale child-centered reform in the country and participatory approaches toward education in general.

Recent international education trends, particularly in developing countries, witnessed a widespread adoption of child-centered approaches to education. India has been attempting a paradigm shift from teacher-centered to child-centered classrooms for over two decades. Two guiding frameworks of education reform in India, National Curriculum Framework of 2005 and the Right of Children to Free and Compulsory Education Act (RTE) of 2009, advocate participatory and child-centered education. The activity-based learning (ABL) program, a pedagogical approach emphasizing skill acquisition through activities and promoting child-centered classrooms, has emerged as a potential model to execute these pedagogic ideals (UNICEF 2013). Large-scale adoption of ABL programs in India creates opportunities and aspirations for meaningful participatory, democratic, and child-centered reform in primary education. Widespread adoption of such reforms not only calls for a better understanding of design and implementation of the programs adopted but also a deeper inquiry into factors that enable participation at various levels.

The chapter is divided into four sections. The first section presents the conceptual framework and the literature review on which we base this evaluation. Section 2 details the methodology used including sampling, evaluation framework, and approach to data analysis. The third section presents the evaluation of ABL as a means to child-centered reform. This is divided into subsections, each delineating the programmatic forms and the practice of participation. A detailed discussion is included on factors identified critical to participatory and child-centered classrooms. Section 4, the conclusion, summarizes the evaluation results and points to key recommendations.

Conceptual Framework and Literature Review

Education practitioners using participatory action research are commonly inspired by the ideas of critical pedagogy, committed to emancipatory action formulated by Freire (Hall et al. 1982). Consequently, participatory education focuses on dialogical reflection and proposes that education must belong to a democratic process (Freire 1993). As Skovsmose (1985) described, "[I]f a democratic attitude is to be developed through education, education as a social relationship should not contain fundamentally undemocratic features. It is not acceptable that the teacher (alone) has the decisive and prescribing role" (p. 340).

Participation of learners is also central to the ideas of learner-centered or child-centered education. Most closely identified with the work of Dewey (Chung and Walsh 2000), the child-centered view advocated that education should emanate from students' interests, participation, and active investigation. Dewey (1916) aimed to integrate school with society and the processes of learning with life problems by application of the principles and practices of democracy. Often defined in opposition to teacher-centered pedagogy, where students take a more passive role as teachers transmit knowledge, child-centered approaches to teaching are based on the assumption that people learn best when they are actively engaged in the curriculum and when their interests form the foundation for curriculum building (Paris and Combs 2006). Centering students in the learning process, this pedagogy suggests that learners are "constructing and assimilating knowledge" instead of merely absorbing "discrete facts [from] an existing store of knowledge" (Mtika and Gates 2010, p. 396).

Although education scholars identify putting learner-centered pedagogy and social transformation in both participatory and learner-centered approaches, they (particularly scholars of adult learning) also draw some important distinctions. Auerbach (1993) drew this distinction through the nature of participation in choosing the curriculum. She noted that learner-centered orientation gives primary emphasis on participants' involvement with curriculum development *processes* while participatory approaches emphasize drawing curriculum *content* from the social context of learners' lives along with involving them in curriculum development processes. This distinction, however, gets blurred for younger children in primary grades. In describing the learner's viewpoint in what is worth teaching, Kumar (2004) noted that children cannot be expected to articulate their view of an abstract concept like knowledge and may not be capable of deciding what they should learn. What, then, is the nature of *participation* sought from young children? Kumar (2004) concluded that "our best chances lie in agreeing to think on behalf of children rather than in trying to find out what they think" (p. 4). How does this process of thinking on behalf of children and their participation unfold, and how do national projects of public education articulate such an educational reform?

Existing Literature

There is an emerging body of work analyzing pedagogic reform through child-centered education in the developing countries. Child-centered pedagogies have become a part of education policy reform in developing countries as diverse as Botswana (Tabulawa 1997, 1998, 2003), Tanzania (Barrett 2007), Uganda (Siraj-Blatchford et al. 2002), Tibet (Carney 2008), Guinea (Anderson-Levitt and Diallo 2003), Mongolia (Steiner-Khamsi and Stolpe 2006), Namibia (Ralaingita 2008), and India (Sriprakash 2012). Some scholars critique the policy borrowing of child-centered education as a one-size-fits-all, decontextualized "best practice," and question whether it should indeed be recommended as a policy choice in these countries. These scholars revealed numerous stories of failure in its implementation in and the apparent lack of conclusive evidence for child-centered education resulting in improved learning outcomes (Tabulawa 2003; O'Sullivan 2006; Nyambe and Wilmot 2008; Vavrus 2009; Schweisfurth 2011; Sriprakash 2012). Scholars identified various constraints that may render such an approach inappropriate in these contexts, including: limited resources; unrealistic policy expectations; conflicting pedagogic frameworks; incompatible examination and curricular systems; inadequate teacher training; and differences in cultural beliefs that may conflict with the assumptions of a child-centered paradigm.

Relatively few studies directly evaluate the performance of child-centered programs in terms of their effectiveness. These studies reveal a mixed picture of student learning gains. For instance, while a Department for International Development study in Ghana noted a positive relationship between the child-centered program and student achievement gains (Coffey and University of Cape Coast 2012), a longitudinal study in the state of Karnataka, India, pointed toward positive effects on language test scores but insignificant effects on mathematics test scores (Gowda et al. 2013). Another evaluation of the child-centered multigrade, multilevel program in Chhattisgarh, India, noted low performance of children on mathematics and language respective of the approach. There was no difference noted in performance of Grade 3 children while a multigrade, multilevel effect was noted for Grade 2 children (Sarangapani and Mehendale 2013). Similarly, Little's (2005, 2008) reviews of international research on multigrade pedagogy (similar to many child-centered programs) indicated no clear pattern of results either (i.e., students in multigrade classes performed no better or worse than monograde students).

Existing literature on such programs in India is scant and limited in scope. Most studies are based on implementations in individual states, particularly Tamil Nadu and Karnataka.[2] A desk review by UNICEF (2013) of action research on child-centered programs in India noted several limitations of the existing studies particularly around lack of rigor. In terms of capturing processes, it noted that "many of the studies focused mostly on observing whether materials and processes were being followed as they had been prescribed; however there was very little critique of the pedagogy, curriculum or materials in themselves" (p. 51). A significant gap in the current literature concerns understanding participation in the child-centered reforms. For instance, what are the forms and nature of participation in child-centered classrooms? What is the extent of participatory and child-centered practices in large-scale implementations, and what teaching/learning practices and/ or other factors ameliorate or exacerbate this participation?

Research Questions

The aforementioned guiding frameworks of education reform in India, the National Curriculum Framework and the RTE, recommended a focus on "primacy to children's experiences, their voices, and their active participation" (National Council for Education Research and Training [NCERT] 2005, p. 13), and mandated "learning through activities, discovery and exploration in a child-centered manner" (RTE Act 2009, p. 9). In the last two decades, over 250,000 government primary schools with more than 10 million children in 13 states in India have implemented a version of child-centered reform program from primary grades, more commonly called ABL[3] (UNICEF 2013). State-wide, large-scale implementations of ABL programs represent a significant shift for Indian primary education characterized by rote-based, textbook-centered, exam-focused, and authoritarian instruction. Widespread implementation along with the gaps identified in the literature, underscores the need for the evaluation presented in this chapter. We focus our attention on student and teacher[4] participation through an evaluation of ABL as a means to child-centered education in seven states in India. Specifically, we explore three research questions:

1. How are the ideas of participatory and child-centered education embedded in the programmatic form through ABL?

2. What practices of participatory, child-centered education are seen on the ground? How prevalent are these practices?
3. What other factors outside the classrooms are critical to participatory and child-centered classrooms?

METHODS, SAMPLE, AND DATA

The evaluation focused on primary grades[5] in seven states in India: Gujarat, Rajasthan, Madhya Pradesh, Jharkhand, Karnataka, Andhra Pradesh,[6] and Tamil Nadu. The data collection and analysis was divided into three integrated stages.

Stage I (August–November 2013) of the study comprised reviewing existing literature, developing an understanding of ABL as conceptualized by different states through discussions with multiple stakeholders at various levels (state, district, subdistrict), and exploration of learning material and training modules.

Stage II (December 2013–June 2014) and Stage III (July 2014–March 2015) comprised quantitative and qualitative data collection, respectively, with an aim to understand current ABL practice. Stage II included a large-scale quantitative exploration of 857 schools in the seven states through classroom observations and teacher questionnaires. Stage III involved in-depth qualitative study of the nature of classroom processes and relationships in a smaller subsample (110 classrooms) selected from Stage II, in order to identify factors contributing to success of the program. An assessment of student learning outcomes through a standardized test on language and mathematics was also included in Stages II and III.

Participatory Nature of the Evaluation

This evaluation aimed and planned for participation of stakeholders at several levels. An advisory committee with representatives from Ministry of Human Resource and Development, National Council for Education Research and Training, participating state education leaders who had implemented ABL, pedagogy experts, and academics guided the activities of the evaluation from its inception and met periodically. Stakeholder consultations were held in each state to understand the program's evolution. These consultations were comprised of people who were involved in state policy making, administration, curriculum design, and implementation aspects of ABL and nonstate personnel who played a key role in the evolution of ABL. Group consultations with support personnel[7] and teachers were also done in some states.

Both quantitative and qualitative tools were piloted in select schools and went through multiple feedback and revision rounds with the assistance of state officials, pedagogic experts, and academics. Some of the data collection was done by state personnel in addition to the research team at Educational Initiatives. Evaluators appointed by the respective state/district government bodies were primarily involved with the quantitative survey work and learning assessments for students. The evaluators were trained on the survey conduction processes through a two-day training conducted in the local language. A total of 16 trainings were conducted across the seven states, training nearly 600 state personnel.

Similarly, the analysis framework, although proposed by the core research team, was vetted through other experts in the advisory committee. Involvement of stakeholders in dissemination of findings was a critical component of the evaluation. A daylong workshop was organized in each state with participation of members from the state Sarva Siksha Abhiyan office, District Institutes of Education and Training, and State Councils for Educational Research and Training. Select teachers and support personnel were also invited to share their experiences and reflections. Recommendations were discussed across leadership levels, implementation personnel, and teacher trainings to ensure relevance.

Even though we mention the participatory nature of evaluation, we remain keenly aware of its limitations in our case. For instance, due to the large scale of the evaluation, participation from all levels was impossible. Hence we relied on a select number of expert judgments in each state. Participation of state personnel for data collection also involved high costs in terms of both time and resources. Finally, like Probst (2002), we acknowledge that the applicability of participation for research purposes is limited to long-term action research approaches where research goes hand in hand with processes of social and institutional change.

Sampling

For each state,[8] a representative district selection was made using a population-weighted average of the human development and education indices. Inclusion of districts with high educationally backward blocks, and tribal population (scheduled tribes) were also factored in. (See selected districts in Table 5.1) The selection of 120 schools from each

Table 5.1 Sampled districts in the evaluation

State	District
Andhra Pradesh	Chittoor
	East Godavari
	Mahabubnagar
Gujarat	Mehsana
	Rajkot
	Valsad
Jharkhand	East Singhbum
	Gumla
	Ranchi
Karnataka	Bagalkot
	Tumku
	Udupi
Madhya Pradesh	Bhopal
	Seoni
	Shivpuri
Rajasthan	Alwar
	Tank
	Udaipur
Tamil Nadu	Chennai
	Cuddalore
	Salem

state (80 ABL and 40 non-ABL schools in states where ABL is not statewide) included proportional representation of boys and girls, children from urban and rural areas, different types of schools (primary only, primary with upper primary), and different blocks (depending on maturity of ABL implementation, educational backwardness). Stratified two-stage cluster sampling was adopted for school selection using the probability proportional to size method. Stage III school selection involved purposive sampling at the state level to include schools with high and low student outcomes along with high and low adherence to ABL processes as per Stage II data. This sample consisted of 110 classrooms with 15 to 20 classrooms from each state.

Evaluation Framework and Approach to Analysis

The differences in the conceptualization of ABL and the absence of documented log frames necessitated a common ground for the evaluation.

This was achieved by identifying the common underlying principles for child-centered and participatory education. The next 12 principles—referred to in this chapter as principles of Child Friendly Learning Centered (CFLC) education—were derived through extensive discussion with the advisory committee and this evaluation's lens.

1. Meaningful, learning-oriented activities
2. Variety of learning materials in use
3. Provision for self-paced and individualized learning
4. Opportunities to learn through different modes
5. Scope for higher-order thinking and critical questioning
6. Every child engaged or student engagement
7. Continuous assessment integrated with the learning process
8. Democratic processes/relationships in the classroom
9. Equitable and inclusive learning environment
10. Contextualization to children's everyday world and community
11. Physical environment conducive to learning
12. Attention to holistic, all-round development

Guided by the principles of CFLC education, the framework for analysis assumes classrooms and teachers are central to the evaluation. The data from various stages have been explored through these two strands to begin with. Classrooms and teachers are understood within the context of school, the support received from the school and the headmaster/mistress, to appreciate the school environment and its influences on the classrooms. Schools are considered a part of the larger ecosystem comprising of various implementation aspects, state mandates, training and support, and learning materials provided.

Factors critical to answering the evaluation questions were identified through a detailed mind-map of variables. Broad factors considered were at the level of classroom and teacher (i.e., student learning outcomes, teaching attributes, and resources), training and support, curriculum and pedagogy (ABL material), implementation (administrative), and overall vision of the state program to some extent. Each of these factors was further broken down into parameters (details in Appendix) upon which data were collated and organized from various stages. The classroom was considered as the unit of analysis, although we situate it in the larger context of the school and state bureaucratic system.

Evaluating ABL as a Means of Child-Centered, Participatory Education

Child-centered reform in India progressed through a national policy discourse, an international development discourse, as well as conceptualization and evolution of the ABL program at state levels. These discourses and program evolutions have taken their own course and likely influenced each other as the reform progressed. In this light, we present the child-centered reform in India within the three overlapping policy levels of policy, program, and actual practice.[9] Borrowing from the policy discourse and Stage I discussions, the results to be presented focus on various aspects of programs and practice through the identified underlying principles of CFLC education.

Programmatic Form of Child-Centered Reform: Activity-Based Learning

Although several small interventions in India used child-centered, activity-based pedagogies, programs adopted by the states under evaluation, at least initially, borrowed heavily from the Rishi Valley Institute for Educational Resources (RIVER)[10] model practiced at Rural Education Center of the Rishi Valley School.[11] Next we briefly describe key features of the ABL programs. This is followed by a critique of the program in light of its underlying principles.

Key Features and Expectations from ABL Programs

Stage I discussions revealed the initial ABL pedagogy as adopted by the various states had some common features, such as mixing students of different ages or grade levels in a single classroom and students sitting in small groups and carrying out independent learning through activities with support of their teacher and/or peers. Another common feature was that curriculum in each subject was broken down into small, manageable learning units, usually a competency, called milestones, which were arranged in a logical sequence from simple to complex in the form of a learning ladder for each subject. The sequence of tasks/activities within a milestone was such that a child typically went through introductory, practice, evaluation, and enrichment or remedial activities. Each activity was recorded in the form of learning cards, labeled with symbols and colors. The classroom environment was colorful and stimulated by the presence of a number of teaching learning materials and displays of student work. In addition to developing the students' abilities to learn independently and collaborate with each other, this model was also expected to address critical problems in the Indian education scenario, such as high absenteeism, multigrade classrooms, and low levels of learning (Herzerberger n.d.). Further, it was found during Stage I discussions that, over time, state models evolved but continued to be referred to as ABL. Key elements of implementation in each state under evaluation are listed in Table 5.2.[12]

Programmatic Form of Child-Centered Reform: A Critique
A review of the RIVER model and initial state models revealed features allowing for an environment encouraging child participation and autonomy. Unlike a conventional classroom, where children sit in rows with restricted movement, children in ABL classrooms sit in groups and help each other while the teacher sits amid the children. This seating plan not only bridges physical distance between the teacher and children but also presents opportunities for breaking down the structure of the teacher as the center of authority. The cards and materials are (ideally) arranged in a way that the child can access them without much adult assistance. Once children complete an activity card, they can easily find the next card and move to another group. Thus, children participate in and take charge of their learning to some extent. The provision for movement in the classrooms potentially prevents biases in children's seats allocation by teachers. There are low-height blackboards on which children can practice writing. Student work, written work, drawings, or other crafts are displayed in the classroom. Having a space of their own can give children a sense of confidence and participation.

State models that continue to follow grouping of students based on cards use of a variety of materials and encourage peer learning. However, these opportunities might be limited in regions where the state models are conceptualized with textbooks and very little additional learning material is available (as in Andhra Pradesh and Rajasthan). Such areas may tend to fall back on the conventional structures inside classrooms. Furthermore, in textbook-based models, teachers may have to explicitly create the provision for self-paced learning and opportunities for collaborative learning, unlike models where these styles of learning are designed within the pedagogy.

Table 5.2 Key features of state ABL models

	Andhra Pradesh	Gujarat	Jharkhand	Karnataka	Madhya Pradesh	Rajasthan	Tamil Nadu
Grades	1–4	1–5	1–4	1–3	1–4	1–5	1–4
Subjects covered	Telugu, Math, EVS, English	Math, EVS, Gujarati	Hindi, Math, EVS	Kannada, English, Math, EVS	Hindi, Math, English, EVS	Math, English, Hindi	Tamil, English, EVS (science and social studies in grades 3, 4), Math
Year of start	1997	2010	2009	1995	2008	2008	2003
State-wide Implementation	2011	In process	Implementation stalled	2009–10	In process	2015	2007–08
Major changes to the model	No. of cards reduced Reverted to textbooks	No major changes to model as yet	No major changes during pilot phase	No. of cards reduced	Time-bound assessments introduced No. of cards reduced Logo system changed	No. of cards reduced Eventually moved to textbooks	Textbook introduced under *Samacheer Kalvi**, in addition to card and ladder Trimester system introduced No. of cards reduced Logo system changed

Key aspects of the current model	Activity-based textbooks No card/ladder Grouping of students not mandated No provision for extra material by state	Card and ladder for students Additional learning material like math kits, workbooks, etc. Grouping of students based on activity type Prescribed set of activities to cater to development of multiple intelligences	Program no longer functional New program with activity-based learning and ability-based grouping in practice Card and ladder and other learning materials for class 1 and 2 when functional Self-learning material with learning cycles for classes 3 and 4	Card and ladder for students Additional learning material like math kits, etc. Grouping of students based on activity type Monthly guidelines on milestones to be covered	Card and ladder along with some cards incorporated into a workbook Grouping based on activity type Monthly and term-wise assessment schedules	Activity-based textbooks No specific mandates on grouping Elaborate formats for CCE Teacher diary and reflection formats	Card and ladder along with textbook Additional learning materials including 3-D math kits and language readers Grouping based on activity type Trimester system dictating curriculum to be covered CBSE recommended CCE formats

*Samacheer Kalvi is the School Education Department of the Government of Tamil Nadu.

Assessment in the RIVER model is built into the cards in the learning ladder, where completion of a milestone is indicative of the competency being attained. No marks or grades are assigned after a card is complete, thus making working the cards potentially nonthreatening for children. However, with the introduction of CCE mandates and feedback from stakeholders on the need for a more formal assessment, Tamil Nadu and Madhya Pradesh implemented new assessment formats in addition to the ones implicit in the ladder. Rajasthan and Andhra Pradesh developed their own systems of assessments and evaluation. Some of these are formal assessments and not integrated into learning.

The model offers the scope to learn through multiple modes: individual learning; learning through interactions with peers; learning through experimentation; and learning by making and doing things. However, for this learning to happen, the quality (and availability) of materials also seems critical (in addition to the teacher), such that activity cards that enable multiple modes of learning should be reflected in their design. If the materials do not support the intended processes, the modes of learning available to children could be restricted. The most significant changes in all the states' models has been observed in the learning material used by students. Over time, Andhra Pradesh and Rajasthan completely reverted to textbooks, and Tamil Nadu supplemented cards with textbooks. As a possible consequence, the nature of the material provided could limit the flexibility available to children to learn through different modes and at their own pace.

Although there is scope for nonlinear ladders in the RIVER model, none of the states under evaluation implemented them. Thus, each child is expected to go through largely the same set of cards in nearly the same sequence. As Shukla (2009) noted in the context of Tamil Nadu's implementation, for ABL to be truly 'differential' education, there needs to be scope to adjust the sequence, repeat/reiterate or bypass certain things, and use learning methods with some children that are not being used with others. The differentiation in ABL programs seems largely around the pace at which students learn. This flexibility is also limited by the normative mandates of progressing students to the next grade. The original ABL model, best represented by the RIVER model, does provide for opportunities to create a fear-free and inclusive environment and different modes of learning. At the same time, different program implementations can create conditions that deviate significantly from the underlying principles and at times go against the philosophy of child-centered education.

Practice of Participatory, Child-Centered Education in the Seven States

In order to understand the nature and forms of participation inside the classrooms, we focused on defining parameters of classroom environment as well as student and teacher participation. The parameters of participation were identified by how policy articulates child-centered learning, inputs from quantitative data analysis in Stage II, and iterative analysis of Stage III qualitative data. Broadly divided into two categories, these parameters included, at the classroom level, (1) fear-free environment, (2) inclusive environment, (3) student engagement, (4) opportunities for self-paced learning, and (5) peer learning opportunities.[13] Specific to teachers and teaching, these parameters included (6) organization of students (grouping based on ability, activity, etc.), (7) availability and usage of a variety of learning materials, (8) teacher understanding of the state ABL program, (9) teacher effort, and (10) teacher buy-in of the program. The degree of alignment of each parameter was coded through a categorization into high, medium, or low buckets. Next we discuss the classroom practices and prevalence of these parameters for 110 classrooms (and 110 corresponding teachers) considered in the qualitative analysis.

Classroom Parameters and Classification

From the detailed observations, 75% of the classrooms (n = 82/110) were found to be reasonably fear-free (high to medium classification). This was indicated by students' physical movement in the classroom, their voluntary and active participation in classroom activities, students assuming responsibility for their learning (e.g., taking card and/or teaching learning material alone), and the absence of physical punishment. Although these classrooms also included ones where the atmosphere was casual and not oriented toward learning, these results show a significant positive step toward "a warm and welcoming" environment as imagined in the policy documents (Government of India 1992). We considered inclusive practices in classrooms: the effort that made to integrate all students in a class and if there are any discriminatory practices on the basis of caste, community, gender, learning ability, grade level, and the like.[14] We took note of teachers admonishing, beating, or making deprecating comments. Our observations revealed practices of gender segregation in seating arrangements in many classrooms in Rajasthan, which was observed rarely in classrooms in other states. When they were present, children with special needs were rarely given full attention. Typically, these students were not engaged in activities, and only negligible effort was made to include them with the rest of the class.[15] Despite the prohibition on corporal punishment in India, light beating and threatening by teachers was found in classrooms across the states.

Besides classrooms being fear-free, student engagement in learning activities was found to be high in 27% of classrooms. This was analyzed through signs such as students asking questions or responding to teachers' questions, students interacting with peers or teacher about a task/learning activity, and interest shown to students while doing classwork. Students taking charge of their own learning was observed in only 13% of classrooms. This was understood through signs of student independence, whether they went about doing their activities even in the absence of a teacher or volunteered to help their peers. High to medium levels of peer interaction and self-paced learning were observed in these 13% classrooms; low levels on these parameters were found in all other classrooms. Opportunities for self-paced learning were understood through students' ladder positions (the exact milestone/card position where each student was on the days of observations) and if they were doing different activities at any given point of time. We studied the spread and/or clustering of ladder positions whenever data were available. Opportunities for peer learning, in contrast, were observed through planned and unplanned interactions between peers. Students' initiatives to voluntarily help their peers were taken as a strong sign.

The analyzed classrooms were classified based on the ratings on the abovementioned classroom parameters and divided into classroom types. The purpose of this classification was twofold: (1) to see the degrees of alignment with some of the underlying principles of child-centered education, and (2) to identify critical differentiating factors where this alignment was found to be high. Only 30 parameters (Type 1 and 2) were observed to be reasonably well aligned to underlying principles of child-centered education. These results are summarized in Table 5.3.

Teacher Participation and Teaching Parameters
Different states under evaluation mandated disparate ways of organizing the classrooms in terms of groupings students based on activity or ability. In the states that mandated activity-based grouping—Karnataka, Tamil Nadu, Gujarat, and Madhya Pradesh—only 23% (n = 17/73) actually practiced it. In Rajasthan, which mandated grading with ability, four out

Table 5.3 Types of classrooms in the study sample

Classroom type	Student engagement	Fear-free and inclusive environment	Opportunities for self-paced and peer learning	Number of classrooms (out of 110)	Percentage of classrooms
Type 1	High	High	High to medium	14	13%
Type 2	High	High to medium	Medium to low	16	14%
Type 3	Medium	Medium	Medium to low	25	23%
Type 4	Medium to low	Medium to low	Low	37	34%
Type 5	Low	Low	Low	18	16%

18 classrooms observed actually practiced it. The remaining classrooms practiced either the conventional, whole-class teaching (where the teacher addressed the class as a whole and students sat in rows) or groupings based on other criteria.[16] Similarly, the availability and usage of classroom learning materials varied by state. In Tamil Nadu and Madhya Pradesh, schools had a variety of learning materials and resources; in Gujarat, schools were provided with funds to purchase materials as needed. Most states also encouraged teachers to use locally available materials and create their own learning resources. High material availability was observed in 38% of classrooms (n = 42/100). Most of these classrooms (n = 28/42) were in Karnataka and Gujarat. Despite the presence of a variety of learning materials in these classrooms, students and teachers were observed using them only in 16 cases. The effort enacted by the teacher was observed to be high for 23% (25/110). These teachers: noted errors that students made and gave appropriate feedback; took a learning process to completion with each child; made their own materials; kept an eye on and assisted all students in clearing doubts with respect to their classwork/homework; maintained a student diary using multiple strategies to teach; and/or gave different homework to different students.

Teacher knowledge of their state's ABL program was found to be largely procedural (which included knowledge of grouping children, ladder, built-in assessment, etc.). Few teachers understood the underlying principles of the program. Procedural understanding of the model also differed by state. For instance, in Karnataka and Gujarat, most teachers interviewed in Stage III (19/19 in Karnataka and 13/15 in Gujarat) and were able to explain how ABL should work in their classrooms. In Madhya Pradesh, well over 50% of the teachers interviewed during Stage III were not clear about the state-mandated methodology, and grouping and processing according to the state model was practiced in only one classroom. In Rajasthan, more than half of the 18 teachers interviewed had only a broad or superficial knowledge of the state-run CCE program. Tamil Nadu has had a statewide implementation since 2007. However, as the model has seen significant change since 2011, voices from the field (teachers, trainers, and Block Resource Teacher Educators) indicated a low degree of confidence in the current state model and conflicting messages from state officials. Only one out 16 classrooms observed in Stage III was practicing activity-based grouping as prescribed by the state. In Andhra Pradesh, teachers typically did have a procedural understanding of the state model. It is noteworthy that the current model in the state is a simplified version and does not involve the use of card and ladder or grouping of students. Apart from this, teachers' perceptions that the method was not "serious enough" as it had little provisions for disciplining children, and their divided opinion on their own roles in the classroom as mere facilitators versus enhanced roles, further confirmed a deeper disconnect with the underlying principles of child-centered education. For instance, a teacher in Madhya Pradesh insisted that he preferred the traditional method of teaching since "children do not take continuous evaluation seriously." Raising the issues of discipline and authority, another teacher mentioned that "earlier children used to be under discipline. Now children don't ask anything from the teacher; a teacher is not respected anymore." Articulating their new role, some teachers mentioned that their role in ABL methodology is only to facilitate, to help only if children are unable to do something; otherwise children should drive their own learning. They also sensed a loss of agency in the ABL method. This view was more prominent in classrooms observed in Gujarat and Tamil Nadu. Teachers also strongly felt that they have to take care of every child and how their workload in the classroom has increased as a result of ABL.

Teacher buy-in was understood based on the views expressed on desirability of ABL, the kind of benefits and challenges that they saw in implementing it, and to some extent their beliefs in principles of child-centered education. This was also matched against teachers' classroom practices. Analysis revealed that only 21% teachers had a high buy-in to the ABL model of their state. Teachers with high buy-in were strongly associated with Type 1 classrooms (highly fear-free, high child engagement, with children taking charge of their learning). Teachers with low buy-in into the program did not feel involved in the state program, felt a loss of agency, and/or felt confused by the changes brought into the model. For instance, a teacher in Rajasthan articulated her dissatisfaction with the changes brought to the state program in this way:

> Let any program come, but for it to be successful, let it run for a long time. CCE is also a good program except it has more written work. LEHAR [Learning Enhancement Activity in Rajasthan] was stopped abruptly and CCE was started, and now I do not have material or full information to do CCE.

Factors Critical to Participatory and Child-Centered Classrooms

Even though we limited the practices of participation to the classroom in this evaluation, we understand that the teacher and classroom contexts are situated within the larger ecosystem of school and government support and the implementation system.

Basic Implementation Factors

Several challenges faced by teachers were exacerbated by the lack of basic administrative factors. Pupil–teacher ratio in 24% of observed ABL classrooms in Stage III was above 35 to 1, which led to difficulty in classroom management. Teachers across the states mentioned that the method is almost impossible to implement if class size is too high. Similarly, delivery of learning materials for ABL was reported to be delayed by one to two months in 37% of the schools visited.

Pedagogic and Teacher-Related Factors

Stage II and III data analysis pointed toward key pedagogic and teacher-related factors that led to both improved student learning outcomes and positive classroom practices. Particularly, activity-based grouping and high usage of a variety of teaching/learning materials were associated with better learning outcomes. From iterative analysis of qualitative data, teacher buy-in was found to be instrumental. Classrooms where activity-based grouping was followed by using cards and ladder were 0.5 standard deviations ahead on student learning outcomes compared to classrooms where whole-class teaching was practiced. (See Fig. 5.1.) This difference is statistically significant with medium effect size (using Cohen's d metric) indicating meaningful differences between the two groups. Similarly, use of a variety of teaching learning materials appeared to be one of the key differentiating factors between the top and bottom 15% of classrooms ranked on student

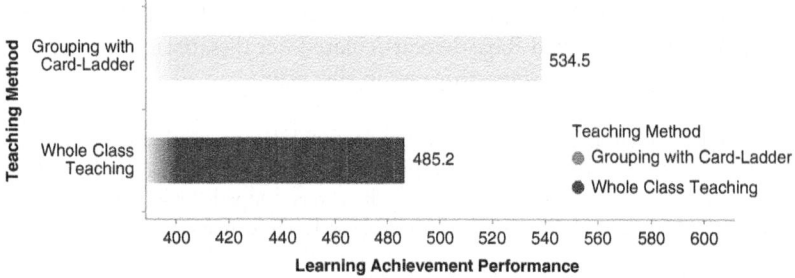

*All raw scores have been scaled to a mean of 500 and SD of 100
**'Grouping - Any other' and 'Grouping- Ability' not considered for analysis due to heterogeneity, low N, respectively
Data presented here is at student level; Grouping with card ladder: 401 students; Whole Class Teaching: 1032 students
Difference between 0.2 SD-0.5 SD-Small effect size; 0.5 SD - 08 SD- Medium effect size; Value greater than 0.8 SD-Large effect size.
This allows us to understand the magnitude of difference between two sets of data.

Fig. 5.1 Student learning outcomes by classroom organization

learning achievement. Classrooms showing high usage of teaching learning materials performed 0.3 standard deviations better than classrooms where low or minimal use of resources was observed. (See Fig. 5.2.) This indicates small effect size and statistically significant differences.

In addition to these differences, both teacher effort and buy-in to the state program was pertinent to creating child-centered classrooms, as shown by the qualitative analysis. The percentage of teachers who put in high effort and those able to keep all students engaged in a classroom was relatively small (about 20%). Almost all of these classrooms fell into Types 1 and 2. The organization in these classrooms was almost equally divided between activity-based grouping and whole-class teaching. This finding highlights the importance of teacher involvement in terms of effort taken and classroom management skills in creating a child-centric classroom, over and above the pedagogy followed or the material used. Teachers in Types 3, 4, and 5 classrooms made medium to low effort in their attempts to follow ABL through activity-based groupingshowed. Although a structural framework in the form of activity-based grouping was present in these classrooms, a child-centered, participatory learning environment was not evident in the absence of teacher effort, involvement, and ability to keep all students engaged.

Further, within the classrooms aligned to child-centered parameters (Types 1 and 2), 17 (out of 30) classrooms followed either whole-class teaching or primarily teacher-decided groups. Thus, even without the adoption of a structural mechanism like activity-based grouping through

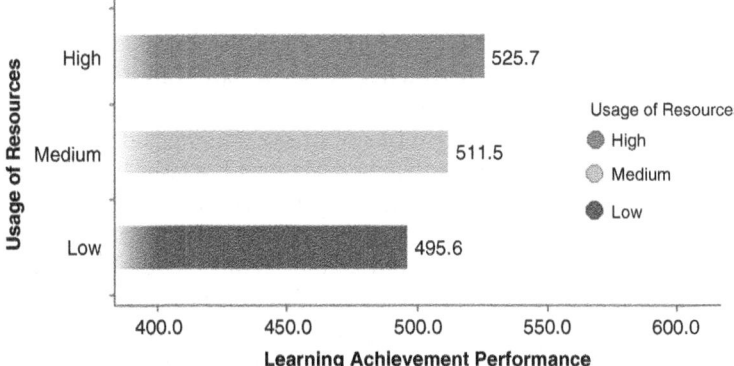

*All raw scores have been scaled to a mean of 500 and SD of 100
Data presented here is at student level; Number of students in classrooms with 'High' usage of resources: 564,
Number of students in classrooms with 'Medium' usage of resources: 1064,
Number of students in classrooms with 'Low' usage of resources: 1415,
Difference between 0.2 SD-0.5 SD-Small effect sizes; 0.5 SD - 08 SD-Medium Effect size; Value greater than 0.8 SD-Large effect size.
This allows us to understand the magnitude of difference between two sets of data.

Fig. 5.2 Student learning outcomes by use of additional learning resources in classrooms

card and ladder, a classroom could display high levels of child engagement, provided the teacher put in high effort. However, greater learner autonomy was observed in classrooms that did follow activity-based grouping (13/30) as conceptualized in the original RIVER methodology. Despite teachers' high efforts, those 17 classrooms remained somewhat teacher-centric and showed relatively lower opportunities for self-paced learning and peer learning. Additionally, use of a variety of learning materials (outside the regular textbooks, cards, etc.) was found to be higher in classrooms following activity-based grouping.

Teacher buy-in to the state-mandated model was crucial to the degree of student participation. Teachers who put in high efforts but were not following the state-mandated grouping did not buy in to the model. Even though aligned to most classroom parameters, the key differences between these classrooms (where teachers put in high efforts but did not follow the state-mandated grouping) as compared to the ones where teachers put in high effort and followed the state-mandated grouping were children taking charge of their learning and participating in learning activities without the teacher's insistence. These differences were noted by children continuing to work in the absence of teacher, taking a break from work and returning to it without intervention, and even going out of their way to help peers.

Programmatic and Design Factors
Since certain parameters of child-centered education discussed thus far show significant variations by state, a discussion of state contexts and how they impact classroom practices is imperative. Weak understanding of the ABL model by teachers pointed to a lack of strong training and support in certain states, particularly in Rajasthan and Madhya Pradesh. In Stage III teacher interviews, 10 out of 18 in Rajasthan and six out of 20 in Madhya Pradesh shared that they do not consider themselves proficient in the method. About 20% of teachers interviewed in Madhya Pradesh reported large group sizes (up to 250) for training. Trainer proficiency and lack of clarity in delivery was mentioned by 45% of teachers interviewed in Rajasthan. Further, even though management of training and support was perceived to be better in Gujarat, Tamil Nadu, Andhra Pradesh, and Karnataka, teachers there had gained only a procedural understanding of ABL. A discussion with an ABL trainer from Tamil Nadu underscored the point that training rarely covers underlying principles of ABL in sufficient depth. The trainer mentioned: "Teachers undergo some ABL training which is at the level of answering exam questions ... they never understand the why of it."

In addition to lack of appropriate training, support activities provided by cluster and block resource persons primarily focused on record keeping and data collection, and teachers did not cite support personnel as a source for resolution of academic issues. Some teachers even expressed negative opinions of support personnel, believing that their visits focused on monitoring. As a teacher in Madhya Pradesh said, "I believe that these visits are aimed to just find flaws in teachers because most of these people don't give us any helpful suggestions." At the same time, support personnel may not have the required skills or experience to provide the necessary academic support. Support personnel generally had qualifications that equipped them for secondary school teaching. Most were recruited with limited or no teaching experience. In some states, entry criteria for support personnel were less stringent than for teachers. For example, in Gujarat, support personnel and teachers are recruited based on the same eligibility test, where higher-ranked candidates are offered teaching positions and lower-ranked candidates are recruited as support personnel. Cluster-level meetings for teacher training and support were not reported as fora of support in any state except Karnataka. Teachers in Karnataka reported that cluster-level teacher meetings and consultations every one to two months were useful in resolving academic issues and implementing ABL better.

As discussed earlier, teacher buy-in was quite low overall. This statistic was, however, highly skewed by state; Karnataka had high buy-in (78%) compared to less than 10% in all other states. Comparing the state histories of implementation, our analysis revealed that continuous involvement of teachers, continuity of the program over a period of time, and broad alignment with other programs run by the state were significant design factors for successful implementation. A study of program evolution and teacher interviews in Karnataka revealed much higher involvement of teachers in making materials, decisions related to ABL implementation, and the detailed modalities of implementation. In comparison, there was poor communication to teachers in Tamil Nadu, Madhya Pradesh, and Rajasthan about significant changes made to the materials and their involvement in making those changes. For instance, implementation of ABL in Madhya Pradesh ceased between 2012 and 2014. When training for ABL was announced in 2014, a teacher recalled, "When no trainings happened after 2012, we thought the ABL program had been stopped. When we were called for trainings in 2014, this came as a shock to us."

Significant successive changes in Tamil Nadu's ABL model along with misalignment with other programs have also resulted in low buy-in (6%), despite the state having a 10-year history of ABL implementation. For instance, along with ABL documentation requirements that already include formative assessments, Tamil Nadu required teachers to fill in additional forms to comply with CCE requirements; Karnataka and Gujarat do not require such additional documentation. Hence, although the program is participatory to some extent, good governance (Neef 2003) in its implementation is required. Some teachers and the education bureaucracy might be willing to learn and participate, but doing so would require creating conditions and scope for participation. Appropriate pupil–teacher ratios in classrooms, timely delivery of learning materials, and training of teachers and support personnel need to be addressed before this type of program is implemented. Additionally, if the governing bodies of critical stakeholders (teachers, support personnel, etc.) do not participate in decisions related to major changes in the programs, inequities at the macro level result (Cooke and Kothari 2001).

Conclusions and Implications

Participatory and child-centered education approaches to mass education for primary grades in India have been imagined as multiple participation modes. Most significantly, these modes include: placing the child at the center of learning processes; participation of children in driving their own learning; and, more broadly, participation as means to preserving and enhancing the idea of democracy. When we evaluated child-centered reform through ABL, we noted that some of these possibilities have occurred while some are limited. In most states, evolution of the models tended to move the programs away from the underlying principles of child-centered education. Continuous changes in ABL structure, learning materials, and normative regulations around assessment and syllabus completion have created conditions that exacerbate practices on the ground. A move away from the ideals at the level of conceptualization can lead only to partial practices that lack a sound basis. Through this evaluation, we delineated how the implementation fares in various classroom environments and student and teacher parameters. Only 27% of classrooms in the sample were reasonably aligned with participatory and child-centered principles. Few states have adopted ABL as intended by state models. Fifty percent of classrooms in the sample offered almost no opportunities for self-paced and/or peer learning. The democratic ideals, as expressed through student autonomy and taking charge of their learning, were seen in only 13% of sampled classrooms.

At best, the practice of ABL on the ground can be seen working only in some pockets of large-scale implementations. Although participatory and child-centered classrooms may seem ideal, as Hickey and Mohan (2004) pointed out, an idealistic framework is only as good as its implementation. This fact poses serious questions about program sustainability in India. Low prevalence of classrooms that show alignment with the principles of child-centered education can be understood through a variety of factors that influence implementation. The evaluation identified some factors that are critical to child-centered and participatory classrooms. Contrary to the perception that learning materials are central in ABL, this study found that teacher involvement—in terms of effort taken, teacher preparedness in terms of trainings and support provided, and teacher buy in to the program in terms of participation in various stages of implementation—is critical. Apart from this, it is impossible to imagine successful implementation if basic factors, such as appropriate pupil–teacher ratio and on-time availability of learning materials, are not ensured. A state's commitment to building capacity, keeping the program running without making too many changes, and alignment with other initiatives is of critical importance.

The findings presented in this chapter have important implications for policy makers and educators who aim to implement child-centered programs at scale. First and foremost, this study maintains that the critical need is to scale up a *mind-set*, not a set of materials and methods. Apart from other things, scaling up a mind-set requires nurturing communities of practice. As our study has shown, teachers are central to these communities of practice. Much like participatory action research, as McTaggart (1994) discussed, child-centered education reform needs a "series of commitments"; it is not merely about learning but also about knowledge production and improvement of practice. This reform demands an evidence-based culture that encourages further research, regular systematic reviews, and documentation of major decisions with substantial evidence. Finally, any implementation of child-centered and participatory education will have to focus on the underlying philosophy rather than the instrumental character of the method. In this light, activities related to monitoring, support, and measurement of outcomes must align with principles rather than mechanics. This focus would mean greater communication of the program goals to teachers and support staff and tracking parameters like student engagement and participation in the classrooms. With these recommendations and findings, we hope this chapter allows readers to reflect on the myriad ways of supporting the promise of child-centered and participatory education.

Appendix

Factors and Parameters for Analysis

	Classroom & Teacher			Training & Support	Curriculum	Implementation (administrative)	Vision & Buy-In		
Outcomes	Teacher	Resources					Leadership	Functionaries	Community
Academic outcomes • Stage 2 scores • Stage 3 scores	Buy-in Attentiveness to all students	Availability		Quality Quantity & recency	Alignment to CFLC principles	Training on time Material on time	Understanding of top level Coherent vision for primary education	Understanding of principles Views on desirability and challenges	Buy-in to ABL
Classroom environment • Student engagement • Fear free environment • Self-paced learning • Peer learning • Inclusive environment	ABL understanding Effort by teacher Teaching method	Usage (teacher/ student)		Support quality Support quantity	Coherence	Planning for ABL introduction/ scaling Consistency over years Funding	Consistency in direction across leadership changes	Perception of support from top	What they want from schools

Notes

1. The authors were part of the core research group, at Educational Initiatives for this evaluation. Educational Initiatives is a leading education research organization based in India. Authors are thankful to UNICEF, the Ministry of Human Resource Development and the state governments for commissioning the study on which this chapter is based.
2. For studies in Tamil Nadu, see: NCERT 2011; Srivastava 2010; Akila 2009; Shukla 2009; Mahapatra 2008; Anadalakshmy 2007. For Karnataka, see: Gowda et al. 2013; Sriprakash 2012; Annigeri et al. 2010; Kaul 2004; Usha 2004; Lalitha 2003.
3. Although the program has different official names in some states (e.g., Nali Kali in Karnataka, Pragna in Gujarat), ABL is the more commonly used term.
4. In this chapter, we limit the idea of participation to children and teacher participation. Community participation, even though a part of some policy documents and some program implementations, is not reviewed here.
5. Grades 1 to 3 in Karnataka, 1 to 5 in Rajasthan and Gujarat, and 1 to 4 in the remaining states.
6. The state of Andhra Pradesh was undivided (i.e., included the current states of Andhra Pradesh and Telangana) when the evaluation started.
7. Education support personnel cover a broad range of professional, administrative, technical, and general staff working within the education bureaucracy.
8. Selection of states was subject to considerations of the coverage and duration of their ABL programs, ensuring adequate diversity in the sample, a state's willingness to participate, costs, and available resources.
9. For the purpose of this chapter, by the term "policy," we refer to the intent and basic principles by which the government is guided toward educational initiatives. "Program" refers to the guidelines, formulated and enforced by the governing bodies, that set the blueprint of implementation, ideally as per the policy principles; and "practice" describes the implementation *as observed* during the period of this study.
10. In articulating their programs, all the states under evaluation made either a direct reference to Rishi Valley's RIVER methodology or mentioned Tamil Nadu's ABL program, which in turn borrowed from RIVER. Some states (e.g., Gujarat) also reviewed certain other child-centered programs in the state.
11. Rishi Valley is an Indian boarding school, founded by the philosopher J. Krishnamurthi. It is located close to the town of Madanapalle in the state of Andhra Pradesh.
12. In Jharkhand, the pilot ABL program was introduced in 235 schools in 2009 and had become nonfunctional at the time of this study. Hence, the state was excluded from the qualitative study, and a dipstick review was conducted instead.

13. Several other parameters related to teacher classroom management skills, overall experience, qualifications, and the like were considered, but only parameters important in our analysis are discussed in the text. Also, we understand these categories to be overlapping, such that classroom parameters (such as fear-free classroom environment) could be influenced by the teacher/teaching parameters (such as understanding of ABL) in the classroom and vice versa.
14. For this study, we limited the data for inclusive environment to the classrooms. We understand that subtle exclusive practices may extend beyond classrooms. Even within the classrooms, these practices may not be very evident in the three days of observations. In-depth identification of inclusion/exclusion practices could be a study in itself, and our inability to do this is one of the limitations of this study.
15. This may partly be because the ABL model itself does not have explicitly formulated methods to handle such children. Teachers in some states did appreciate the training they had received in integrating children with special needs into the classroom.
16. Grouping based on other criteria included static groups decided either by the teacher or by student's convenience. In many cases, groups of friends sat together.

References

Akila, R. (2009). *A trigger for change in primary education: An evaluation of ABL in Tamil Nadu, 2009.* Government of Tamil Nadu.

Anandalakshmy, S. (2007). *ABL: A report on an innovative method in Tamil Nadu.* Retrieved from http://www.ssa.tn.nic.in/docu/abl-report-by-dr.anandhalakshmi.pdf

Anderson-Levitt, K. M., & Diallo, B. B. (2003). Teaching by the book in Guinea. In *Local meanings, global schooling* (pp. 75–97). Palgrave Macmillan US.

Annigeri, V. B., Kulkarni, A. R., & Revankar, D. R. (2010). *Evaluation of effectiveness of Nalikali program in Karnataka.* Dharwad: Centre for Multi-Disciplinary Development Research.

Auerbach, E. (1993). Putting the P back in participatory. *TESOL Quarterly, 27*(3), 543–545.

Barrett, A. M. (2007). Beyond the polarization of pedagogy: Models of classroom practice in Tanzanian primary schools. *Comparative Education, 43*(2), 273–294.

Carney, S. (2008). Learner-centred pedagogy in Tibet: International education reform in a local context. *Comparative Education, 44*(1), 39–55.

Chung, S., & Walsh, D. J. (2000). Unpacking child-centredness: A history of meanings. *Journal of Curriculum Studies, 32*, 215–234.

Coffey, & University of Cape Coast. (2012). Synthesis report. Retrieved from http://r4d.dfid.gov.uk/pdf/outputs/misc_education/61003-IDEVREAN11016GH_ABL%20Report_Final_with_appendices_300413.pdf
Cooke, B., & Kothari, U. (2001). The case for participation as tyranny. In B. Cooke & U. Kotari (Eds.), *Participation: The new tyranny?* (pp. 1–15). New York: Zed Books.
Dewey, J. (1916). *Democracy and education*. New York: Macmillan.
Freire, P. (1993). *Pedagogy of the oppressed* (Rev. ed.). New York: Continuum, 1970.
Government of India. (1992). *National policy on education programme of action*. New Delhi: MHRD.
Gowda, K., Kochar, A., Nagabhushana, C., & Raghunathan, N. (2013). Curriculum change and early learning: An evaluation of an activity based program in Karnataka, India. Stanford: Stanford Center for International Development.
Hall, B., Gillette, A., & Tandon, R. (1982). *Creating knowledge: A monopoly*. New Delhi: Society for Participatory Research in Asia.
Herzberger, R. (n.d.). Features: History of MGML pedagogy at Rishi Valley. Retrieved October 9, 2014, from Rishi Valley Education Centre Website: http://www.rishivalley.org/features/History%20of%20MGML%20at%20Rishi%20Valley.pdf
Herzerberger, R. (n.d.). *Rationale for multigrade pedagogies*. Retrieved October 9, 2014, from Rishi Valley Education Centre website: http://www.rishivalley.org/features/Rationale%20for%20a%20Multi-Grade%20Multi-Level%20Pedagogy.pdf
Hickey, S., & Mohan, G. (2004). *Participation—From tyranny to transformation?: Exploring new approaches to participation in development*. London: Zed books.
Kaul, A. (2004). *Nalikali: Innovations in primary education in Karnataka*. Government of Karnataka.
Kumar, K. (2004). *What is worth teaching?* New Delhi: Orient Blackswan.
Lalitha, M. S. (2003). *Evaluation of Nalikali approach under Janshala Programme in Karnataka*. Mysore: University of Mysore.
Little, A. W. (2005). *Learning and teaching in multigrade settings*. Unpublished paper prepared for the UNESCO.
Little, A. W. (2008). *Size matters for EFA. CREATE pathways to access*. Research Monograph No. 26.
Mahapatra, A. (2008). *ABL: Effectiveness of ABL under SSA*. Tamil Nadu: SSA.
McTaggart, R. (1994). Participatory action research: Issues in theory and practice. *Educational Action Research, 2*(3), 313–337.
Mtika, P., & Gates, P. (2010). Developing learner-centred education among secondary trainee teachers in Malawi: The dilemma of appropriation and application. *International Journal of Educational Development, 30*(4), 396–404.

NCERT. (2005). *National curriculum framework 2005*. New Delhi: NCERT.
NCERT. (2011). *Programme evaluation of ABL in Tamil Nadu*. NCERT.
Neef, A. (2003). Participatory approaches under scrutiny: Will they have a future. *Quarterly Journal of International Agriculture, 42*(4), 489–497.
Nyambe, J., & Wilmot, D. (2008). *Bernstein's theory of pedagogic discourse: A framework for understanding how teacher educators in a Namibian college of education interpret and practice learner-centred pedagogy*. Cardiff: Cardiff University School of Social Sciences.
O'Sullivan, M. (2006). Lesson observation and quality in primary education as contextual teaching and learning processes. *International Journal of Educational Development, 26*(3), 246–260.
Paris, C., & Combs, B. (2006). Lived meanings: What teachers mean when they say they are learner-centered. *Teachers and Teaching: Theory and Practice, 12*(5), 571–592.
Probst, K. (2002). *Participatory monitoring and evaluation: A promising concept in participatory research?* Weikersheim: Margraf Verlag.
Ralaingita, W. D. (2008). *Re-making the Namibian teacher: A study of teacher reflection in an era of social transition and policy reform*. ProQuest.
RTE Act. (2009, August 27). *The right of children to free and compulsory education act*. Ministry of Law and Justice, Government of India.
Sarangapani, P., & Mehendale, A. (2013). *Multi-grade Multilevel (MGML) programme in Chhattisgarh: An evaluation*. Mumbai: School of Education, Tata Institute of Social Sciences.
Schweisfurth, M. (2011). Learner-centred education in developing country contexts: From solution to problem. *International Journal of Educational Development, 31*(5), 425–432.
Shukla, S. (2009). *Draft report on implementation review and theoretical analysis of ABL*. unpublished.
Siraj-Blatchford, I., Odada, M., & Omagor, M. (2002). Supporting child-centered teaching under universal primary education in Kampala, Uganda. In S. E. Anderson (Ed.), *Improving schools through teacher development: Case studies of the Aga Khan Foundation projects in East Africa*. Lisse: Swets & Zeitlinger.
Skovsmose, O. (1985). Mathematical education versus critical education. *Educational Studies in Mathematics, 16*(4), 337–354.
Sriprakash, A. (2012). *Pedagogies for development—The politics and practice of child-centred education in India*. Springer.
Srivastava, A. B. L. (2010). *Time-on-Task of teachers and students in primary schools of Tamil Nadu*. RESU, ED-CIL.
Steiner-Khamsi, G., & Stolpe, I. (2006). *Educational import: Local encounters with global forces in Mongolia*. New York: Palgrave Macmillan.

Tabulawa, R. (1997). Pedagogical classroom practice and the social context: The case of Botswana. *International Journal of Educational Development, 17*(2), 189–204.

Tabulawa, R. (1998). Teachers' perspectives on classroom practice in Botswana: Implications for pedagogical change. *International Journal of Qualitative Studies in Education, 11*(2), 249–268.

Tabulawa, R. (2003). International aid agencies, learner-centred pedagogy and political democratisation: A critique. *Comparative Education, 39*(1), 7–26.

UNICEF. (2013). *Activity-based learning in India: Overview strengths and challenges.* New Delhi: UNICEF.

Usha, M. N. (2004). *External evaluation of Janshala: Karnataka state report.* Bangalore: Institute for Social and Economic Change.

Vavrus, F. (2009). The cultural politics of constructivist pedagogies: Teacher education reform in the United Republic of Tanzania. *International Journal of Educational Development, 29*(3), 303–311.

CHAPTER 6

Learning and Evolving in Hybrid Learning: A PAR Perspective

Rajarshi Singh, Neha Sharma, and Ketan Verma

INTRODUCTION

Evolution has mandated a lengthy childhood for the human species, during which children undergo rapid physical and mental development. The rate of mental growth slows down by the onset of the juvenile stage, ultimately becoming very limited when an individual reaches adulthood. The completion of adolescence is culturally marked with the end of the 'nesting' period, a phase congruent with the schooling years, when children are expected to face some of the biggest challenges, ranging from learning new languages, imbibing social skills, absorbing mathematics, inculcating scientific thinking, discovering their own artistic creativity to developing critical thinking. Post-industrial societies have deemed schools as places for such learning, teaching, discovering and developing in spite of the non-uniformity of learning processes and their rate of learning.

R. Singh (✉) • K. Verma
ASER Centre, New Delhi, 110 029, India
e-mail: rajarshisingh@gmail.com; ketan.verma@asercentre.org

N. Sharma
Pratham, New Delhi, 110 029, India
e-mail: neha.sharma@pratham.org

Despite the cultural acceptance of school-based instruction as the common norm, we at Pratham[1] question 'schooling' that is accepted as almost sacrosanct, but not without reason. In this chapter, we share our learning and experiences from the Hybrid Learning Program, a large-scale learning experiment involving 26,000 empowered children and their communities following a Participatory Action Research (PAR) framework. The name, "Hybrid Learning" symbolizes a mixed or hybrid strategy where the interaction of children, community partners, local populaces, technology, and researchers are combined to plan for action.

Schooling Status in Rural India

Beginning from the centrally sponsored District Primary Education Programme (DPEP) in 1994, and its latter evolution, the Sarva Siksha Abhiyan (SSA), the flagship program for Universal Elementary Education (UEE) after 2000, the Government of India has successfully promoted the culture of 'schooling' by investing intensively on school infrastructure and enrolment[2] improvement schemes. However, the focus on quality of schooling and the learning achievements of children is absent. As a result, despite a high enrolment of over 96% children (between the ages of 6 to 14) in school[3] the *Annual Status of Education Report* (ASER)[4] has demonstrated a consistent decline of learning outcomes over the last decade. The proportion of children in grade 5 who can read a grade 2 level text, has dipped to less than 50% (ASER 2016). Today almost all of India's 200 million children are in school, but as economist Lant Pritchett characterizes it, the country is in a "big stuck" as far as children's learning outcomes are concerned (Pritchett et al. 2016). We note that 20% of those children who discontinue their education, do so because they are not interested in studies (Central Statistics Office 2011), implying schooling that is not engaging enough, or fails to generate enough interest. The currently prevalent "banking model of education" (Freire 1993, 2000), is plagued by insufficient learning outcomes in schools. Further, Mukherjee and Sikdar (2012) show that in contrast to 'enrollment increasing' schemes, which have received approximately 98% of the funding, 'quality improvement' schemes have seen an increase from 0% support in 2007–2008 to 0.31% in 2011–2012, demonstrating an overwhelming negligence of the quality of education. The Hybrid Learning experiment aims to fill this gap of quality education at the grassroots levels.

Learning and Participation

In this section we explore the semantics of PAR in the context of children growing up in the largest democracy[5] that is rapidly becoming a knowledge economy. We begin with a working definition of participation in the Indian context first and then take up issues of learning, followed by a more detailed discussion on PAR.

Defining Participation

Participation in its broadest form is natural and intuitive. A newborn cries and demands to be fed or be attended to, thus participating in its own development by capturing the attention of a provider and obtaining nourishment. In similar fashion, developmental participation is concerned with the involvement of communities and people in decisions that have a potential of impacting their lives through a formal or informal framework. The socio-political and cultural underbelly of communities introduces heterogeneous flavors to participation. Despite the variations in both settings and approaches in different cultural contexts, the themes of empowerment and freedom are constants. Simply put, participation is a necessary condition for people to realize and act upon their freedom. Such a view of participation is not new, and perhaps its biggest proponents in modern Indian history were leaders and participants of India's struggle for independence. Although introducing political shades to a term now often used to characterize "development" may seem far-fetched, it is appropriate if not essential to do so to understand what 'participation' means and can mean in India, the largest democracy, which obtained its freedom by capitalizing on the most powerful democratic tool—participation. "Independence" is bottom up, and in conceiving of the utopia of the Village Swaraj (self-governance by a village) as extolled by Mahatma Gandhi, every village is a republic unto itself, self-dependent and responsible for basic needs, such as education and employment of its populace (Gandhi 1942). The *Panchayati Raj*[6] is a participatory democratic system, where rural voices are heard and action is taken in accordance. We thus define "participation" as the right and freedom of any and all individuals to voice and exercise their opinions for their personal development as well as the good of their local community and its members. In this definition, the opportunity to realize one's voice and vision is implicitly understood, given the intimate relationship between rights and opportunities in a democratic setting.

Participatory governance often faces the threat of oligarchy, where a few among the many usurp positions of power to push their own agenda. Thus, development oriented democratic participation demands inclusivity, wherein all voices are encouraged and considered, "weaker" sections of societies are given equal standing, and actions are taken first for the greater good of the local community while also respecting the freedom of an individual. It is not sufficient to include the masses only once for action; it is necessary to create a system of continuous participation where the people have a perpetual say. Given that children are the most underrepresented members of a democratic society,[7] it is therefore important to comprehend the nuances of participation of children who grow up with two most complex realities—their developing mind and the growing realization of existence of a complex social structure around them—powered by norms of languages and culture. Although there are those who believe that children are not fully capable of taking 'adult' or 'matured' decisions or should not be burdened with the responsibility of making decisions (Hart 1992), we see that children in rural India are capable of accepting the challenge of decision making, which is an amalgamation of multiple components: establishing objectives, ranking and classification of desired objectives, development of alternatives and their evaluation, evaluating probable consequences of a decision, and translating decisions into action iteratively and effectively. Participation of children is therefore not of one kind but many, where children have the freedom to exercise their say in the multiple steps of decision making. Hart (2008) describes this gradation of participation through the "ladder of participation," laying out a practical design to begin understanding the value given to children's voices in programs for children.

Combining all these ideas, we define participation of children in the Indian context as the right of children to play a key role of informed decision makers in their own futures in collaboration with adults and other children who are willing to listen to their voices.

The Hybrid Learning experiment uses the above ideas of participation and builds upon the earlier strategies of Learning to Read pedagogy[8] that follows the philosophy of Teaching at the Right Level (TaRL) (Banerji and Duflo 2015). Although the school system follows a rigorous curricular framework that expects children to "read to learn," the resounding consensus from children, their parents, and communities engaged in traditional knowledge-imparting systems, and our own experience suggests a need to focus on "learning to learn." It is with this conviction and realization the Hybrid Learning program spans multiple cognitive and non-cognitive skills, utilizing the potential of children, local communities and spaces, trained facilitators, and audio-visual content on a digital platform to create a village-level learning atmosphere that is democratic—by the children, for the children, and of the children.

Defining Learning

De Houwer et al. (2013) define learning as an "ontogenetic adaptation," where "learning" becomes a survival mechanism that helps children explore the uniqueness of their environment. The innate urge to explore creates further opportunities for learning. Integrating the above definition of learning with constructivist theories, we see that learning happens not in isolation but in association with multiple environments; Piaget's close work with children demonstrated how they build on existing schemas, an internal store of knowledge and conceptual understanding. The social aspects of learning, where key actors are identified from the immediate surroundings (namely, other children or teachers—broadly any adult with some knowledge to offer) demonstrate the innate participatory nature of learning and knowledge acquisition. Finally, we note that motivation plays a major role in a child's participation. A recent study shows that children are dissatisfied with their ability to bring about changes in their local and school settings. As Davey et al. (2010) reported a child saying:

> "Teachers don't want to listen to you anyway...We were doing it the teacher's way for five minutes but then stopped; and said its boring. So the teacher stopped the lesson and said everybody has to go home." (p. 12)

It is evident that social participation not only leads to greater learning and development of children but also of those adults who wish to help children in their growth. A program that is self-learning and self-informed through the creation of a cyclical loop of learning, implementation, and reformulating its learning is inherently intelligent.

Next we review PAR, a participatory approach to actionable research, and explore how the concept of intelligent programming and design is used in this new experiment.

Review of Participatory Action Research

Traditional research is concerned with recognizing a problem through observation and devising solutions that aid the researcher in understanding the cause and effect of the observed phenomenon, ultimately leading to an "improved theory." This methodology is, however, insufficient to bring about actionable change in the lives of persons in a society for two reasons: (1) The question itself may not be the right question to ask, given local realities; and (2) the answer may not be sufficiently robust to bring about a positive transformation in the lives of persons living in that particular social reality. The PAR methodology combines "social investigation, educational work and action," (Hall cited in Brown and Tandon 1983, p. 279), where the collective participation of researchers and community members drive the "process of mutual learning where the local people have control over the processes" (Cornwall and Jewkes 1995, p. 1669). In PAR, the local community transforms itself into an active participant in research rather than being the object of research, thus enabling equitable participation, redistribution of power, and the inclusion of contextualized knowledge throughout the research. Freire (2000) noted that participatory research

> "requires that the investigators and the people (who would normally be considered objects of that investigation) should act as *co-investigators*. The more active an attitude men and women take in regard to the exploration of their thematics, the more they deepen their critical awareness of reality and, in spelling out those thematics, take possession of that reality." (p. 106)

The PAR schema thus provides opportunities for traditionally neglected voices to be heard so that they are included in decision-making processes that have the capacity to bring in changes in their lives. It also "engages young people in active organizational decision-making regarding institutions and systems that directly impact them" (Wright 2015, p. 23). In PAR, external actors (researchers), work in conjunction with local participants to problematize a social issue through the following steps: (1) Identifying the social domain and existing conditions/fact finding, (2) articulating the assumptions of the operational model/conceptualization of the issue, (3) developing alternative hypotheses/planning solutions and implementation processes, and (4) implementing and re-evaluating the hypothesis[9] (Alvesson and Sandberg 2011) through a continuous feedback loop following the intelligent programming and design philosophy.

History of Participatory Action Research

PAR approach owes its origins to the fields of adult education, international development and social science, which paved the way for "bringing participation into research" (Elden & Levin cited in Khanlou and Peter

2005, p. 2334). PAR is the marriage of Action Research (AR), postulated by Kurt Lewin (1946) as a theory of social action that intimately ties research to action through a "spiral of steps, each of which is composed of planning, acting, observing, and evaluating the result of action" (McTaggart 1991, p. 170), and Participatory Research (PR), which "attempts to present people as researchers themselves in pursuit of answers to the questions of their daily struggle and survival" (Tandon 1998, p. 7).

Both AR and PR are committed to bringing about social changes through the action oriented questioning and study of an inclusive group that would include outsiders to the problem and insiders with intimate knowledge of the challenge. As a synthesis of the two modes of research, PAR utilizes the spiral actionable structure of AR and community participation of PR through a "group activity" (McTaggart 1991). Here, the systematic collaboration between communities and researchers is fostered to actualize an iterative means of bringing about informed change for the benefit of the community. However, some critiques of PAR have raised the issue of "tyranny of participation" (Cooke and Kothari 2001), where modes of participation insufficiently vary to accommodate different social factors under this approach.

These objections provide a segue to develop the PAR framework further, where the nature of participation is understood contextually and the heterogeneity within marginalized communities is recognized, where empowerment through citizenship10 becomes a common standard (Hickey and Mohan 2005). Hence, in the following section we explore the Hybrid Learning experiment and devise a working understanding of PAR applicable to a scalable educational intervention across three states in rural India.

HYBRID LEARNING PROGRAM AND PAR

Pratham has been committed to improving learning outcomes through digital literacy and the use of user friendly and engaging, scalable and cost effective technology since 1998. The synthesis of our experiences with computer-aided learning, experiments with novel technology initiatives, such as the Digital Read Aloud to improve reading; the Beehive Project, a community driven project aimed at creating physical and virtual resources for sharing and learning; and Learn Out of The Box, a low cost digital classrooms project, and the lessons from Sugata Mitra's "Hole in the Wall" experiment (Mitra 2000) inspired the seed thought of the Hybrid Learning experiment. We note that quality content and dialogue with children are critical factors to "hook" children and sustain their participation. Digital technology, albeit not the solution to the woes of non-learning across rural India, can serve as an effective mode of delivering engagement.

The Hybrid Learning Program is a digitally-aided group based "learning to learn" oriented intervention facilitated by Pratham in partnership with 400 local communities to encourage discovery based learning of children in grades 5 through 8 across the states of Uttar Pradesh, Maharashtra and Rajasthan in India. Hybrid Learning is Pratham's effort to facilitate educational participation across rural communities to enable children's learning through a digital platform.[11] Children and their advocates in the village are encouraged to take ownership of the program.[12] Pratham carries all financial burden of the experiment, thereby creating a "compulsion free" atmosphere where children are free to either participate or not participate in the endeavor. Considering that there is no timetable or structured timeline to follow, children feel empowered to participate (if they choose to do so) variably over the course of the experiment. Even though such a lack of structure and the availability of freedom and choices vis-à-vis participation make the results not easy to compare and compute, this is perhaps the basis of PAR as envisioned in Hybrid Learning, which allows researchers to track the organic participation of children. The digital platform records the children's content usage and attendance, so as to inform content generation. Furthermore, audio-visual tools such as cameras, help children create their own video content, which they share amongst themselves. Although an apps-based facility for children to indicate their choices or create their own contents is revolutionary in remote rural areas, the availability of tablets offers opportunities and challenges for the young as well as the experienced participants. The next sections touch upon the ways in which children, communities and researchers negotiate with these opportunities and hurdles.

'Building' Towards Children's Participation

More than 26,000 children, their guardians, and their communities, have joined hands with Pratham to evolve the open school model[13] wherein any and every child in the village is welcome, without any restriction. The participants and Pratham work together to help children create their own learning environment—effectively redefining the concept of "child-friendly" environment as the space where what, how much, and how they learn is left up to the children. The underlying philosophy of such community based research is succinctly summarized by Hall (2005, p. 19) as "a proposal for action that focuses on transformed understandings of the creation of knowledge human beings." These empowered learners from low-income rural areas design their own learning path by navigating across a bouquet of scientific, math, general knowledge, and conversational English audio-visual content.

The first hurdle participants face is the crunch of resources—there are far tablets than participating children in the village. Tablets are indivisible resources that cannot be equally divided among children—and here lies the conundrum for children: a questions of mapping resources to their own numbers. If anybody has seen children playing a game of cricket, or football in the villages or observed older children taking care of their younger siblings, the solution to the problem of not having sufficient resources (in this case tablets) becomes trivial. Pratham's facilitators brought to the fore such pre-existing behavior of children to facilitate a solution; children banded together in small groups in the proximity of their homes or any other space that suited them to use the tablets. A parent who had volunteered to keep the tablet safe, ensured the groups could use it by making sure it was charged and available solely for the learning activities of children.

The children grouped themselves in many ways. During the first few weeks a higher prevalence of intergroup movement of children was observed, which reduced drastically at the end of this "shuffling" period, when they adjusted and bonded with their group members. As it stands today, approximately 10 children are mapped to one tablet. These children are the primary custodians and users of a particular tablet. On average there are five children in one group. Thus, two groups have "ownership" of one tablet. Groups sharing a tablet have devised multiple ways of allocating access to the devices: most of the groups exchange tablets every day, while some use it on alternate days. Considering the gender divide in rural India, it is quite encouraging to see mixed-gender groups. This is not to say that there aren't any single-gender groups; there are. But even these single-gender groups see boys and girls working together in other groups.

The children in the program have agreed to the idea of membership. A group has members—children who "belong" to the group, and "guests" who sit in. The guests include children who are members of other groups with tablets and children from the community who were either too young or too old to formally sign up for the program. The flexibility of having guests has helped the program go beyond a "beneficiary" model, which now seems constricting to us. Here lies a critical example of programmatic decision-making through empowered children: most group members have opened up access to other children from their community who would not have access to the tablet otherwise. Through this we realize the potential of child participation, as children are not bound by rules and strictures that generally dictate the capacity of adults. The open invitation to a larger population created two distinct challenges for children: (1) How does a group instill a sense of belonging and adopt an identity, and (2) how does a larger group of children use a tablet, which has a screen size of 7.19 × 4.72 × 0.31 inches? We noticed that names provide a concrete identity to cement a sense of belonging and say as much about the entity as about the one naming them. The children have adopted a variety of names for their groups across the villages. For example, groups have been named after regional and national heroines and heroes (Rani Laxmi Bai, Shivaji, Mahatma), geographic regions (Bharat, Lucknow), after cricketing nations (Australia, New Zealand), Goddesses and Gods (Saraswati, Allah), and local flora and fauna (Gulab, Orange), among others.

Given that children drove the choice of group members and adoption of group names, the experiment has gone beyond tokenism or manipulation—it has become a tool for exercising power to leverage their positions in society. An example of this shift could be seen when children negotiated with their guardians and the local community to solve the "charging issue" through practical means, by getting their tablets charged in the homes of friends with power backups, paying the local *kirana* (general store),[14] or buying personal solar power cells.

Having solved the challenge of charging their tablets, children faced the problem of managing the screen-to-face distance (König et al. 2014) during their tablet sessions, especially given the variation of their eyesight, screen resolution, brightness, and text size. We were privileged to see children tackle this problem of human-technology interaction head on in the Bharat group from Ograpur village, where a young man named Sudhir and his friends placed the tablet on a chair and arranged the other group members and guests around it cascading out in a crescent. Shorter children were up front and taller ones in the second and third rows. Other groups solved this problem using a variety of geometric seating arrangements to increase ease of viewing and to pack in all interested parties as close to the tablet as possible.

These are but a few examples in which children are working and managing their own groups. As we move ahead in the chapter, we will explore some critical issues of group participation: engagement, content "stickiness" (how much a particular content is used by the children), child leadership, and the interaction across groups, within groups and between children and researchers.

Children and Their Engagement

The Hybrid Learning program spans seven blocks[15] in four districts across three states, essentially covering a diverse range of geographical, socioeconomic, cultural, and linguistic terrains, probably making it the largest and most heterogeneous educational PAR experiment in Asia.[16] Here we step back to consider what we understand and mean by "children" and their "culture(s)." Unlike the scientifically traditional view of universal personhood, we believe that the consciousness and behavior of children is dependent on their local culture; thus, we do away with the practice of viewing children as a homogenous group that shares "psychic unity" (Shweder 1990, p. 22). Children are active participants who have their own contextualized realities. As a result, their culture is not one whole but a mosaic of many fractional realities. Capturing, documenting, and exploiting these multiple cultures and their effect on the participation is biggest challenge of this experiment.

Nonhomogeneous children and groups of children working in a variety of cultural contexts to learn together necessitate the creation of naturalized learning spaces, where children freely work through the set of resources in a nonlinear fashion. It is in these spaces, or zones of proximal development that children internalize cultural contextualized meanings and understanding of activities and knowledge (Vygotsky 1978). Children collaborate with each other, with children in other groups, and with other more competent members of societies, such as guardians or older children and Pratham facilitators, learning the essence of the content as well as gauging how to participate and use the resources at their disposal. They partake in discovery-based mimicking play as well, which enables them to learn what they deem worthy of learning by themselves (Goncu and Becker 1992). The interaction of children occurs across multiple planes (Rogoff 1998) within and across their corresponding cultures—personal, interpersonal, and institutional. Children thus freely learn on their own terms in the Hybrid Learning experiment; flipping and shifting across the available content, until settling down on a point of beginning they decide themselves. The choice of content in any session is left up to the children.

The freedom of choice based on localized priorities, perspectives, and processes (Cornwall and Jewkes 1995) enables the participants to realize the full potential of PAR.

Children often choose their topics through the iterative process inherent to the PAR methodology. The content on the tablets is updated every 6 to 8 weeks—based on the responses and feedback of children, which is culled through the analysis of their usage data stored in the Pratham App and from discussions where Pratham facilitators talk to children. For example, on a visit to the village of Neemtikar, we asked the young women of the Gulab group what they liked most, and liked least, and why. The group members, mostly Muslim girls, expressed their dislike for a video titled, "Golden Girls", which showed an Indian champion sprinter winning a medal for her performance in a running race at the Asian Games. We finally found that for the girls of Gulab group, the objection had to do with the champion athlete in sporty clothes, because after all she was a woman. At the end of the discussion among themselves, the girls decided not to watch this particular video. This incident demonstrates the collegiate participatory mechanism in place and provides an example of an otherwise marginalized group asserting their opinion. It is thus critical that the PAR framework considers the various heterogeneities of its participants.

Wide and in-depth participation, where children fix their own timetables and lesson plans has added a richness to the experiment. As the groups are of many kinds, varying with respect to their gender composition, age, enrolment in private or public school, reading levels, and other socioeconomic factors, their means of working through the content is varied as well. The only absolute commonality is the freedom to work through the lessons; some groups have an internal consultative process to come to a consensus. A few groups are driven by their leaders convincing the others around, while in others each child is given a chance to pick one lesson turn by turn. And then, there are groups that follow a lesson plan set by an older child who has taken the responsibility of guiding younger children through the content. We asked one such child in Lamangaon village, why he was helping younger children work on the tablet. His answer surprised us: "Why shouldn't I do it? It feels good." Community members, particularly the youth and guardians, especially mothers, have responded positively, adopting the role of change makers and transforming themselves into agents of change who want to alter the reality of the children's learning environment. Consider another example, where a mother was keeping an eye on the group while going about her daily chores. "I am illiterate, how can I help?" she asked us rhetorically before smiling and bringing out a model-lung that her daughter's group had made. When the child fumbled to explain the workings of the human lung, this mother, a self-proclaimed illiterate, helped her daughter through the conceptual explanation. She listened in while the children used the tablet. Thus, even mothers and other adults who support the children are gaining from the experiment. Probably the biggest change from the viewpoint of the community is that members have begun to realize the possibility of playing an influential role in the educational development of their children. Although a school's doors are closed for the majority of guardians, the Hybrid Learning program has opened windows. This has made the participation genuine, a bottom-up phenomenon instead of a consequence of top down planning (Tandon 1998).

Having covered the "what" and "how" of participation and engagement, it is imperative that we investigate *why* some content is more child-friendly and inspiring than others? No sophisticated tools are used to extract responses from children; instead, Pratham facilitators simply open up a dialogue with children. This way, children not only connect with Pratham's field staff, but they also actively evaluate their choices more consciously. In addition to enabling our understanding of what makes a lesson "sticky" (popular and viewed widely by children), facilitators are able to encourage children with quieter dispositions to speak up. For example, on the videos on conversational English, the children said that they wanted to learn English because they believed it to be very valuable. Furthermore, the child actors in the videos looked and felt like the participants themselves. Upon asking children if they would like to make such videos themselves, we learned that they were already making videos—in fact, they were making stylized films that initially began with a reproduction of the tablet content and evolved into interviews of each other (including their own background stories) and their advocates. Children were involved in creating content iteratively. They planned their shoots, evident from the set design and movement of the camera that zoomed in or out, and undertook multiple takes, experimenting with lighting conditions (early morning, later in the day, evening, etc.), ultimately keeping the best files on top of their folder. Through open conversations with the field staff and among themselves, children are now utilizing the cyclical nature of PAR, namely, planning, action, observation, and reflection.

With the help of some child participants, the content team ultimately developed a richer set of conversational videos, including *Mummy's Interview*, where the interaction between an English-speaking mother and child was recorded and touched up later by specialists. The participants themselves are growing into producers of knowledge—in this case, a video that is good enough to aid in the English-language development of these children. This strategy of involving all created a healthy symmetry across many participants in the spirit of PAR (McTaggart 1991). Compare this with the traditional chalk and duster methodology, where the students remain dependent on the teacher who writes the answers on the board for children to copy. They are rarely encouraged to think beyond the prescribed syllabus or ask questions.

Throughout this section, we discussed how the Hybrid Learning program successfully brought children into the fold of program design and management. The next section explores further details of the PAR nature of the experiment.

An Evolving Program and Evolution of PAR in South Asia

The evolution of India as a knowledge economy is changing what is required of learning, with the emphasis now on problem solving and going beyond teaching-learning of subjects from textbooks. Although children in schoolrooms are forced to play catch-up to the curriculum,[17] the curriculum itself is stuck with its practice of age-grade knowledge acquisition, which does not recognize nonlinear learning trajectories. The Hybrid Learning program problematizes education in rural India by recognizing that learning is not bound by walls or pages and that there exists multiple cultures of knowledge within societies. By building a bridge between the children's learning and their everyday life through contextualization of knowledge and subject matter, the model empowers young citizens to transcend traditional standards of knowledge generation and acquisition (Hall 2015). The experiment learns from the varied experiences of its participants, thus "incorporating the dynamics of knowledge into democracy…where the citizen as trustee and inventor visualizes and creates a new self-reflexive idea of democracy around actual communities of practice" (Visvanathan 2009, para. 38). Throughout this section, we chart the evolution of the experiment, bringing up challenges of PAR and scope for further development of its practice.

Inclusivity, Ownership, and Empowerment

The ASER tool was used in the preliminary phase of the Hybrid Learning program to gauge the basic reading and numeracy skills of children in the villages. The household-based assessment aided in informing the guardians and community members about the status of basic literacy. One in three children between grades 5 through 8 (or 10–14 years of age) could not read a 20-word paragraph in their school language. Having been hosts to Pratham's "Read India" camps where children learn to read,[18] the communities wanted a program that was more participatory and focused on skills beyond the basic foundations of literacy and numeracy. Children wanted to learn science, math, and communicate in English. We realized that audio-visual resources would overcome the hurdle of reading and enable an inclusive learning atmosphere. Parents were drawn into a discussion about learning through easy to understand, yet substantive evidence, of the challenge facing their children—schooling without sufficient learning. When a community is grappling with a malady such as non-learning in schools, it is important to make the problem visible and enable citizens to diagnose their condition, which is what this experiment has done.

Hybrid Learning gives primacy to the children's experience, because children understand the hurdles of other children the best. This empowering and inclusive participation of children is congruent with the practice and philosophy of "collaborative research designed to promote social change through equal partnerships between researchers and participants" (Kim 2016, p. 39). Noting the variety of participants (Hickey and Mohan 2005), in their discussions, Pratham facilitators included children, their advocates, and community leaders to understand the demands of each group (for instance, parents who pushed for a modicum of formality through "homework").

Follow-up activities are conducted across villages in the form of fairs, called *melas*, that bring all the groups together to participate in quizzes, activities, role-plays, and presentations. Children's inputs were used to pick themes of these fairs, which organized by the children that showed their enthusiasm for Science and English. The pride of the children in their handiwork was publicly displayed before a sizable crowd, which led them to increase their participation. Designing these fairs gave children a local, direct access to their role as key decision-makers. Perkins et al. (2007)

noted that fun and enjoyable activities are crucial drivers of youth motivation. The involvement of children also helped build substantial trust between them and adult participants. As children in India are not used to being heard and considered, their sustained participation is built on mutual trust (Cornwall and Jewkes 1995).

Village-level subject-specific fairs were used during the initial phase of the experiment. Considering the constraint of capacity and time of guardians, especially mothers, we noted that a local community *mohalla*-based[19] fairs were more participant-friendly. Demonstration and learning exercises designed around village games are more engaging than subject-specific fairs. For example, it is easier to help children discover the concept of distance, displacement, speed, and velocity through a running race that they themselves participate in than by presenting the same concept in a theoretical manner. The children actively engage in a running race; only now they are armed with borrowed tape measures and wrist watches to time and analyze their performance, thereby learning in the process. The spirit of localization converts an otherwise "distant" scientific concept closer to participants' turf (Cornwall and Jewkes 1995; Hall 2015), thus promoting participation and action through the act of local activity based knowledge creation.

As the children's guardians wanted "homework" to be introduced and were concerned that their children were spending much of their time on digital devices without the traditional "pen and paper" practice, group and individual worksheets were distributed to help children in self-assessment. It was observed that although the worksheets were being used by children who were advanced readers, children with lower competencies were out using them. "It is too difficult," some participants informed us. "Make it easier," they said. This feedback led to an exercise to simplify the worksheets.

The community's excitement over tablet ownership was palpable, which translated into the guardians personally ensuring that the children were engaging with the device regularly. The idea that there would be no "teacher" to "teach" the children and that they were expected to study on their own was novel. It was observed that children gravitated more toward material that was relatable to their immediate surroundings, characters they could identify with, and videos that went beyond them being mere audio-visual adaptations of their text books. These insights specifically shaped any new content creation.

Participation of Adults and Their Empowerment

Approximately half the Pratham facilitators on the ground were new to Pratham, and several of them were recruited from the participating villages. It is clear why the youth from the villages were willingly participating as key administrative and programmatic point persons in the Hybrid Learning program. A locally recruited field facilitator explained why he joined the experiment: "I was looking for a job. You came to our village and needed somebody like me. I [am to] work for the children of my village and similar villages. This is good. Very good. I am respected. It's better than working in a factory." Pratham's field staff understand the local pulse. They know the children and the context. Furthermore, the children know their "Sir" or "Ma'am," as they refer to their facilitators, as gentle guides who help them learn new ways of looking at the world. The only way to be accepted by children and the community is by listening to them and helping convert their concerns into action.

In the absence of the traditional teaching-learning atmosphere, Pratham facilitators helps groups of children navigate through the program. Facilitators help empower participating children in creating a ground-up and child-friendly learning environment in their villages, thereby creating a community-level ownership of children's education.

Community members are free to participate and help their children learn. So far, their participation has been limited and more along the lines of monitoring children's progress. Considering the low levels of literacy among villagers and how busy they are, it is difficult to expect much more at present. It is possible that program participants have not realized the full potential of their possible contribution in improving the learning atmosphere of their communities. Despite this limitation it is encouraging to observe parents who are otherwise conscious of their socio-economic and cultural realities, encouraging their children to work together in groups. We believe that this program may be altering the adult consciousness at some level. The experiment has proven that because the whole community is involved, the whole community learns.

Empowering Through a Digital Platform

Direct access to interactive multimedia interfaces not only opens new avenues for children to delve deeper into their creativity but also provides them information in a nondoctrinal fashion. Their cognitive skills and interest levels are targeted on three levels: familiarity, knowledge, and understanding. Concepts emerge from the everyday lives of children, and they raise questions about things they come across daily. These questions are interesting as well as thought-provoking, ranging from "Why is the sky blue" to "Why do we yawn when we get tired?" These questions tap into the natural curiosity of children and encourage them to learn more.

Last, the digital platform empowers researchers to take up what we could call a fail-forward (Maddock 2012) stance when it comes to design elements, which is aligned with the PAR philosophy, as it is a reflective practice where failure of desired outcomes leads to rethinking of possibilities for achieving outcomes instead of abandoning efforts as sunk losses. For example, considering the large number of guests who join in the sessions, designers introduced the feature of guest log-in to capture how many children or other community members were using the resource when the group was not around. Incidentally, the guest log-in enabled quicker access to content, which the children recognized and utilized. Despite the cost of not having group-level data for a period of time since the spread of this behavior, it provides us two key facts, namely—that children are experimenting and that they are eager to access the content. Field observations are backed up by the fact that children in groups are logging in as guests simply because it is easier to do so—a path of least resistance. The experimental nature of the research along with a fail-forward philosophy helps us design our application better, given this behavior.

Working together, outside the school system, and within a known environment of their own choice, children are able to freely express themselves—and absence of any penalty of failure encourages children to experiment without fear. The group empowers individuals as much as individuals empower the group. Experience clearly shows that children stop being afraid of asking questions about what they have not understood. They discuss and negotiate, and the group moves ahead once everyone has understood the concepts. They make models, act out videos, take notes, and fill in worksheets mapped to the content all on their own. They move beyond the Pratham app and explore other features of the tablet; shoot their own videos, add external applications to the tablet and personalize their tablets with photographs and music.

As part of our continuous learning, it has been observed that in some locations, a select few youth from higher grades are helping the children by providing locally sensitive guidance—this is but a step away from recognized structures such as *graameen* forums and self-help groups.

Working together with the community, we realize the value of education and the amount of engagement of children and communities through observations that not only focus on scholastic aspects of learning but nonscholastic aspects such as team work, negotiation, presentation skills, and group management skills. Dr. Chavan (2013) summed up this outlook of child-friendly learning and education: "We should move away from the age-grade system.... Instead we need an age-stage system that allows children to meet learning goals in both the social and academic sphere when they are ready, transitioning to each stage at their own pace" (p. 224).

Conclusion

The Hybrid Learning experiment aims to discover contextual solutions to overcome the two primary barriers of quality learning across rural parts of India—poor access to materials and the absence of a learner-centric learning environment by leveraging a PAR methodology. We understand access not just as the availability of physical materials but also improved usability of teaching-learning materials that are aligned with the learners' educational competency.

Considering the experimental outlook of all the participants, the program itself has a flexible design that has helped it evolve continuously. Experiences from Hybrid Learning program adds new dimensions to the PAR framework in two ways:

1. The modes of participation vary not only across age groups, gender, and socio-economic classes, but they also change depending on the field of enquiry; for instance, PAR pertaining to education ought to be different from PAR for agriculture.
2. Even while innovating localized solutions heterogeneity among various groups should be kept in mind to ensure continued participation.

In conclusion, the participatory design of Hybrid Learning program encourages discovery-based learning, which has helped children to realize the value of asking questions, working in groups of their choice, selecting the pace of learning, getting their communities involved in their learning, and getting back to researchers with clear responses as to what is working and what is not—thus empowering the most underrepresented section of our democratic society, exercise the single most tool of democracy; channeling their voices for beneficial action for improved learning.

Notes

1. Pratham Education Foundation (www.pratham.org) is India's largest non-governmental organisation in the education space that focuses on high-quality, low-cost, and replicable interventions. It is an innovative learning organization created in 1995 to improve the quality of education in India.
2. Enrolment has been equated to 'access' although it is not so.
3. Attendance in primary schools is about 71% and varies across states.
4. Facilitated by Pratham, ASER (www.asercentre.org), India's largest citizen-led household survey, with more than 25,000 volunteers every year, has brought the learning gap in basic reading and numeracy to light over the past decade. The survey has successfully demonstrated the phenomenon of 'not learning enough' across schools and communities and made it visible not just at the policy level but at the local village level as well.
5. With 41% of populace below the age of 18, India has the largest youth population in the world.
6. Panchayati Raj is a system of governance in which *gram panchayats* are the basic units of local administration at the village level. A panchayat is a village level council.
7. Indian Citizens below the age of 18 do not have the right to vote, isolating them from the democratic process.
8. As practiced in Pratham's Read India program to equip all children with foundational skills of literacy and numeracy.
9. Hypothesis of the intervention or action leading to required outputs, outcomes resulting in desired goals.
10. Reflecting the idea behind the "Village Swaraj" described previously.
11. As much as we know, it is indeed a unique experiment in Asia.
12. Through a process of continuous dialogue between project staff and children and community members.
13. Fondly described as "open is cool" by Pratham's co-founder Dr. Madhav Chavan.
14. In some cases the local stores stopped charging children to power their tablets.
15. Sub-district unit of administration.
16. As far as we are aware, Hybrid Learning is the only educational PAR program covering such a wide geography in Asia.
17. Despite gaps in learning levels of children, teaching in Indian schoolrooms is solely guided by the textbooks for the grade prescribed by the curriculum. In this approach majority of children who haven't acquired grade specific ability usually struggle to follow the curriculum being delivered by the teacher.

18. This reading program was run in schools and covered only selected school-going children. In contrast, Hybrid Learning is a community program and involves many children who were not part of the previous reading program.
19. Cluster of a few homes.

References

Alvesson, M., & Sandberg, J. (2011). Generating research questions through problematization. *Academy of Management Review, 38*(2), 247–271.

ASER. (2016). *Annual Status of Education Report*. New Delhi. Retrieved January 18, 2017, from http://img.asercentre.org/docs/Publications/ASER%20Reports/ASER%202016/aser_2016.pdf

Banerji, R., & Duflo, E. (2015). Teaching at the right levels. *Solutions for low learning levels in India*. Retrieved June 3, 2016, from http://www.ideasforindia.in/article.aspx?article_id=1541

Brown, D., & Tandon, R. (1983). Ideology and political economy in inquiry: Action research and participatory research. *Journal of Applied Behavioral Science, 19*(3), 277–294.

Central Statistics Office. (2011). *18th Conference of Central and State Statistical Organizations; Agenda-4: Education statistics-issues*. Government of India, Ministry of Statistics & Programme Implementation, Bhubaneswar, Odisha.

Chavan, M. (2013). Who needs classrooms? In C. Chandler, A. Zainulbhai, & McKinsey & Company (Eds.), *Reimaging India: Unlocking the potential of Asia's next superpower* (pp. 221–226). New York: Simon & Schuster.

Cooke, B., & Kothari, U. (2001). *Participation: The new tyranny?* London: Zed Books.

Cornwall, A., & Jewkes, R. (1995). What is participatory research? *Social Science & Medicine, 41*(12), 1667–1676.

Davey, C., Burke, T., & Shaw, C. (2010). Children's participation in decision making. A children's view report. *Children's Rights Alliance for England*. Participation works. Retrieved June 3, 2016, from https://www.childrenscommissioner.gov.uk/sites/default/files/publications/Childrens_participation_in_decision-making_-_A_childrens_views_report.pdf

De Houwer, J., Barnes-Holmes, D., & Moors, A. (2013). What is learning? On the nature and merits of a functional definition of learning. *Psychonomic Bulletin & Review, 20*, 631–642.

Freire, P. (1993). *Pedagogy of the city*. New York: Continuum.

Freire, P. (2000). *Pedagogy of the oppressed*. New York: Continuum.

Gandhi, M. K. (1942). My idea of Village Swaraj. In H. M. Vyas (Ed.), *Village Swaraj. (1962)*. Ahmedabad: Navajivan Publishing House.

Goncu, A., & Becker, J. (1992). Some contributions of a Vygotskian approach to early education. *International Journal of Cognitive Education & Mediated Learning*, 2(2), 147–153.
Hall, B. L. (2005). In from the cold? Reflections on participatory research 1970–2005. *Convergence*, 38(1), 5–24.
Hall, B. L. (2015). *Beyond epistemicide: Knowledge democracy and higher education*. International Symposium on Higher Education in the Age of Neo Liberalism and Audit Cultures, 21–25 July, University of Regina.
Hart, R. A. (1992). Children's participation: From tokenism to citizenship. *Innocenti Essays No. 4*. UNICEF, International Child Development Centre.
Hart, R. A. (2008). Stepping back from 'The Ladder': Reflections on a model of participatory work with children. In A. Reid, B. B. Jensen, J. Nikel, & V. Simovka (Eds.), *Participation and learning; perspectives on education, and the environment, health and sustainability* (pp. 19–31). New York: Springer.
Hickey, S., & Mohan, G. (2005). Relocating participation within a radical politics of development. *Development and Change*, 36(2), 237–262.
Khanlou, N., & Peter, E. (2005). Participatory action research: Considerations for ethical review. *Social Science & Medicine*, 60, 2333–2340.
Kim, J. (2016). Youth involvement in Participatory Action Research (PAR): Challenges and barriers. *Critical Social Work*, 17(1), 38–53.
König, I., Beau, P., & David, K. (2014). *A new context: Screen to face distance*. 8th International Symposium on Medical Information and Communication Technology (ISMICT), Firenze, Italy, 1–5.
Lewin, K. (1946). Action research and minority problems. *Journal of Social Issues*, 2, 34–46.
Maddock, M. (2012). If you have to fail-and you do-fail forward. *Forbes*. Retrieved February 20, 2017, from http://www.forbes.com/sites/mikemaddock/2012/10/10/if-you-have-to-fail-and-you-do-fail-forward/#355ceb937a9a
McTaggart, R. (1991). Principles of participatory action research. *Adult Education Quarterly*, 41(3), 168–187.
Mitra, S. (2000). *Minimally invasive education for mass computer literacy*. CRIDALA 2000 Conference, Hong Kong.
Mukherjee, A. N., & Sikdar, S. (2012). *Public expenditure on education in India by the Union government and roadmap for the future*. India Infrastructure Report. Retrieved June 3, 2016, from www.idfc.com/pdf/report/2013-14/IIR-2013-14.pdf
Perkins, D. F., Borden, L. M., Villarruel, F. A., Carlton-Hug, A., Stone, M. R., & Keith, J. G. (2007). Participation in structured youth programs: Why ethnic minority urban youth choose to participate-or not to participate. *Youth & Society*, 38(4), 420–442.
Pritchett, L., Andrews, M., & Woolcock, M. (2016). *The big stuck in state capability for policy implementation*. Working Paper No. 318. Center for International Development at Harvard University.

Rogoff, B. (1998). Cognition as a collaborative process. In W. Damon (Series Ed.) and D. Kuhn & R. S. Siegler (Vol. Eds.), *Handbook of child psychology, cognition, perception and language* (Vol. 2, pp. 679-744). New York: Wiley.
Shweder, R. A. (1990). Cultural psychology—What is it? In J. W. Stigler et al. (Eds.), *Cultural psychology* (pp. 1-44). Cambridge: Cambridge University Press.
Tandon, R. (1998). Social transformation and participatory research. *Convergence*, 21(2/3), 5-18.
Visvanathan, S. (2009). *The search for cognitive justice*. Retrieved July 8, 2016, from http://bit.ly/3ZwMD2
Vygotsky, L. S. (1978). Interaction between learning and development. In *Mind and society* (pp. 79-91). Cambridge, MA: Harvard University Press.
Wright, D. E. (2015). *Active learning: Social justice education and participatory action research*. New York: Routledge.

CHAPTER 7

Reclaiming the Collective: Challenging Neoliberal Ideology Through PAR

Shabnam Koirala-Azad

WHAT IS PARTICIPATORY ACTION RESEARCH?

In social science research, participatory action research (PAR) signifies an alternative paradigm of knowledge production in which groups who are adversely affected by a social problem undertake collective study to understand and address it. PAR is not just a method involving participation by research subjects. It presents people as researchers in pursuit of answers to questions of daily struggle and survival, breaks down the distinction between researcher and researched, and returns to the people the legitimacy of the knowledge they are capable of producing (Koirala-Azad and Fuentes 2010). It is based on the assumption that people are capable of understanding the social forces that shape the conditions of their lives (Tandon 2002). Research questions then speak to the needs of the group because they emerge from their shared experiences.

PAR pushes academic research to be more democratic and meaningful and of service to communities, especially those that traditionally have been marginalized. It believes in the organic process of knowledge generation.

S. Koirala-Azad (✉)
Univeristy of San Francisco, School of Education, San Francisco, CA, USA
e-mail: skoirala@usfca.edu

© The Author(s) 2017
H. Kidwai et al. (eds.), *Participatory Action Research and Educational Development*, South Asian Education Policy, Research, and Practice,
DOI 10.1007/978-3-319-48905-6_8

Orlando Fals Borda said, "Through the actual experience of something, we intuitively apprehend its essence, we feel and understand its reality and we thereby place our own being in a wider more fulfilling context (Fals-Borda and Rahman 1991, p. 4)" It believes that academic knowledge combined with popular knowledge and wisdom can result in new scientific knowledge that can break commonsense assumptions that are embedded and perpetuated due to a monopoly on knowledge generated by a powerful few. PAR is often referred to as a people's science. The production and diffusion of new knowledge produced collaboratively is integral to the research process because it is a central part of the feedback and evaluative objective of PAR (Koirala-Azad and Fuentes 2010).

Community-based research approaches like PAR allow individuals and communities to look closely at reality; to question our surroundings and to "see" how social, political, and economic issues take shape in surroundings; and to engage in a process of further inquiry and analysis around these issues with the intention of using the knowledge generated to find relevant solutions. The process of participatory research happens in three simple phases that symbolize the reading, analyzing, and transforming of reality.

Developing capacity to do research among all participants is critical. Participants often learn how to do research by *doing it* in the process of researching their everyday lives and community. They then analyze collectively to make sense of shared experiences. Collective analysis includes a series of practices that are transparent and collaborative and facilitate group ownership and collective negotiations. This analysis then feeds into research questions and becomes the basis of an inquiry. Infused in this process are systematic dialogue, reflection, and informed action.

Participatory Action Research in the Nepali Context

The study on which this chapter is based was a four-year participatory research with Nepali students in secondary and tertiary educational institutions in Kathmandu. The purpose of the study was to explore student experiences in Nepali schools as a way of better understanding the inability of higher education institutions to retain students. Participatory research was chosen as the methodology for this study for some of the reasons discussed earlier. As an educational researcher and based on prior research experiences in Nepal, where I found a dearth of qualitative studies on the education system, I was committed to adding the voices of the education community to the large body of existing quantitative studies and statistical reports. I was also intrigued by the idea of conducting "democratic" research in a young, chaotic democratic state. With my authentic experience of many "educational problems" as a student in the Nepali education system and my strong network of family, friends, educators, and activists, the idea of engaging in a "rigorous [collaborative] search for knowledge ... with a renewed commitment, an ethical stand, self-critique, and persistence" (Fals-Borda and Rahman 1991, p. 4) was not only appealing but also in line with my commitment to "doing things differently" (Koirala 2004, p. 24). Since the main purpose of the study was to examine some of the most significant gaps in the country's education system, it seemed fitting to choose a research approach that would allow me to engage with those who are arguably the most silenced within the educational institutions: the students. The task of forming a research group was made easy when a student whom I had interviewed in a previous study enthusiastically asked to be included when I explained to her why I was back in Nepal. Immediately, she recruited three other students who were interested in "doing research." Of the three additional students, only two were active in the research process. In addition, I invited a friend who was a college graduate and was then teaching at a new private college to join the group. This group (see Table 7.1), albeit small, reflected Nepali diversity, especially in terms of caste and gender. Although this chapter does not specifically focus on the coresearchers and their specific roles, I would like to recognize their contributions to data collection and to articulating some of the findings presented in this paper.

Table 7.1 Coresearchers

Name	Age	Gender	Educational level	Type of institution attended
Shradha	18	Female	High school (10+2)	Private school
Arjun	27	Male	MA	Government school through high school; private engineering college
Ram	20	Male	IA (intermediate of arts degree or high school equivalency)	Public College
Shweta	17	Female	High school (10+2)	Public college

Source: Koirala-Azad (2008)

All coresearchers identified themselves as Nepali even though they came from different ethnic or caste groups. Arjun was especially interested in the study because he felt that, being from what is considered a lower caste and lower socioeconomic class, he had defied all odds by not only in receiving an MA degree but also by going on to teach at a private college. My own positioning in the research and among my coresearchers was probably the most complex. I was both an insider and an outsider—an insider in the sense that I shared cultural and linguistic characteristics with them as well as the experience of attending Nepali schools. However, I was very explicit about the fact that I had lived abroad for eight years preceding the study and that I was also connected to an institution of higher education in the United States. Interestingly, our commitment to participatory research and to this participatory process allowed us to engage in honest dialogue so that all personal intentions were vetted prior to the study; this helped us to find specific ways in which the study could be mutually beneficial to all involved.

We chose our research sites based on: (1) the type of institution (private, government run, parochial); (2) the demographics of students (urban elite, urban poor, middle class, working students); and (3) location in the Kathmandu Valley. In most cases, the type of institution usually correlated to the socioeconomic class of the students attending it. For instance, a government-run school in Lagankhel that was visibly run down catered mostly to students from poor families in the area. In contrast, many of the private schools cater to upper-middle-class families who can afford to pay the hefty tuition fees. For the purpose of this study, we also decided to focus on schools within the Kathmandu Valley, since most educational institutions are concentrated in urban areas and also because there has been significant urbanization since the intensification of the Maoist conflict since the mid-1990s, creating new challenges for urban schools, which now have to deal with an influx of students from rural areas (from various ethnic and linguistic groups). After a grueling process of gaining entry into the institutions, our research team went into eight institutions with the intention of "talking with students." In each institution, we had at least one contact person, usually a faculty member, who allowed us to speak with a group of students. In one instance, the principal had the students line up outside the library so that we could speak with them during their recess. There were three main methods of data collection:

1. *Higher education questionnaire.* All students who were interested could fill out a questionnaire that asked general questions about their background and their satisfaction or dissatisfaction with their education. Since this was an anonymous questionnaire, we found that students were not only willing but also honest and detailed in their responses. Each student who filled out a questionnaire was then invited to an individual interview, although not all of them participated in this.
2. *Individual interview.* These interviews lasted about half an hour and were taped and transcribed.
3. *Group dialogue.* Although we invited all interviewees to join our biweekly "reflections," most of those who attended were students who were friends with the coresearchers. These discussions usually took place outside of schools, in cultural spaces or even eateries popular among the youth. All conversations were recorded. The data for the study came from the ideas, reflections, and field notes of the coresearchers as well as the interviews with the larger student body in schools. Without downplaying the limitations and challenges of using participatory research as a methodology, it became increasingly clear through the process that including student voices in educational research was critical not only in creating a more authentic and realistic understanding of the realities of schooling but also in enabling the students to perceive themselves as active agents in their own educational process (Nygreen et al. 2006).

Reclaiming the Collective

Communities that have inherently functioned as collectives, like many in Nepal, have been torn apart in the past three decades due to civil strife, an increasingly divided economy, natural disasters, and unprecedented immigration and forced displacement (Gilligan et al. 2014). Nepali social discourse currently centers on a changing value system, which refers to the replacement of a sense of cohesion, trust, reciprocity, and loyalty with mistrust, individualism, deeper class divides, and a sense of entitlement and meritocracy. This internal disintegration of the social, economic fabric of the country is further exacerbated by external influences from, most prominently, Western media and its values of globalization that push a specific neoliberal agenda. Among many of the students with whom I conducted research, extensive knowledge of US television shows was often connected to a need to acquire many of the products seen on television in order to gain status among friends. One student, specifically referring to this growing sense of need, said, "People are willing to kill for cell phones these days. It really happens, I'm not kidding. People steal, hurt, kill to pull themselves up in this society. My father said things like this would never ever happen when he was growing up."

Stories like these gave me, as the institutional researcher, room to engage with my coresearchers in conversations about what they saw as root causes of these shifts in society. Their thinking ranged from the inability of the education system to instill collective values to hopelessness around a "selfish" dominant culture that was usurping Nepali traditional values of loyalty and camaraderie. When asked to further reflect on the constituents of this dominant group, a few marked them as those who had "made it," often insinuating that they belonged to a subcategory of those who have not made it.

The further we deconstructed these notions, the easier it was to unravel the more insidious aspects of a pervasive global neoliberal ideology based on rule of market, increased competition, and individual gain. These conversations became critical to our understanding of the significance of PAR in Nepali society. In one session, prior to beginning our research project, we drew out a list of all the values that students identified as problematic in efforts toward positive change. These included greed, inability to see the needs of others, *arka ko tauko ma tekera aghi badne bani* (a habit of stepping on other people's heads to get ahead), lack of trust, and inability to share. After talking through some of the points on this list, we drew up another chart to think about how we could engage in "democratic research" as "coresearchers" in a context where these negative values seemed so pervasive. As we read together "knowledge and participatory research," students started identifying key ways in which engaging with PAR *could* perhaps counter these identified values. Three ideas most resonated with the team:

1. *Collaboration*—Understanding that those most affected by a problem work together to resolve it. By entering a study in a spirit of learning, coresearchers were able to see themselves as producing knowledge together rather than holding specific types of competing expertise. Starting with the assumption that knowledge that is systematically co-created through inquiry and based on lived experiences is more likely to lead to practical solutions. Working with one

another creates the human resources necessary to commit to a process of sustainable and long-term change.
2. *Capacity*—Recognizing that individuals have capacity to transform a society. The coresearchers all identified with being in an educational system that assumed ignorance and was quick to consider them failures. Shared experiences of rote learning, highly authoritarian classrooms with strict teachers, an exam-based merit system, and extremely high cases of "failure" on examinations were at the root of these insights. Students were drawn to the idea that lived experiences and existing knowledge could be seen as capacity for further production of knowledge.
3. *Cyclical process*—Our work in community building and change is cyclical and ongoing. The coresearchers appreciated a nonlinear way of looking at a change process. We talked about development in Nepal in the 1980s and 1990s, when change meant working quickly toward an outcome. We reminisced about funds that came into the country for infrastructure development and how projects were deemed complete if a school or bridge was built, sometimes half built. "When we work in community, we are always involved in building as we see necessary," said the youngest member of the group. The linear, counterproductive approach to change, which we all agreed had created greater harm than good, was contested through this organic cyclical process of developing questions, engaging together in inquiry, making meaning of information gathered, creating new knowledge geared toward transformative actions, and then revisiting and refining the questions.

Identifying specific aspects of participatory research that resonated with the team in their respective contexts was an important step in ensuring a process of reimagining how we could engage in a process of investigation toward change. Given the earlier identified manifestations of neoliberal ideology, a strong collective intention to engage in an antihegemonic, anticolonial, and informed approach had to be created for us to start the project in a unified manner. This was especially important given the co-optation of terms such as "participatory," "democratic," and "authentic" in development discourse and practice of neoliberal change agencies in Nepal. The more we talked and worked through these ideas, the more unified the group became on the idea of addressing issues of "selfishness" and individual gain by engaging in a process where we held ourselves and each other accountable to *being* and *doing* differently. As one researcher stated, "Anyone can go out and interview people, it's *how* we do it, *how* people feel when we ask them questions and *how* we interact as a group that will ultimately shape this research." This was one important step toward recognizing capacity, engaging in a collaborative process marked by a humble posture of learning and creating humanizing relationships, and, essentially, reclaiming a sense of the collective.

Demystifying the Expert

The domination of neoliberal agencies over change processes in the Third World has created a competitive market for experts. In Nepal, the general sentiment that expertise can only come from the outside has been pervasive for a long time. The habit of reliance on foreign experts became a topic of national debate following the devastating earthquake in April 2015. As the country was reeling from damage, the government's immediate reliance on outside aid and expertise of relief consultants was disputed by rising voices of younger generations committed to rebuilding efforts and quite confident in their abilities to contribute. The nation is at another crossroads where we need to figure out how to tap into this rising collective of change makers from the grassroots. The shift from deep insecurities around "local" knowledge and ability to one of grassroots movements has been apparent following every crisis in Nepali history. Without clear alternative methods of building new knowledge and transformative actions, history has shown that even the best intentions fall prey to old habits. PAR, for us, posed an alternative method that allowed us to question, systematically explore, and share knowledge in a way that challenges some of these habits and assumptions.

As we explored various Nepali educational institutions, the habit of accepting reality as absolute truth was glaringly apparent. The learner's mind is seen as an empty vessel into which the riches of approved knowledge are placed. Freire (1994) argued that this type of education "inhibits creativity and domesticates (although it cannot completely destroy) the intentionality of consciousness by isolating consciousness from the world, thereby denying people their ontological and historical vocation of becoming more fully human" (p. 65), that is, to creatively transform reality based on critical perception. Our own experiences and our observations in current Nepali classrooms showed that the authority of the teacher is firmly established and classroom learning and practices allow little to no room for engaged pedagogy. Several students affirmed this observation:

SK: Yahan ke padirahanu bhaeko chha? (What are you studying here?)
Rajan: Commerce.
SK: Yo college man pareko chha ta? (Do you like this college?)
Rajan: [smiles] ... Uhh ...
SK: Thikei chha, sochna time lagchha ... malai thaha chha ni. (It's okay, I know you probably need time to think about it.)
Rajan: Uhm ... haina, kuro ke bhane ... maila kahilepani sochekei chhaina. Malai ke man parchha ke man pardeina koseile soddha pani soddheina kaseilai pani matlab pani chhaina. Tyasele chupa lagera baschhu. (Uhm, the thing is that ... I've never thought about whether I like it or not ... no one asks and no one cares. That's why I keep silent.)

Rajan continued participating in follow-up interviews and focus group dialogues and became increasingly vocal in the process. He identified "rote learning" as a key reason behind his initial silence and spoke extensively about it during subsequent dialogues. In her extensive research on literacy programs in Nepal, affirmed that the "traditional model of rote learning in schools [does] not encourage students to criticize or challenge ideas" (p. 4). Lost in this type of education are the feelings, opinions, and critiques of students, and, more important, their recognition of themselves as active beings. The pedagogy allows very little room for the validation of their own knowledge and experiences. Further analyses of these students as historical beings and as "subjects" within their social contexts provide other evidence for the roots of this learned silence. One example is Nepal's history of *bikas* (development) and dependency on external or foreign aid, which, I assert, has created a habit of dependency resulting in stagnant passivism. Others include deeply entrenched inequities based on caste, class, and especially gender that give voice to the privileged few; and most currently relevant is the extremely unstable political situation that places all attention on political parties and very little on the people. In our analysis, we felt that this acceptance was very much related to a learned passivism and dependency often stemming from two distinct historical experiences: first, that someone else, perhaps with more power, has more valuable knowledge than one; and second, not questioning the locations and enactments of this power.

It may not be surprising then that we found that institutions of secondary and tertiary education in Nepal ignore and fail to demonstrate any accountability to students and their families. At the institutional level too, we often encountered administrators who, perhaps rightfully, felt their institutions were doing the best they could, given lack of financial and other support from the government and a lack of pressure from their own constituents to change in any way. One administrator said, "We aren't even on any higher education map, no one cares, we have a long way to go before anyone really cares about our standards." Several layers of power dynamics were clearly at play, including one in which educational institutions measured their worth against those in the global competitive market of higher education institutions. It was not surprising then that students also internalized this idea that in order to get a good education, they must aspire to enter better-known institutions in other countries, once again creating different classes of students: the successful ones who leave the country and enter institutions abroad, those who can afford private education in Nepal, and those who expressed feeling "stuck" in Nepal. Philip Altbach (2004) referred to this hegemony of context-specific education and training as the "new neocolonialism," or the exacerbating of value differentials in locations of knowledge production and ownership. The emancipatory nature of PAR and its aim to "help people recover, and release themselves, from the constraints of irrational, unproductive, unjust, and unsatisfying social structures that limit their self-development and self-determination" could be a significant way of challenging this new neocolonialism (Kemmis and McTaggart 2000, p. 597).

Many of the students we interviewed in Nepali higher education institutions, especially the ones I personally interviewed, would answer questions with the same initial words: "What can I tell you that you don't already know? You're studying in America." However, as students began interviewing each other, collecting stories, analyzing data, and generating findings, it became clear that what we were learning together was new knowledge, some of which none of us could have foreseen at the beginning of our work together. Our finding on "learned silence," for instance, generated discussions among the coresearchers and several other students about nationalism, power, the history of Nepali monarchy, forms of government, and other topics that elevated the discourse of a simple reoccurring experience in our research—initial silence.

Reimagining Development

The knowledge gained from PAR is focused on action, not understanding alone. When development becomes synonymous with failure, corruption, oppression, and half-completed initiatives, alternatives are sought. The preceding sections provide some reasons for why PAR provides a methodological alternative to reading reality, analyzing its possibilities and determining the tools and methods necessary to find solutions to commonly experienced problems. To this end, although they may seem obvious, several key assumptions of PAR, in contrast to those of traditional development methods, need to be stated.

Knowledge from Community Informs Institutions

Instead of governments and institutions imposing blueprints for change, communities and groups identify needs and potential solutions. Institutions, then, take on a different role. Rather than being enforcers of development, they become supporters and provide the structural support necessary for communities and groups to engage in long-term change processes. It may be hard to imagine this shift in our current hierarchies, but the fragmentation and disintegration of governments and institutions, as in Nepal, is making these shifts seem more realistic and necessary. Our research team, through the study, was able to identify some key issues in Nepali higher education (Koirala-Azad 2008), one of which included the overt exclusion of Dalit castes from access to educational institutions. The team had an opportunity to present its findings to the then minister of education, which led to a policy change mandating several seats in government institutions to those who identify as Dalit. This was one small but significant example of how the grassroots can inform institutions and enable change.

Even though the government of Nepal has ensured free primary education to all children of primary school age with the provision of free textbooks and stipends of Rs.400 a year to all Dalit students, formal education is still unaffordable for Dalit children, given the historical economic and social exclusion of Dalit castes in Nepal. The literacy rate among Dalits is 52.4% compared to the national average of 65.9%, and it is 34.5% for Tarai/Madhesi Dalits. Only, 24.7% of Hill Dalits and 11.8% of Tarai/Madhesi Dalits complete eighth grade, a rate is far behind the national average of 41.7%. Dalits comprise only 1.6% of those with a 10th-grade education (the school leaving certificate) and above and only 0.8% of those with a bachelor's degree. The low educational status of Dalits has a multifaceted impact in their socioeconomic and political lives. When these rates are further disaggregated by gender, an even more significant gap in Dalit girls' education is evident.

The exclusion of Dalit populations from formal schooling was a blind spot for our research group until we met Narayan at Namuna school. We walked into a classroom with broken windows and wooden benches and sat with Narayam, somewhat naively, to hear about his schooling experience. He smiled and pointed to his clothes and said:

> Look at me. Look at this dirty shirt and my torn tennis shoes. Poor people in Nepal don't have options to do anything. We have no choices. If I had a choice I wouldn't stay in this country, I would leave too. I don't want to stay here ... [points at the window. The glass is visibly cracked with a small part of it missing], look at the window. Why would any of us want to stay here? It's because we have no options. None! And still my parents tell me I should be happy to be in school because so many other Dalit children cannot go to school. We are treated badly out of school, in school, everywhere.

When we looked deeper into government provisions for students like Narayan, we noticed that even the funds allocated for Dalit education very rarely reach students. The improper and untimely distribution of scholarships by the government offices and then schools further excludes Dalit children from being properly benefiting from funds. Lack of resources, coupled with discriminatory admissions practices, meant extremely limited options for Dalit students in formal schools (Dalit Civil Society Organization Coalition 2015). Two other students who identified as Dalit shared stories of overt discrimination from teachers and fellow students ranging from disrespectful language to being prohibited from drinking water from the communal water fountain.

The research group collected quantitative data as well as the narratives of Narayan and other students to present to personnel at the Ministry of Education. Although the then minister chose to act immediately with a policy change toward inclusion, the change has not been sustained due to the many changes in government and the constant political unrest in Nepal. For many of the students, our ability to collect and share information on neglected realities provided hope for how consciousness raising from the bottom is possible and necessary for change.

Power Is Located in Multiple Places

The language of empowerment has been co-opted extensively in the neoliberal enterprise. Instead of "shifting power," "distributing power," or even "empowering," it may be more helpful to think about locating and defining power in different ways. In PAR, the power to learn, the power to produce knowledge, the power to engage in reciprocal relationships and to transform allow us to think of ways in which power is situated in individuals and collectives but also how it has to be honed in order to achieve the collective good. Members of our research team often discussed how enacting power for the common good was different from enacting power for personal gain. One example was this was our findings on the mass emergence of private schools in Kathmandu and the complexities of how power played out in this privatization of education.

A male student at a government high school in Lalitpur explained:

> 50 rupees ... that's how much I pay in fees every month. I go to school here because my family cannot afford to send me to a boarding school. There are 58 of us in one class and 10 of us share one desk and bench. I get angry because even though they say it's a government school and it's cheaper I still have to buy books. Then they tell us to buy 20 notebooks for all the different subjects. If we don't buy what they tell us to buy, we get thrown out of class. Last week, they said that every student had to make a donation so that the school can replace the windows. I haven't told my parents yet. They'll scold me if I ask for more money.

Our research team decided that these public government schools could hardly be blamed for these fundraising attempts. In a prior study on the effects of political instability on the education system, I interviewed teachers and principals at three government schools. Mrs. Sarala Bhattarai, principal of the Dhumbarahi School, picked up the tape recorder I had placed on the table, held it to her mouth, and started listing the numerous broken promises the government had made to these schools. Her justified tirade included this statement: "What happened to all the books that we were supposed to get? Last year I bought books out of pocket because my only other option was to cancel school and close it down".

With the growing number of schools in the Kathmandu Valley, one would think that access to education would grow along with it. Why then have we created a society that idealizes private schools yet prevents most of the population from even entering their doors? Purna, a housekeeper, sends her granddaughter to Future Pillars School, an "English boarding school" that makes children wear uniforms and a tie and charges thousands of rupees every year as nonrefundable deposits. One of the coresearchers asked the principal about the purpose of this "nonrefundable" deposit. Even after probing for an hour, the answer was only "We have many expenses." Meanwhile, Purna works extra hours in order to make those payments. This issue resonated with many students in our interviews. Nina, a female student at a private school, elaborated:

> Anyone can open a school in their home and call it a private school. Then comes the uniform fees, the book fees, donations ... you know what I mean by donation, right? [She smiles, I nod.] It is never-ending. I really don't think what I learn is more valuable than what I would learn at the government schools. It is just that I ride to school in a nicer bus and wear a tie. My parents are just tired of it. I have come to realize that the need to attend an English-speaking boarding school is directly connected to social status.

In the research team's informal conversations and daily interactions, it was clear that most parents and students were very aware of the business mentality of the educational institutions that are sprouting up all over the major cities. They recognized that the quality of education does not match the schools' monetary demands. And yet they struggle to find a way to gain admission into these institutions. This was one way in which power and empowerment was understood in relation to the commodification of knowledge, the yearning for social status and financial goods.

Another way in which we experienced empowerment was by unpacking the concept and practice of accompaniment—the very act of supporting and collaborating with one another toward a common goal. This experience provided a stark contrast to concepts of individualism that students had previously identified as problematic in Nepali society. Identifying power in terms of agency also allowed for students involved in the project to think about the prevalent dichotomy of power and powerlessness and where they would situate themselves and why.

For some of my coresearchers, assuming the identity of a researcher enabled them to transition from passive recipients of knowledge and information to active producers of new knowledge that was relevant to their lives. In their reflections, they talked about how they would locate themselves differently in the conversations around power and powerlessness. Standing in front of their classmates and teachers to share their research findings enabled them to overcome their own habits of learned silence. Arjun's reflection on the research process from field notes of August 10, 2003, provided one example of this assertion:

> As a student and as a teacher, I want to challenge myself to be more active and more vocal. After this research, I realize that I have never thought about how I teach my students. I am teaching them the way I was taught, and I don't like the way I was taught. I am realizing that I am always doing what is expected of me and not what means most to me as a student, teacher, human being, Nepali. There are so many other possibilities.

Engaging in Inquiry Is at the Heart of the Educational Process

The shift from recipient to producer of knowledge, especially in the Nepali context, was significant. For the four youthful researchers on the team, the fact that the process of investigation "was based on their own experience lent their research its power and authenticity". Developing research questions based on identified problems; long periods of interviewing, documenting, reflecting, and refining data collection methods; transcribing and analyzing data enabled all of us to develop research skills that could be transferred into other projects. Every time we got stuck, we developed new questions that we would have to pursue in order to advance our work. For example, when we first started the interview process, we often were met with long periods of silence from our participants. We initially had decided to keep the questions broad and open ended and therefore began our questions with "How do you feel about your schooling experience? Do you like being at this school?" After our first round of interviews, the research team delved deeper into this silence. We attributed the silence to two potential causes: (1) the type of authoritarian education we are accustomed to where no one asks questions, especially about your own thoughts and feelings; and (2) the abruptness of our questioning style. We decided at that meeting that we needed to tweak our interview strategy in two distinct ways: by finding points of connection with participants to have "normal" conversations that would put them at ease without making them feel like they were being questioned and, on a higher level, by being cognizant of "learned silence" and the dynamics of power and authoritarian traditions latent within this concept. In many ways, the obstacles and challenges we faced gave us pause and allowed us to affirm that our chosen methodology for this study was most appropriate in our context, primarily because it helped in the "unlearning" of silence (Koirala-Azad 2008, p. 14).

This iterative and cyclical process was very new to students, and they often commented on how different it was from how they learned in school. Of the students we interviewed in schools and universities, the majority commented on the stress associated with examinations such as the school leaving certificate and its inadequacies and inaccuracies in measuring learning. Success on the exam, the main determinant of future plans and educational and career paths for many students, is based on students' ability to memorize content. For students who can afford it, private tutoring outside school has become a way to better prepare for this exam. For others, like Sarita, this system of learning is much more of a struggle:

> This is my third time taking the [school leaving certificate] exam. Third time! I've already lost a whole year because I'm failing in optional maths. [I intervened to ask why she was taking "optional" math. Shouldn't it be "optional?"] No, in high school we have to take compulsory math and optional math. Optional math is trigonometry, calculus, and really hard things like that. I don't understand any of it and my teacher doesn't explain anything. When I asked him for help after class, he said to memorize everything and I would pass. He said I wasn't working hard enough. To tell you the truth, I have been working very hard. I really want to go to nursing [school] and become a nurse but I cannot do anything until I pass.

These stories stood in contrast to our sometimes-bumpy but fairly consistent process of asking questions, finding answers, analyzing their meaning, and asking new questions to better understand the state of Nepali education. For us, these practices allowed for real conversations on the difference between the production of knowledge based on lived experience versus the transmission of static knowledge and the roles each could or could not play in consciousness raising and social action.

One particular weekend was dedicated to practicing interviewing skills. Almost all of us chose to practice on a family member. We were all struck by how much we did not know about our own families and how even those practice interviews were unintentionally relevant to our study. Engaging in inquiry also meant that we were in a dynamic process that allowed us to question our own assumptions and "truths" while increasing our understanding on a variety of topics. The concept of inquiry and related tools that we acquired in the PAR process had long-term effects as well. Two years after we had completed our research project, two members of the original research team had started their own PAR projects on educational inequities. At the end of our original research process, we had identified areas that needed further inquiry. One area was based on the experiences shared by girls in co-ed schools and narratives of disrespectful treatment from some male teachers and peers. The two young women on our research team decided to pull in several peers to investigate theses experiences further. Arjun, from our original research team, leveraged his role as a faculty member at the engineering college to provide support for this research team.

Conclusion

For the past three decades, Nepal has shifted quite drastically from a totalitarian, hierarchical, and stable monarchy to a country wrought with internal conflict, political instability, natural disasters, and economic decline, leading pundits to declare it a "failed state." Some would argue that these crises have allowed us to witness forces of both disintegration and integration at the same time. This chapter builds on the latter—a reemergence of the grassroots, a yearning for alternative approaches, and a desire to retain the authentic collective nature of Nepali social fabric. The ideas presented in this chapter are based on a four-year study by a team of Nepali high school and university students exploring nuances in their educational system based on the experiences of students like themselves. The study led to discoveries that were commonly experienced in the Nepali educational system but never articulated. These included the prevalence of discriminatory practices based on caste and class, the emergence of private schooling as commercial enterprise, and, most significantly, an increasing value of meritocracy and a greater divide between success and failure for students. In the team's initial conversations about using PAR as an approach, the most attractive aspects were those that seemed to counter emerging negative values of competition and self-promotion (in contrast to Nepali cultural concepts of community)—these included PAR's focus on collaboration and accompaniment, on seeing and leveraging existing individual capacity, and the nonlinear approach to knowledge production and change that allowed for a dynamic process.

The team experienced some significant triumphs in the research process, such as an opportunity to present findings at the Ministry of Education, leading to some tangible policy changes in favor of Dalit students. Dalit students also were offered platforms at their own schools and universities to share some insights and were able to work through some of the discomforts to make sure their findings, which reflected the experiences of much larger groups of students in Nepali schools, were heard. Two members of the team also branched out and created their own PAR projects after ours was complete. Despite these triumphs and many challenges, probably one of the most important aspects of the work for the team was to *be* and *do* differently. Attributes of the research process—such as learning to engage in a consultative process that meant stating individual opinion clearly but also to knowing when to step back, listen, and be detached from one's own ideas to allow for group consensus; respecting one another's ideas but also presence; practicing patience with each other and the process; developing bonds of friendship; and learning to be lovingly honest with each other in resolving tension—allowed us to better understand that engaging in collective work meant we had to learn to *be* different and to practice these attributes that allowed us to have a collective identity.

To us, this intentionality around recognizing, learning, and practicing attributes conducive to collaborative work was where we had the greatest ability to counter some habits of a neoliberal history of development. Challenging neoliberalism meant transforming our imagination and challenging our own assumptions. PAR allowed us to do this through its dialogical and reflective process. PAR often runs the risk of claiming too much (Koirala-Azad and Fuentes 2010)—that the mere adoption of PAR as an approach deterministically leads to individual and social transformation, that PAR necessarily promotes universal participation and democratic practices, or that the knowledge production dimension of PAR is always useful to social change efforts. There are many challenges in PAR as an alternative paradigm of social science or educational research that are just beginning to emerge in literature (Koirala-Azad and Fuentes 2010). However, context-specific gleanings from experiences in PAR, such as those shared in this chapter, are valuable in helping us determine what aspects of PAR allow for a paradigm shift.

References

Altbach, P. (2004). Globalization and the university: Myths and realities in an unequal world. *Tertiary Education and Management, 1,* 3–25.

Cammarota, J. (2005). *Reflections on the field: Anthropology and education—Past, present, and future.* Washington, DC: American Anthropological Association.

Cammarota, J., & Fine, M. (2007). *Revolutionizing education: Youth participatory actions research in motion.* New York: Routledge.

Fals-Borda, O., & Rahman, M. A. (1991). *Action and knowledge: Breaking the monopoly with participatory action research.* New York: Apex Press.
Fine, M. (1994). Dis-stance and other stances: Negotiations of power inside feminist research. In A. Gitlin (Ed.), *Power and method: Political activism and educational research* (pp. 13–35). New York: Routledge.
Freire, P. (1973). *Education: The practice of freedom.* New York: Seabury Press.
Freire, P. (1994). *Pedagogy of hope.* New York: Continuum.
Gaventa, J. (1991). Toward a knowledge democracy. In O. Fals-Borda & A. Rahman (Eds.), *Action and knowledge: Breaking the monopoly with participatory action research* (pp. 121–131). New York: Apex Press.
Gilligan, M. J., Pascuale, B. J., & Samii, C. (July 2014). Civil war and social cohesion: Lab-in-the-field evidence from Nepal. *American Journal of Political Science, 58*(3), 604–619.
Kemmis, S., & McTaggart, R. (2000). Participatory action research. In N. K. Denzin & Y. S. Lincoln (Eds.), *Handbook of qualitative research* (2nd ed.). Thousand Oaks, CA: Sage.
Koirala, S. (2004). *Exploring solutions at the intersection of education, immigration and transnationalism: Efforts of the diaspora in Nepali social change.* Unpublished doctoral dissertation, University of California, Berkeley.
Koirala-Azad, S. (2008). Unraveling our realities: Nepali students as researchers and activists. *Asia Pacific Journal of Education, 28*(3), 251–265.
Koirala-Azad, S. (2010). Exploring the intersection of philanthropy, research and scholarship in a 'third world' context. In S. Koirala-Azad & E. Fuentes (Eds.), *Activist scholarship: Possibilities and constraints of participatory action research.* Social Justice, 36(4), 84–98.
Koirala-Azad, S., & Fuentes E. H. (Eds.). (2010). Activist scholarship: Possibilities and constraints of participatory action research. *Social Justice, 36*(4).
Nygreen, K. (2006). Reproducing or challenging power in the questions we ask and the methods we use: A framework for activist research in urban education. *The Urban Review, 38*(1), 1–26.
Nygreen, K., Kwon, S. A., & Sánchez, P. (2006). Urban youth building community: Social change and participatory research in schools, homes and community-based organizations. *Journal of Community Practice, 14*(1–2), 105–121.
Park, P. (1999). People, knowledge, and change in participatory research. *Management Learning, 30*(2), 141–157.
Rahman, M. A. (1993). *People's self-development: A journey through experience.* Dhaka, Bangladesh: University Press.
Robinson-Pant, A. (2001). Development as discourse: What relevance to education? *Compare, 31*, 311–328.
Smith, S., Willms, D., & Johnson, N. (Eds.). (1997). *Nurtured by knowledge: Learning to do participatory action-research.* New York: Apex Press.
Tandon, R. (2002). *Participatory research: Revisiting the roots.* New Delhi, India: Mosaic Books.

CHAPTER 8

Applying Participatory Action Research to Program Evaluation in Education Policy

Mary Vayaliparampil

INTRODUCTION

As the world works toward development goals, participatory action research (PAR) becomes increasingly relevant to international development in general and education policy in particular. The United Nations General Assembly (2015), for example, calls for "all countries and all stakeholders, acting in collaborative partnership" (p. 1) to implement the United Nations 2030 Agenda for Sustainable Development. Against this backdrop, the values of participation, democracy, and inclusion that PAR approaches espouse assume added significance in policy processes. In the realm of education policy, the participation of stakeholders can take place at any and every stage of policy development, ranging from conceptualization to implementation to evaluation. This chapter provides an example of how PAR can be used for evaluative purposes to examine the program effectiveness of education policy. Specifically, this chapter is based on a dissertation research study undertaken by the author. The chapter is structured into four sections. The first section describes the relevance of stakeholder perceptions to program evaluation. The second section introduces Photovoice as the

---

M. Vayaliparampil (✉)
Institute for Multi-Track Diplomacy, Arlington, VA, USA
e-mail: vayaliparampil.mary@gmail.com

© The Author(s) 2017
H. Kidwai et al. (eds.), *Participatory Action Research and Educational Development*, South Asian Education Policy, Research, and Practice,
DOI 10.1007/978-3-319-48905-6_9

PAR methodology used in the study. The third section presents the research study undertaken on India's Education for All Program. Finally, the fourth section discusses potential applications of Photovoice to the education policy process in the South Asian context.

STAKEHOLDER PERCEPTIONS IN PROGRAM EVALUATION

Crafting education policy involves a complex process that policy makers often discuss as a series of stages (Kelly and Maynard-Moody 1993). Indeed, the policy cycle primarily consists of five stages: (1) agenda-setting, (2) policy formulation, (3) public policy decision making, (4) policy implementation, and (5) policy evaluation. The final stage of policy evaluation is one of the most crucial phases. It is necessary to examine the extent to which the policy and its related programs have been effective to, affording for further improvisation of policy. Research into policy effectiveness traditionally has relied on methods that have roots in scientific positivism.

However, there is increasing recognition that quantitative analyses alone cannot capture a holistic understanding of the effectiveness of programs in mitigating problems faced by the target population. The identities, perceptions, and beliefs of the beneficiaries are indispensable. Perceptions of the target population are also a critical factor that determines the continuity of participants in the program as well as the potential for recruiting new participants to the program. Experts such as Kelly and Maynard-Moody (1993) advocated enhanced engagement by policy analysts in promoting dialogue among insiders to gain their interpretation in policy evaluation. Therefore, to improve the effectiveness of programs implemented toward a policy goal, it is essential to understand the perceptions of every stakeholder involved in the policy process. PAR methodologies, such as Photovoice, provide the ideal platform to facilitate stakeholder participation in the policy process.

PHOTOVOICE METHODOLOGY

PAR is an approach to research that is characterized by the participation of communities, reflection of theory and practice, and collaborative action for change among stakeholders and the researcher. PAR encourages education planning and administration process to be more participatory, democratic, and inclusive. Photovoice is an innovative PAR method developed by Caroline Wang and Mary Burris in 1992. It is a participatory analytic process by which people use photography to identify, represent, and enhance their community through social action in collaboration with policy makers and researchers. Photovoice has its origins in community health, documentary photography, and Paulo Freire's (1970, 2001) ideas of empowerment, feminist theory, and education for critical consciousness. Jay Ruby (1991) explained that Photovoice provides researchers "the possibility of perceiving the world from the viewpoint of the people who lead lives that are different from those traditionally in control of the means for imaging the world" (p. 50). More recently, Photovoice has been used by Newman (2010) to examine how community participation by spinal cord injury survivors was influenced by environmental barriers and facilitators. Other projects involving Photovoice include a study by Booth and Booth (2003) to determine how mothers with learning difficulties viewed themselves and how the mothers perceived they were viewed by others. Booth and Booth found that their study's participants used Photovoice to capture multiple "angles of vision on the world" (p. 440) in relationship to the participants' individual self-perceptions and their collective identity in the communities where they were situated. Another study by the research team of Mitchell, Stuart, Moletsane, and Nkwanyana (2006) found that Photovoice was an ideal methodology to engage and empower their rural South African participants in participatory action in their community. The research team found that participants used Photovoice to identify and display images that captured the dynamics of cultural production within the community governance structure.

Although Photovoice has a much longer history in community health, when applied to education policy research, it can be a potent tool to promote more immediate policy or program changes for the stakeholders involved. For example, Matt Streng and his colleagues (2004) applied Photovoice to immigration issues and identified factors that influenced the adaptation and quality of life for new adolescent Latino immigrants in their schools and communities. An immediate outcome of this Photovoice project was that the school changed its policy to assign a full-time advisor for the AIM (Acción, Inspiración, and Motivación) Club and listed the club on the school's website. Attempts were also being made by organizations to elicit funding for developing youth programs to support trauma-affected Latino youth. Photovoice coupled with PAR was the impetus for such action. Indeed, there is a powerful relationship between Photovoice and PAR when it comes to affecting policy on the ground. A qualitative review of Photovoice research by Hergenrather, Rhodes, and Bardhoshi (2009) found that nine studies reported changes in program or policy. Some of the changes were in terms of partnerships between the community and organizations, improving HIV prevention activities, and providing healthy choices in school vending machines. Hergenrather et al.'s literature review highlights the positive impact of Photovoice in bringing about change. Such change aligns with PAR as Photovoice is a methodology for involving members of the local community and stakeholders in capturing the impact of policy on the community.

Photovoice Research Study

This section describes and reports on a research study that employs Photovoice for evaluative purposes in order to examine program effectiveness of India's Education for All policy in urban and rural areas. Throughout India, the Education for All program is known by the Hindi phrase Sarva Siksha Abhiyan (SSA), which means "education to all." SSA is the Indian government's flagship program for achieving universal school enrollment. Eight specific interventions within SSA target disadvantaged population subgroups:

1. Midday Meal
2. Stipend for Girls
3. School Sanitation and Hygiene Education
4. Madrassa Modernization
5. Civil Works
6. Village Education Committee
7. Residential Hostel for Girls
8. School Supplies

The disadvantaged subgroups in the general population included Muslims, scheduled castes, scheduled tribes, and girls. Stakeholders under consideration were the state government, international nongovernmental organizations (NGOs), local NGOs, teachers, and parents. The primary research question for this study was: What are the stakeholders' perceptions of the effectiveness of the SSA in increasing school enrollment in India? This central question was explored through three specific secondary research questions:

1. To what extent did the various stakeholders attribute the increase in school enrollment since 2004 to the SSA?
2. What difficulties did stakeholders experience in implementing SSA, and how did they impact the effectiveness of the SSA?
3. What are the inadequacies of the SSA in addressing the challenges to secondary school enrollment, according to the stakeholders?

Method

The research design of the study involved a multiple case study approach. Three UNICEF education officers, nine state government officers, six representatives of local NGOs, 18 teachers, and 135 parents comprised the participants of the study (n=171). The research methodology included Photovoice to collect data from parents and interviews to collect data from all other stakeholders. The Photovoice methodology described by Wang and Burris (1997) was adapted to consist of four steps:

1. Training the participants on the topic of the study, the Photovoice methodology, the goal of recording photographs, and the ways to use the cameras
2. Devising the initial themes and taking pictures
3. Facilitating group discussion for critical reflection and dialogue based on the pictures taken
4. Dissemination of information to policy makers, funders, media, and others who may be mobilized to advance reform

The training session took approximately one hour. Taking photographs took approximately one hour as well, and the focus group discussion took approximately two hours. Digital cameras were provided to the participants to take pictures. The focus group discussions were recorded using a digital recorder. The validation of data is inbuilt into the Photovoice methodology. The participants themselves selected the photographs, issues, and themes that best represented the community's perceptions during the focus group discussions. The dissemination of information was done through the presentation of the findings at seminars organized in each state by the researcher in collaboration with the respective state governments. The data collected consist of documents, semistructured interviews, photographs, and focus group discussions related to the photographs.

Data Analysis

The study employed thematic analysis in interpreting the transcripts of the semistructured interviews and focus group discussions compiled during Photovoice. The data reduction process began simultaneously with the data collection process. Field notes and audio recordings were reviewed on a day-to-day basis to identify emerging themes and questions for further clarification. Summaries of the researcher's overall impression of the encounters were prepared and provided to the participants to get their feedback as a way of "member checking" (Carlson 2010). In the case of the Photovoice material, the initial analysis was carried out by the participants themselves by identifying the photographs that best represented the community's perceptions during the focus group discussions. The analysis of data after data collection was carried out in two phases. In Phase 1, the thematic analysis described by Braun and Clarke (2006) was employed in analyzing the data. In Phase 2, the data analysis proceeded from noting patterns and themes to determining cross-case explanations. This was done by identifying the similarities and differences between the themes that emerged out of the three cases. The findings of the study are presented next.

Findings

To introduce the findings, Fig. 8.1 presents a thematic map summary. There were three main findings from the participants' data. The participants perceived that SSA led to an (1) increase in school in enrollment, but there were (2) implementation difficulties with SSA and (3) overall program inadequacies.

Effectiveness in increasing school enrollment

As Fig. 8.1 shows, the participants perceived that SSA was effective in increasing school enrollment. With regard to the extent to which stakeholders attributed the increase in school enrollment to the SSA, three major findings emerged: (1) the individual intervention as contributor, (2) the combination of interventions as contributors, and (3) non–supply-based interventions as contributors. The participants captured these interventions with their Photovoice images. For example, Photo 8.1 shows an image of the Midday Meal intervention.

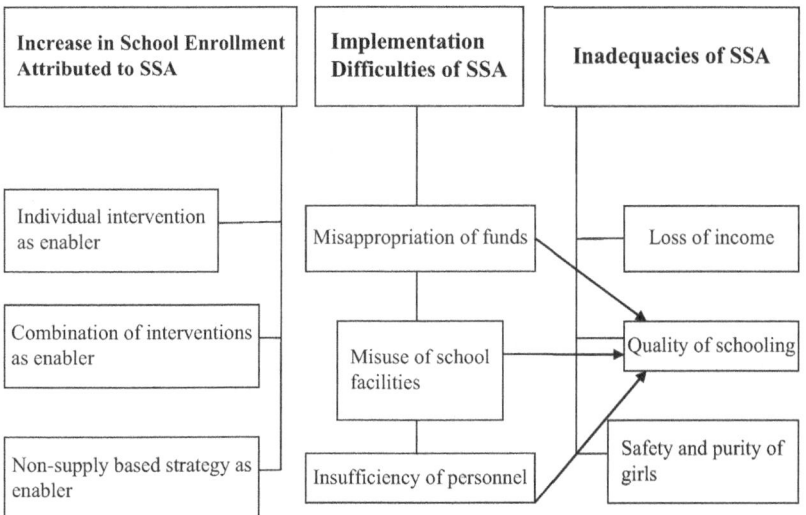

Fig. 8.1 Thematic map of the study's findings

Photo 8.1 Midday Meal photographed by Parent 93

Individual Intervention as Enabler

As Photo 8.1 shows, the Midday Meal intervention was found to be the most effective intervention in increasing school enrollment. The intervention enabled school enrollment figures to grow irrespective of whether other interventions were implemented or not. This individual intervention was perceived favorably and as indispensable to increasing school enrollment. Parents and other stakeholders were of the strong opinion that if the Midday Meal intervention was discontinued, there would be a dramatic drop in school enrollment. Intervention indispensability was highlighted by a district education officer in a rural Jharkhand in the following manner.

Education officer:	In the beginning they used to distribute raw food to parents who would cook it at home but then often the child would not get sufficient food. The parents would share it among all the members or give more to those who go to work. So from 2004 the children are given a cooked meal in school. This Midday Meal has been very effective. Now children are coming to school, parents are sending them just for the meal.
Interviewer:	What if the Midday Meal had not been implemented?
Education officer:	If the Midday Meal was not implemented, nothing would have worked. Everything else would have been useless. Parents would not have sent their children. Even now with the Midday Meal, the attendance drops in the afternoon. Some children go home after they eat.

Combination of Interventions as Enabler

Some interventions in combination with other interventions were perceived to act as enablers in increasing school enrollment. These interventions were appreciated and perceived as having been useful in increasing enrollment but lacked the ability to draw children to school on their own. The participants also perceived that if these individual interventions were not implemented or were discontinued, it would make no or very little difference to student enrollment. An example of an intervention that, though useful, was not indispensable is illustrated by the following conversation:

NGO 2: In the SSA program, one of the most effective interventions is the appointment of parateachers.... When parateachers started to come, the schools benefited a lot. It not only provided extra staff but also the parateachers are of the same community and it removed the language barrier. So the enrollment and retention of children has increased.

Interviewer: What do you think would happen if the appointment of parateachers was not implemented?

NGO 2: Hmm ... I don't know. I am not sure. Maybe fewer number of children would have joined but I think they might still come for the midday meal.

Interviewer: What about the other interventions? How effective have they been in increasing enrollment?

NGO 2: The role of the VEC (Village Education Committee) has also been very good. In some areas when the money given by the government falls short, the VEC goes around and collects donations for the school and fills all the potholes. In another place, they built many taps and put up many fans. All this was done due to the initiative of the VEC in collecting donations from the villagers. All these SSA programs are good. They have definitely helped in bringing the children to school but I am not sure of their individual effectiveness. If any one was not implemented and the others continued, I don't think there would be a big effect. As long as the Midday Meal is there, I am sure the children will come to school.

Non–Supply-Based Strategy as Enabler

Strategies that did not involve the supply of any kind of resource to students were also found to have played an important role in increasing school enrollment. Expanded responsibilities requiring school teachers to take a census of school-age children in the village to identify those not enrolled in any school was perceived to have helped increase school enrollment. When a child not attending school was discovered, teachers were expected to work out a solution that addressed whatever prevented the parent from enrolling the child. The next example demonstrates the role of this noninterventional aspect of the SSA program.

We go to guardians and convince them, tell them to send the children—you say that because of poverty you cannot send the children, they go to break rocks, because of poverty you cannot send the children, they go to do manual labor, if they don't go they won't get money, from where will we get rice and how will we eat—they tell us all these reasons so we tell them okay then in a week you send them for three days and then the other days they can do your household work or else you can send them for one half—let them come the first half and the second half they can do housework or take care of younger children, we even tell them to send the younger children to school with the older child and we will manage.

Implementation Difficulties

The misappropriation of funds, misuse of school facilities, and insufficiency of personnel were the three primary challenges in the implementation of the SSA. Photo 8.2 shows a Photovoice image that participants captured to show these implementation difficulties. The photo is of a school's toilet facilities.

Photo 8.2 Dirty toilet facilities photographed by Parent 86

Misappropriation of Funds

Misappropriation of funds was found to have occurred in two ways: misappropriation through systemic corruption and misappropriation through violence. The participants perceived that systemic corruption occurred along different levels of authority within the SSA, ranging from senior administrative officers within the state government to members of the village education committee and contractors involved in the construction of the school building. Misappropriation through violence occurred when personnel controlling SSA funds, such as school principals, were killed if they resisted militant Maoist demands for money. The comments from some parents in a Photovoice focus group discussion accusing another parent, who is the cook for the Midday Meal at the school, of corruption illustrate this problem.

Parent 1: We have got the gas cylinder but nobody knows where the money has gone. Children don't get proper food.

Parent 4: You are the master of the money; you should know where the money has gone.

Cook 1: I kept complaining that the cylinder hasn't come; I can't cook on the mud burner. Then after two months I asked him where has the money gone, and he said he has put it in the account.

Parent 3: Have you seen the money in the account? If the money is in the account, why are the children getting bad food? They are supposed to get eggs and milk but there is only rice gruel everyday. They think "These are poor children, nobody will question" and the 1 lakh, 2 lakhs disappears for their own service. There are only 50 glasses for 300 children. We tell them oil and dal is over, and they tell us to make do with what is there. The money comes in advance into the account, and then it disappears.

Misuse of School Facilities

Members of the larger community in which the school is located misused the facilities in various ways. For example, because the community lacks running water and sanitation facilities, some people utilized the school's facilities. The next excerpt shows the extent to which children were disturbed by the misuse of the school facilities.

You look around; you can see the mess here. You think this is made by the children; it is not. Children don't bring alcohol bottles to school. The bad elements from the *basti* (slum dwelling) come here in the night. They play cards, get drunk, make the toilet dirty and go. It stinks so bad my daughter tells me you have to hold your nose even if you are 10 meters away. Who will clean it? Teachers tell the children they should keep the school clean, but I won't let my child clean other people's mess. They come here to learn or to become servants?

Additionally, in the state of Jharkhand, the military misused school facilities to store ammunition and house soldiers. As a result, the schools were severely damaged when Maoists attacked the army. Photo 8.3 is a photo of a damaged school.

Photo 8.3 Caught in the Maoist conflict by Parent 17

Insufficiency of Personnel

The schools are not equipped with administrative staff or provided with external personnel. Therefore, the teachers are assigned various additional responsibilities. A major nonteaching responsibility for teachers in the three states is the management and supervision of the SSA interventions. For example, teachers were responsible for maintaining daily records of details, such as the materials used and the number of students for the Midday Meal intervention. Besides this, they were also responsible for supervising the helpers in preparing the Midday Meal. Parents complained that teachers spent a lot of time on the SSA programs instead of teaching. This creates an undue burden on the teachers, as described next.

> The burden on teachers is becoming more. Because the burden is more, teachers cannot pay attention to quality, it is difficult. They have to write reports because the cooks are illiterate. Teachers spend 25% of their time in nonteaching activities in this and that. There are arguments with the cooks also sometimes over how much to cook and how to cook. I think these jobs should be given to the *panchayat* [village council]; then the harassment of the teachers will be less.

SSA Inadequacies

The third finding centered on SSA inadequacies. The participants perceived the SSA to be inadequate in addressing secondary school enrollment challenges of loss of income, poor-quality schooling, and the safety of girls.

Loss of Income

Loss of income was a major theme that emerged from analyzing participants' perceptions of the inadequacies of the SSA program in addressing the challenges to secondary school enrollment. Participants perceived loss of income to be of two types: loss of indirect income and loss of direct income. Loss of indirect income results from the loss of labor. Labor involves the work that school-age children could do for their own families, such as working on the farm or taking care of younger siblings so that the mother can contribute to the family income. The role of household labor as a factor preventing boys from enrolling in school is illustrated in the next case.

> Some childrens [*sic*] are there but they need to get education but the family is not helping. In our school only Wasim is there. Night nearly one o'clock two o'clock water will come it seems. He has to collect water for the house ... then he helps his father in the harvest time. He won't come to school harvest time. They need help to cut the crops; extra hand means extra money.

Loss of direct income is the failure of a family to continue to have the additional income that is earned by a child family member. It refers to the inability of a child to contribute directly to the family income by engaging in a form of labor as a direct consequence of being enrolled in school. Photo 8.4 is a parent's representation of this problem.

Photo 8.4 Loss of income captured by Participant 68

According to participants' perceptions, the SSA program in India addressed some life and schooling concerns for parents, such as providing healthy food and minimizing school expenses. However, it failed to address certain other life concerns, such as the loss of labor for the care of small children, household chores, and farming support. The SSA program did not have a mechanism to provide parents with a substitute for the loss of labor; nor did it compensate parents for the loss of income.

Poor Quality of Schooling
"Quality of schooling" refers to the stakeholders' perceptions that the quality of the educational experience in school was inadequate. As a result, parents did not see much benefit in having their children enrolled in school. Quality of schooling was perceived to be inadequate primarily with regard to two aspects: the personnel providing educational experiences and the physical facilities in which the educational experiences were provided. Photo 8.5 portrays the poor physical facilities of a school in Karnataka.

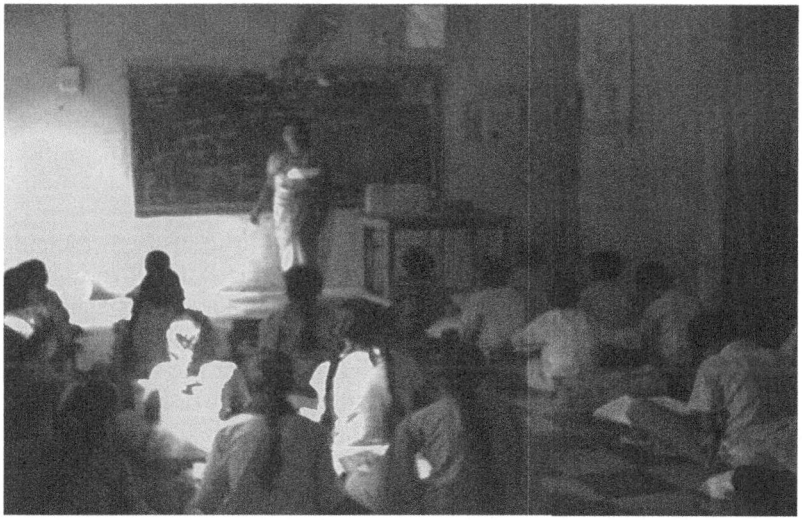

Photo 8.5 Poor school facilities captured by Parent 102

In addition to the substandard facilities, parents also complained about the teachers. One parent had this to say about the teachers: "No studies happen in school. They don't do anything; they often gossip among themselves. They come, sign, and go; one teacher often sits in his chair and dozes and the children make noise; he is newly married. Some teachers come from far, traveling two, three hours, and they are tired and they don't teach."

The following is an excerpt from the Photovoice focus group discussion with parents about the school facilities and the teachers.

Interviewer: Okay, so tell me why you chose to click the picture of the school building?
Parent: Because till now it is not final, and there are so many problems because of it. The school building is not final. It is stuck since 1998 or '99. But we thought our children's lives will be destroyed so we forcibly opened the locks. This is a middle school so there are big, big girls. Where is the bathroom? There is so much difficulty with the latrine; I keep telling it should have a boundary and gate and there should be a latrine, bathroom inside so that girls do not have to go outside and they remain safe.... Cows and goats also wander in; you saw one when you came, didn't you? Also, in the classrooms—two classes, three classes sit in one room; we keep asking for some more classrooms on the top but nobody listens.
Interviewer: What about the water pump?
Parent: We have a water pump, but it is outside the school boundary; nor is the room for making rice gruel inside the boundary. The latrine is also outside and it is so dirty that nobody uses it. I have taken a picture and given you. The girls are hardnosed; they will go far away and hide behind the trees to relieve themselves but they will not use the toilet; it is very problematic. The water pump is working at present; oftentimes it is not and you have to go far for water. You have to be after them for so long to get it fixed.

Safety and Purity of Girls
Safety and purity emerged a theme specific to the secondary school enrollment of girls. "Purity" refers to the virginity of female children. It was per-

ceived that a major concern of parents was to ensure the physical safety, reputation, and purity of their girl children. Secondary schools in rural India are often more than a reasonable walking distance from children's homes. This means that children have to travel long distances on their own, making them vulnerable to physical harassment. For parents of female children, this was a major concern. Also, according to participant perceptions, the marriage prospects of girls depend largely on each girl's reputation. A girl's reputation involves community perceptions about her sexual and nonsexual romantic encounters with the opposite sex, as explained by this parent: "There are boys also in the school; tomorrow if somebody says they saw my daughter talking to boys then her name will be spoiled who will marry her.... Girls are sometimes stupid; they get carried away if some boy gives them little attention. If there are only girls in the school it is okay." The Stipend for Girls intervention provides female children with one rupee for every day of attendance in school. However, this incentive did not override the parents' concern about the safety and purity of their daughters. Participants perceived that the program was inadequate in addressing these concerns. No intervention within the SSA program enhanced the safety or guaranteed the purity of female children when enrolled in secondary school.

Applications of Photovoice

The PAR methodology employed in this study in the form of Photovoice allows for the objects of policy intervention to play an important role in the policy development process. This group of stakeholders is traditionally excluded from having a "voice" in activities that shape their own future. Besides enabling more inclusive, participatory, and democratic ways of policy development, PAR methods such as Photovoice also enhance the credibility and effectiveness of policy interventions. For example, in this study, Photovoice enabled parents to carry their voice to the district authorities. The parents' voice was appreciated equally alongside that of those who developed and implemented SSA policy interventions; the government and teachers. This is important not only because it makes the policy cycle more inclusive and democratic but also because it provides a perspective that is otherwise not valued by policy makers. It is the parents who ultimately make the decision to send their children to school. Therefore, it is useful to understand what inadequacies in the SSA still prevent parents from enrolling their children in school.

Further, Photovoice allowed a direct connection between the policy target and the policy maker, which made the policy process more holistic.

The more popular research methods, such as interviews and focus group discussions, can be inclusive but do not provide policy targets a direct audience with policy makers. The collaboration between policy targets, researcher, and policy makers with Photovoice enabled the policy development process to be more effective. Policy makers received feedback, supported by scientific evidence, about policy interventions from the intended targets of those interventions. Through the photographs collected, Photovoice provided additional concrete evidence of the problems and inadequacies of the SSA interventions.

Photovoice in this case was also empowering for marginalized communities in that it allowed them to dialogue with those in authority about policy concerns. In the normal course of events, marginalized populations, such as scheduled castes and scheduled tribes or those who have converted from such groups to other religions in South Asia, usually have no influence on policies that impact their lives. Photovoice is particularly useful in non-Western contexts, such as that of South Asia, where cultures are collectivistic rather than individualistic. The individualistic nature of qualitative research methods, such as interviews, is problematic in some ways when collecting data from collectivistic cultures. While conducting interviews for this study with the other stakeholders, some interviewees seemed hesitant, uncomfortable, and not confident when answering questions. In one case, the district education officer called one of his assistants to participate jointly in the interview as the assistant was thought to be knowledgeable about certain statistics. During Photovoice focus group discussions for the study, participants sometimes hesitated to discuss their photographs; with prodding from others, they became increasingly vocal and more confident. Focus group discussions for the study often turned into community events with a lot of nonparticipating community members watching the process from the sidelines and occasionally voicing opinions.

Furthermore, Photovoice allows researchers to build better rapport with the participants as it necessitates researchers spending time in the relatively informal activity of digital camera training and taking pictures. Photovoice was selected by the researcher specifically for this benefit. The researcher needed a methodology that would enable data collection from a relatively larger sample of parents than what interviews would allow. Focus group discussions by themselves make it possible to collect data from larger numbers, but this researcher had misgivings about the extent to which it would be possible to develop a rapport between researcher and participants as well as among participants themselves. Also, being in the presence of a researcher can be an intimidating experience for participants from marginalized communities. They may not quite comprehend the role of a researcher but understand that he or she is engaged in important work rather than a social visit. Most participants in this study were seeing cameras for the first time and were eager and excited to learn a new skill. The process of learning to use a digital camera relaxed the participants and made them less uncomfortable in the presence of the researcher. This is particularly useful, given that researchers are usually outsiders to the community they are collecting data from and are trying to elicit critical reflection and dialogue in a limited period of time.

For this particular study, the researcher, a nonresident Indian, could not adequately carry out the final phase of Photovoice, which is to advance reform. An important implication in the final phase of Photovoice is the mobilization of efforts to advance reform. For this study, the researcher disseminated the findings to a wider audience. The participating parents collaborated with the researcher to conduct an elementary analysis of the data. They identified majority opinions regarding effectiveness, implementation problems, and inadequacies of the interventions and prepared a brief report, which was submitted to the district education officer in person by the participants and the researcher. The researcher also presented the findings at local conferences but ultimately was unable to realize the full potential of mobilizing for the advancement of SSA reforms. Other researchers conducting Photovoice may have the ability to utilize continual in-person follow-up and to push more aggressively for policy reform with those in authority.

In relation to this study on the SSA, reform at the macro level could have involved policy changes if the researcher had been in a position to spend more time within the country. An important finding was that the poor quality of public school education prevented enrollment of children in schools. During Photovoice group discussions, parents overwhelmingly complained that public school education was poor. Parents were vociferous that the poor quality of education prevented their children from being able to compete successfully for spots in higher education and jobs. Their children, they said, would still be left at the bottom of the ladder. The education, therefore, did not provide them with social mobility. For that reason, some parents believed it was pointless to send children to public schools. Rather than sending them to public institutions, they preferred keeping their children at home if they could not afford private education.

The implication here is that the Indian government needs to emphasize quality over quantity. The traditional practice in the context of education is to concentrate public spending on quantity before quality. The larger focus of the SSA has been on increasing school enrollment figures. In spite of these SSA interventions, school enrollment figures at the secondary school level in India have a long way to go. The findings of this study using Photovoice imply that improving the quality of public school education will increase school enrollment as it acts as an incentive for parents to enroll their children. This notion that the poor quality of schools hindered the enrollment of children was more widespread among the parents than among the other stakeholders that were interviewed. This researcher believes that the use of Photovoice with parents helped elicit more active participation and critical reflection from them than other research methods would have.

At the micro level, for example, the researcher could have pushed for reform in the allocation of resources to schools. Findings from Photovoice revealed that parents were inconvenienced when the same quantity of materials, such as school uniforms, were supplied to primary school children and middle school children. The insufficient material was a particularly acute problem when making clothes for older girls with the same quantity of cloth that is provided for primary school children. Reform to provide different allocations of resources customized to the needs of the schools and the children would have improved the implementation of the school supplies intervention.

Beyond the use of Photovoice for a collective evaluation of policy and related interventions, it also has potential as a formative assessment tool. The ability to elicit direct, evidence-based constructive feedback from large numbers of the policy target helps in the process of developing policy and interventions. The use of Photovoice during the early stages of policy development enables improvisation. Photovoice may be conducted at the initial draft stage, when a draft policy or intervention is ready and feedback is being solicited from key stakeholders. Photovoice is also ideal at the pilot stage of a policy intervention to identify fault lines and potential implementation difficulties in the proposed intervention.

Finally, a significant benefit of Photovoice is its ability to promote community ownership of processes that contribute to national development. For policy interventions to be sustainable, communities must take ownership of the associated processes. The processes are to take place locally and resources to be shared among the community members. Altman (1995), for example, opined that "[i]n the absence of community structure or commitment to assume ownership, interventions are unlikely to be sustained" (p. 528). Photovoice brings together community members on a shared platform to identify problems, discuss solutions, and influence the adaptation of solutions with policy makers. When Photovoice is used during the development and implementation of interventions, community members are more likely to protect resources, resolve conflicts, and address implementation problems when they arise.

Although Photovoice has a number of benefits, it can be somewhat more challenging to implement than other research methods. A key challenge in conducting this study was enlisting the participation of community members. Emails and phone could not be employed as these facilities are often lacking in rural South Asia. In-person recruitment efforts during the pilot Photovoice were not particularly successful. Community members apparently were reluctant to make independent decisions. Although some agreed to participate, only a few turned up at the fixed time and date; others changed their minds or forgot to show up. This challenge was resolved by first securing support of a respected community leader. Once the leader communicated his or her approval of the Photovoice activity, community members participated more actively.

Another challenge is that the logistics for organizing Photovoice is relatively more complex than that of interviews or observations in terms of the time, scale, and tools needed. Working through the stages of Photovoice— training participants, taking pictures, facilitating the group discussion, and advancing reform—is a time-consuming process compared to interviews and other research methods. Organizing Photovoice resources, such as cameras, projectors, audio-visual recordings, projection screens, rooms, and the like—can be expensive. Photovoice is used primarily in the context of community development. In South Asia, rural communities often lack regular uninterrupted electricity supplies. This could be a problem when uploading pictures taken by participants to a computer or projector to facilitate focus group discussions. Researchers must organize sufficient power backups and other supplies, as locations may be many hours from stores. In terms of scale, dealing with an entire community, including participants and nonparticipants, presents another difficulty in South Asian contexts.

Researchers also need to be prepared to deal with interruptions due to unexpected events in the community. As South Asian cultures are collectivistic, seemingly unimportant personal events can turn into community events, necessitating the immediate involvement of participants in the midst of the Photovoice process. Nonparticipating community members sometimes may feel the need to voice their personal opinions, and researchers will have to be prepared to deal with the impact of this on institutional review board protocols. The importance of independent opinions to the research process is not always well understood, and conducting focus group discussions in closed rooms may not align well with South Asian cultures. The myriad of benefits associated with Photovoice reveal it to be a critical research methodology in international development. For policy interventions to be positive forces for national development, target populations must be informed, engaged, and active participants in the policy development process. Photovoice is the most appropriate methodology for this purpose.

REFERENCES

Altman, D. G. (1995). Sustaining interventions in community systems: On the relationship between researchers and communities. *Health Psychology, 14*(6), 526.

Booth, T., & Booth, W. (2003). In the frame: Photovoice and mothers with learning difficulties. *Disability & Society, 18*(4), 431–442.

Braun, V., & Clarke, V. (2006). Using thematic analysis in psychology. *Qualitative Research in Psychology, 3*(2), 77–101.

Carlson, J. A. (2010). Avoiding traps in member checking. *The Qualitative Report, 15*(5), 1102–1113.

Freire, P. (1970). *Pedagogy of the oppressed.* New York: Continuum.

Freire, P. (2001). *Pedagogy of freedom: Ethics, democracy, and civic courage.* Lanham, MD: Rowman & Littlefield Publishers.

Kelly, M., & Maynard-Moody, S. (1993). Policy analysis in the post-positivist era: Engaging stakeholders in evaluating the economic development districts program. *Public Administration Review, 53,* 135–142.

Hergenrather, K. C., Rhodes, S. D., Cowan, C. A., Bardhoshi, G., & Pula, S. (2009). Photovoice as community-based participatory research: A qualitative review. *American Journal of Health Behavior, 33*(6), 686–698.

Mitchell, C., Stuart, J., Moletsane, R., & Nkwanyana, C. B. (2006). "Why we don't go to school on Fridays": On youth participation through photo voice in rural KwaZulu-Natal. *McGill Journal of Education, 41*(3), 267.

Newman, S. D. (2010). Evidence-based advocacy: Using photovoice to identify barriers and facilitators to community participation after spinal cord injury. *Rehabilitation Nursing, 35*(2), 47–59.

Ruby, J. (1991). Speaking for, speaking about, speaking with, or speaking alongside—An anthropological and documentary dilemma. *Visual Anthropology Review, 7*(2), 50–67.

Streng, J. M., Rhodes, S., Ayala, G., Eng, E., Arceo, R., & Phipps, S. (2004). Realidad Latina: Latino adolescents, their school, and a university use photovoice to examine and address the influence of immigration. *Journal of interprofessional care, 18*(4), 403–415.

United Nations General Assembly. (2015). Transforming our world: The 2030 Agenda for Sustainable Development. Retrieved February 10, 2017, from https://sustainabledevelopment.un.org/post2015/transformingourworld

Vayaliparampil, M. C. (2012). *Stakeholder perceptions of the Sarva Shiksha Abhiyan effectiveness in increasing school enrollment in India.* Unpublished doctoral dissertation, Pennsylvania State University, State College, PA.

Wang, C., & Burris, M. A. (1997). Photovoice: Concept, methodology, and use for participatory needs assessment. *Health Education & Behavior, 24*(3), 369–387.

Case Study 1

Photovoice and Girls' Education in Gujarat, India

Payal Shah

In this case study, I discuss how Photovoice, a participatory action research (PAR) method, can be used to explore the processes inside schools that affect girls' educational experiences.[1] I implemented Photovoice activities as a part of a 15-month critical ethnography of a public residential school for girls in India from 2008 to 2010. Photovoice is a photo elicitation methodology that seeks to capitalize on the relationship between visual and verbal communication to provide marginalized and less powerful individuals a platform to express themselves and share their experiences. As a more participatory and dialectical method that attempts to give participants more power and control over the research process, Photovoice has the potential to generate new forms of knowledge, skills, and perspectives that can contribute to policy and program development (Anggard 2015; Ross 2008; Wang and Burris 1997). Here I discuss how Photovoice provides one way to fulfill the goals of PAR to equalize power differences, build trust, and create a sense of ownership between the researcher and research participants to bring about social justice and change (Reason and Bradbury 2001).

P. Shah (✉)
University of South Carolina, Columbia, SC, USA
e-mail: pshah@mailbox.sc.edu

© The Author(s) 2017
H. Kidwai et al. (eds.), *Participatory Action Research and Educational Development*, South Asian Education Policy, Research, and Practice,
DOI 10.1007/978-3-319-48905-6_10

The KGBV Program in Gujarat

I implemented Photovoice as part of a project that examined a Kasturba Gandhi Balika Vidyalaya (KGBV) school in the Indian state of Gujarat. The KGBV program has been hailed as a precedent-setting national public residential school program for girls, designed to enable the most marginalized girls to attend school.[2] The KGBV program is primarily concerned with increasing enrollment and follows the national curricula and teacher certification standards. Gujarat was one of the initial seven states across India to implement the KGBV program beginning in 2005. It is also one of the two states (the other being Uttar Pradesh) that partnered with CARE India from 2005 to 2010 to promote empowerment in the KGBV schools. As a result, the KGBV program in Gujarat provides a unique institutional environment that has the potential to go beyond providing access.

This project took place in the KGBV Gharwal school, one of 22 fully residential KGBV schools across the state of Gujarat. The school opened in 2005, graduating its first class of students in 2008. This school enrolls girls from various villages and castes within a catchment area of 80 to 100 km (approximately 50 to 62 miles). The primary scheduled castes, scheduled tribes, and other backward castes[3] found within this region are represented at this school, with the exception of Muslims. During my time at the school, 52 girls were enrolled, all between the ages of 10 and 16, placed by ability (rather than age) in grades 5 to 7.

I sought to design a project that privileged the experiences and perspectives of rural, marginalized Indian school-going girls in order to provide a better understanding of processes of girls' empowerment. The girls studying at this KGBV school represent a marginalized group who have not had sustained or consistent opportunities to express themselves individually. In particular, due to a variety of sociocultural norms regarding the expected subservience and silence of both the young and the female, these girls were not accustomed to engaging in conversations where they were asked to articulate their thoughts, feelings, and/or desires. (See Ross et al. 2011.) To actualize this commitment to PAR, I employed Photovoice to infuse my research with reflexivity regarding power, representation, and voice. By placing the direction of my research in the hands of these girls, I sought to illuminate the "voices" of the girls in sharing their experiences (Ross 2008; Strack et al. 2004; Wang and Burris 1997). In particular, I used Photovoice to enable the girls to articulate their thoughts on the role their educational experiences may eventually play in better understanding, confronting, and challenging their marginalization (Pink 2006; Rose 2001).

Photovoice

As a methodology rooted in PAR, Photovoice echoes many of the basic theoretical and epistemological commitments underpinning PAR—power, trust, and ownership (Castleden et al. 2008). Photovoice is based on the method of photo interviewing first described by Collier (1967), where photographs are used as a part of the interviewing process. In Photovoice, the participants themselves take and select the images as part of an approach referred to as reflexive photography or autodriven photoelicitation; the images then act as the stimulus and guide for discussion (Clark 1999; Lapenta 2011; Wang and Burris 1997). Photovoice is also action oriented, used "to promote critical dialogue and knowledge . . . and to reach policymakers" (Wang and Burris 1997, p. 370). I used Photovoice to gain insight into what types and whose voices were exercised in a particular social and institutional context—a public residential school for rural marginalized Gujarati girls. In designing a project where the girls were free to choose what images to photograph and what to discuss based on the photographs, I sought to challenge traditional discursive practices that do not ask, or "hear," what these girls have to say.

I conducted Photovoice activities with 13 girls between the ages of 14 and 16 who were in the seventh grade. The seventh-grade girls comprised the oldest set of students who would be graduating from the school at the end of the school year. These girls were at a crucial life stage where a major decision immediately awaited them: to continue or to end formal education. This group of girls had also been at the school the longest and had been well exposed to the empowerment-oriented school culture.

The Photovoice Process

I began by facilitating an initial planning meeting where the students and I discussed the overall goal and understanding of the project, including ethics and responsibilities related to participating in the project and taking photographs. I gave the girls disposable cameras, and we conducted Photovoice activities in two separate rounds. The first round focused on orienting the girls to the Photovoice process: the process of taking photographs, engaging in discussions about how to think about what they wanted to portray before taking photographs, and physically taking the girls out in pairs to practice taking photographs. For this round, I gave the girls the following prompt: "Take pictures of anything at the school or in the village, in any way you want, that will help me understand something about your life." This round was loosely structured and was intended to enable me to gain insight into the lives of the girls and the villagers through their pictures of the school and the villages located around the school.

The second round of Photovoice activities focused on the girls' perceptions of women. My prompt to facilitate this round was: "Take photographs that help me understand what women and girls do. This includes depicting the lives, work, daily routines, etc., of women and girls in schools, villages, and farms around the school." I emphasized that their photographs had to help "tell a story" so that anyone could better understand their lives and educational experiences and the lives of girls and women in their communities through the oral explanations of their photographs

After completing each round and developing each set of photographs, I conducted a series of one-on-one and group elicitation interviews with the girls where they contextualized, explained, and described each photograph. I asked each girl to describe the photograph in her words, explain why she took it and what story it told, and talk about whether the photograph fully captured what she had intended and, if not, what she wanted to illustrate. I then asked each girl to choose her favorite five photographs and give them titles, which the girls would share in a group.[4]

Implications of Using Photovoice

PAR methods enable marginalized individuals to engage collaboratively in the research process (Castleden et al. 2008; Reason and Bradbury 2001; McTaggart 1991). By participating in the project, the KGBV girls were able to share, in their own way, their constructions of reality. The various aspects of the process—one-on-one conversations, group discussions, engagement during the exhibit, and the larger critical dialogue—shift the empowerment themes of the KGBV school from a pedagogic space to a personal and public space. As a methodological tool for empowerment, the Photovoice project increased the KGBV girls' confidence and their ability to reflect on their lives and futures, which represent critical dimensions of the cognitive and psychological dimensions of empowerment. By inviting the girls to decide what to talk about and how, the process reinforced the perspective that adolescent girls are competent social actors who internalize and shape their own experiences (Thorne 2010). Importantly, this project provided an opportunity to better understand the unique needs and circumstances of marginalized girls and include them in the development process.

This project also proposes that participatory and collaborative research can have the potential to alter the larger institutional environment within which marginalized populations can exert their voice. Participants can use their voice to engage in critical discussions and help challenge dominant and hegemonic discourses, even if only in certain contexts and at certain times. In allowing alternative voices to be heard, Photovoice can provide researchers a way to delve into the processes that happen in schools to support the emergence of new knowledge, understandings, and perspectives about the specific needs, circumstances, and contributions of girls as active agents in their lives. These insights can help us reimagine girls' education as a space where different voices are heard; unique needs, circumstances, and contributions are acknowledged; and all people can participate. These insights, revealed through the use of Photovoice, have direct implications for policy making and program design targeted at empowering girls through schooling.

Notes

1. See Shah (2015) for a full length article on this project.
2. The KGBV program defines "most marginalized girls" as girls who are lower caste and rural and who have either never attended school before or dropped out more than two years ago.
3. Scheduled castes, scheduled tribes, and other backward castes are the official designated terms for the lower castes that are eligible for affirmative action–like policies and programs.
4. See Shah (2015) for examples of the participants' Photovoice activities.

References

Anggard, E. (2015). Digital cameras: Agents in research with children. *Children's Geographies, 13*(1), 1–13.

Castleden, H., Garvin, T., & Huu-ay-aht First Nation. (2008). Modifying photovoice for community-based participatory indigenous research. *Social Science & Medicine, 66,* 1393–1405.

Clark, C. (1999). The autodriven interview: A photographic viewfinder into children' s experience. *Visual Sociology, 14*(1–2), 39–50.

Collier, J. (1967). *Visual anthropology: Photography as a research method.* New York: Holt, Rinehart & Winston.

Lapenta, F. (2011). Some theoretical and methodological views on photo-elicitation. In E. Margolis & L. Pauwels (Eds.), *The SAGE handbook of visual research methods* (pp. 201–213). London: SAGE.

McTaggart, R. (1991). Principles for participatory action research. *Adult Education Quarterly, 41*(3), 168–187.

Pink, S. (2006). *Doing visual ethnography.* London: SAGE.

Reason, P., & Bradbury, H. (2001). *Handbook of action research.* Thousand Oaks, CA: SAGE.

Rose, G. (2001). *Visual methodologies: An introduction to the interpretation of visual materials.* London: SAGE.

Ross, H. (2008). Policy as practice, agency as voice, research as intervention: Imag(in)ing girls' education in China. In M. Maskak (Ed.), *The structure and agency of women's education* (pp. 233–252). Albany: SUNY Press.

Ross, H., Shah, P., & Wang, L. (2011). Situating empowerment for millennial schoolgirls in India and China. *Feminist Formations, 23*(3), 23–47.

Shah, P. P. (2015). Spaces to speak: Photovoice and the reimagination of girls' education in India. *Comparative Education Review, 59*(1), 50–74.

Strack, R., Magill, C., & McDonagh, K. (2004). Engaging youth through photovoice. *Health Promotion Practice, 5,* 49–58.

Thorne, B. (2010). Learning from kids. In W. Luttrell (Ed.), *Qualitative educational research: Readings in reflexive methodology and transformative practice* (pp. 407–420). New York: Routledge.

Wang, C., & Burris, M. (1997). Photovoice: Concept, methodology, and use for participatory needs assessment. *Health Education and Behavior, 24,* 369–387.

Case Study 2

Utilizing Memoing as a Reflexive Tool in Participatory Action Research

Tahiya Mahbub

INTRODUCING REFLEXIVITY, MEMOING, AND MY PROCESS

When I embarked upon my doctoral research journey, in which I was exploring children's "likes" and "dislikes" at two Building Resources Across Communities (BRAC) primary schools through participatory action research (PAR) methods, one of the paramount issues that concerned me was how I would navigate "the self"—that is, myself and the biases I hold—through the research process. Hence, the central question was: How would I utilize the subjectivity of myself, as a member of the Bangladeshi diaspora in my home country, as a strength in my research process? Although I was born in Bangladesh, I had been living away from home for many years and had been educated largely at Northern institutions. Even if previously I had worked with BRAC, my worldview differed greatly from that of my participants, and I was always the Other. This position brought into the context unique dynamics that I as the researcher wanted to contend with authentically. The best way to do so would be to address my biases. By the time of entry into the field of research, I had read extensively on the tools and processes of reflexivity, and it had

---

T. Mahbub (✉)
Montreal, QC, Canada
e-mail: tahiya.mahbub@mail.mcgill.ca

© The Author(s) 2017
H. Kidwai et al. (eds.), *Participatory Action Research and Educational Development*, South Asian Education Policy, Research, and Practice,
DOI 10.1007/978-3-319-48905-6_11

become clear to me that within the school of qualitative research, in which I belonged, this had been an issue of paramount concern to scholars across the globe.

Reflexivity is a process that allows for "detachment, internal dialogue, and constant scrutiny of the process through which the researcher constructs and questions his/her interpretations of field experiences" (Ahsan 2009, p. 398). In other words, reflexivity involves researchers being honest about contemplating their own feelings, assumptions, biases, and experiences and allowing themselves the space to navigate those in relation to the research process. Reflexivity occurs during and after a certain process in the field, as no researcher can enter a field and be *completely* objective, leaving biases, identities, and personal understandings of the world behind. Thus, during the research process itself, these issues play into how investigators engage with participants. Afterward, reflexivity "on" the research process occurs as researchers go through the process again in their own minds and in writing text, addressing how their "selves" in the moment of fieldwork, and soon thereafter, affected the research process. Reflexivity happens during and after the event, in essence because as researchers interact in the field, they are aware of what they bring to the field, and later on they address those biases in the write-up.

I used memoing to conduct reflexivity during my research process and then wove those reflexive moments into the very fabric—the text and paragraphs—of my dissertation. I discuss significant milestones—important considerations and junctures—of the research later in the chapter. One point to keep in mind, however, is that the reflexive process was very fluid; the need for reflexivity was determined by a particular milestone I was at in the research process and not by reflexivity itself. Hence, I did not "force" reflexivity on my research process but conducted it only at milestones in which it was most needed for the sake of my research and the participants. In the sections that follow, I first list my research milestones and then share memoing episodes from my research journal and how I utilized memoing as a reflexive tool within that significant milestone of my research process.

As explained by Arora (2012), memoing is a practice that helps researchers clarify thoughts about the research. Originally used in grounded theory approaches, memos can help document researchers' journeys by creating a space where researchers can reflect on their reactions, following a certain methodological endeavor, expose personal thoughts and feelings, work with their biases, and reflect on prior or present experience (Birks et al. 2008). A total of three crucial steps occurred as the "reflexive process" within each significant research milestone. Each of these steps was conducted through memoing (as described) and then written up and woven into the text of the dissertation itself. In the paragraphs that follow, I illustrate how I did so with two data analysis episodes, but first here are the memoing steps:

1. The thoughts before the milestone. Hence, the significant thoughts and questions in my mind before I actually embarked on and completed that milestone.
2. The record of the actual milestone itself as a significant point in the research process and memo (formally or informally written reaction) to that event.
3. A formal, final reflexive reflection on the episode.

My Research Milestones

Research milestones, as briefly explained earlier, were the steps I took in my research journey. These involved major steps in any given qualitative research process, such as:

1. Consideration of my research worldview(s)
2. My research purpose
3. Questions
4. Literature review
5. Negotiating access
6. Field considerations of methods and ethics
7. Conducting methods
8. Collecting data
9. Reporting findings
10. Data analysis
11. Data presentation
12. Recommendations
    However, reflexive memoing were mostly conducted and needed during milestones 5 through 11. The two milestones with the largest number of reflexive memos were 7 and 10.

Next I present episodes of reflexive data analysis—my memoing process during two data analysis episodes embedded within significant milestone 10.

Milestone Ten: The Data Analysis Process

As mentioned in Chapter 3 of this book, where I discuss my data collection processes, I conducted phenomenological analysis of the findings of this study.

These first research question guiding my data analysis was:[1]

What do children in nominally inclusive primary schools operated by the nongovernmental organization BRAC express when asked what they like and dislike about their school?

This was followed by the subquestion:. What central motifs with regard to inclusive education (IE), emerge from children's pictorial, spoken, and written perspectives?

I deemed phenomenological analysis most suitable to answer these questions because this type of analysis allows for the generation of "common or shared experiences of a phenomenon" and a "deeper understanding of the features of a phenomenon" (Butler-Kisber 2010, p. 53). As clearly outlined in my research questions, I wanted to reach such an understanding of children's experiences of inclusive education at their respective schools. Therefore, the goal of the process of analysis was to uncover the essential characteristics of the children's liked and disliked experiences of inclusive education at the two schools. I would better understand the characteristics of their experiences of inclusive education, as expressed through pictorial, spoken, and written perspectives, by reducing the field data to certain themes generated through a phenomenological analysis. The phenomenological analysis process is iterative and reflective, and includes various continual, recursive, and cyclical stages, but mainly two central periods.

First, I conducted a phenomenological analysis solely on the photos and photo reflections. I had 65 photos and 65 photo reflections from the two schools. Second, I conducted another, more in-depth phenomenological analysis (discussed below) on all the data produced across the two schools compiled into one unit. These included the observations, memos, children's photo reflections, and children's written and spoken (transcribed) data. This included a total of 360 pages of textual data. This analysis did not include the questionnaire, another method I utilized. Each phenomenological stage involved four steps: (1) reading, (2) significant statements, (3) formulated meanings, and (4) exhaustive descriptions. Most of the data were analyzed within the "like" or "dislike" framework; however, reflexivity played a key role once I realized this framework was limiting. Hence, next I have chosen an illustration of reflexive memoing conducted on an in-depth and compiled research analysis episode (step 2 from within the 360 pages of textual data) on a poem and a picture generated by two different students at the two schools. Steps before, during, and after are unpacked in detail.

Step 1: Reflexive Thoughts *Before* the Analysis Milestone

Phenomenological processes are crucial to categorize and thematically understand the vast amounts of information produced in this PAR study. However, the often-stringent adherence to children's "likes" and "dislikes" during the process of analysis may box some of their perspectives into a space that is too limiting for the message they want to convey. This does not mean that their voices are being misrepresented or distorted; rather it means they are being categorized. That being said, sometimes words cannot easily be categorized, and in trying to do so, statements run the risk of losing their nuanced complexity. What children will state can be much more multifaceted than a simple "like" or "dislike." Therefore, I have to adjust the framework I used to analyze the data. Although the statements still definitely can be attributed to either a "like" or "dislike," irrespective of my framework of data collection, some voices from the free associative writings, poems and *adda* (long, informal conversations held between friends) responses suggest much more nuanced and complex perspectives. I have chosen two such pieces (one poem and one photograph) from the raw data to emphasize the ability of children to speak articulately about a given topic, even when the setting is framed in certain prescribed boundaries.[2]

However, what if some of the particularly insightful findings are interpreted in another way, by moving farther away from some of my aforementioned biases, especially that of "like" versus "dislike," in order to see data in a new light? It will be interesting to see how this expands the complexity and nuance of the children's perspectives. I attempt to do that with two such students' perspectives next—one from each of the two schools and produced in different activities. I do not intend to make any claims on the data by such interpretations and displays but rather simply to highlight the extent to which one issue can be interpreted in a multifaceted manner and how that same finding, which was previously categorized as a "like" or a "dislike," can be understood in much broader terms.

Step 2: Data Presentation and Reflexive Analysis *During* and *Continuing* from Data

A Poem

This poem was written by a pupil when asked to write freely and creatively about school. He personally choose the topic of studying due to his own interest.

TITLE: Why I study

> I will be happy by studying.
> If I study well,
> My parents will love me.
> If I study well,
> Father will give me an expensive watch.
> If I go to school by wearing the watch,
> All the students at the school will be surprised.
> I'll tell them, "It's a prize for coming to school and getting mark A!"
> I will gain respect from them.
> Maybe I will be a leader. (Shafin, 12, School "U")

As I reflect on this poem, I find that Shafin speaks more about his own aspirations related to school rather than indicating something he likes or dislikes.

Shafin writes how going to school will make him happy, but, more so, it will allow him to gain his parents' love. He will be happier because his parents will be happier. His parents will then reciprocate by gifting him an expensive watch. Perhaps, for Shafin, the watch was a motivating factor for going to school, but a closer reading of this poem indicates that it was much more. After receiving the watch, he will not only be able to rejoice in surprising his peers but also gain their respect and even become a leader at school.

He does not indicate in the poem why a leadership position is so important to him. However, becoming a leader is linked to being a good student and being respected at school. In his mind, this "upward transition" was possible only by getting an A and displaying a tangible reward for having gotten it. This would then surprise his peers and make them notice and even respect him enough for him to become a leader. He probably senses that the current leader has been chosen because she is respected by others.

Perhaps he respects his team leader and aspires to have others feel that way toward him.

This short poem speaks volumes about the current situation of BRAC School "U." It highlights how the undemocratic way of assigning team leaders impacts the children. It also signals how boys also aspire to be leaders, and, although the aim of BRAC is to put girls in leadership positions, this practice did not always help this particular inclusive classroom. Further, it highlights that, even at one of the most nonformal, flexible school systems in Bangladesh, the focus for children is their grades. In any case, Shafin is happy to go to school but emphasizes in his poem the importance of grades, especially top marks. The reason for his desire may be skewed, but what is interesting is that it is so important to him that it changes how his parents and friends view him. If his father were to buy him a watch for getting an A, Shafin's belief in wanting to receive higher marks would be cemented. Furthermore, the mechanisms of how he got there (i.e., memorizing or just learning facts) would be solidified in his young mind. Would he then be able to break out of this mold of memorization, which so desperately needs to be broken for IE to succeed in Bangladesh? This is an essential question to ask and to ponder. What is also interesting is the intricate ways in which every stakeholder at school is interlinked to Shafin's experiences and aspirations, and each must play a vital role in his ability to make the most of it.

A Photo

Photo 1 was taken by a student at School "M" who was asked to photograph something she liked at her school and to explain her reasons for taking it.

I have taken a picture of the window and painting. My reasons are:

1. The window is my favorite. I look outside it.
2. I like scene very much also because I want to play in field and jump ropes like that girl.
3. My hair would blow in the wind outside. I have long hair like her. I will feel happy.
4. The sun will shine on my face and I can teach my friends how to jump rope.
5. Then everyone in school can learn how to jump rope.

—Zooni, 10, School "M"

Photo 1 Zooni's photo and voice

Interestingly, Zooni, one of the older female students at School "M," pointed out her wish to be outside more often. She very creatively captured two different elements in a single photo to make her point. This is a unique photo, wherein a student captured multiple elements to convey her message, and it was previously categorized as a "like" in the role of the outside in building community at school. However, clearly, interpreting this photo solely within the like/dislike categories would be faulty. A more careful examination is required to unpack the girl's layered message.

It is clear that, for Zooni, the outside is important for several reasons, including the sunshine, the wind, and the space it will give her to jump rope. In school pictures and books, the children read about and discussed the potential of being outside and learning from play but did not practice it very much. It is clear that seeing those images instilled in Zooni an aspiration to go outside and learn a skill she could not master inside the schoolhouse. Furthermore, she did not aspire to learn a new skill only for herself but wanted to be able to share that experience with her peers.

This shows that Zooni may have felt playing outside was not only fun but also an activity for sharing, one that allowed students to be outside more often. Therefore, this photo not only expresses a student's current wish but also her future plans, which are illustrative of this girl's intuitive nature and ability. It also glaringly underlines that, although they would like to, children are not currently able to learn from and teach each other through outdoor activities at BRAC.

STEP 3: REFLECTING ON REFLEXIVITY AND THE DATA ANALYSIS PROCESS

Reflexivity is not a straightforward endeavor. As Mauthner and Doucet (2003, p. 414) explained: "[T]he importance of *being* reflexive is acknowledged within social science research.... however, reflexivity has not been translated into data analysis practice in terms of the difficulties, practicalities and methods of *doing* it" (p. 415). For me, being reflexive in my research process was important. Reflexivity was also important during the data analysis process, as shown in the procedures outlined earlier, in which I tried to interpret the layers of meaning indicated by children's voices with perspectives different from the parameters of "likes" and "dislikes." However, as Mauthner and Doucet discussed, I had to always question whether there was a limit to how reflexive I could be and how deeply I could understand what shaped my research as I conducted it, since such influences might become apparent only later, after I had completed my research.In answering that question, I have to say that I definitely had limitations. First, I was limited by my research questions; second, I was biased because my background as a researcher and teacher is heavily impacted by the literature of the social sciences and inclusive education. I was also limited by additional factors: my emotions and moods.

In terms of social science, although my explicit theoretical and methodological position is one where I reject notions of the detached, neutral, objective researcher, when it comes to analysis, I prefer the kind of organization and framing opportunities that more detached and mechanical forms of data analysis procedures allow. In other words, I value the messiness that reflexivity provides while conducting research but cannot always cope with the messiness of reflexivity when analyzing data. Thus, I tend to gravitate toward analysis procedures that allow the data to be streamlined. This could be attributed to Mauthner and Doucet's (2003) point that little guidance is available in regard to reflexive data analysis. As a "reflexive" researcher, I was unclear on where I should draw the line.

In terms of the literature on IE, I am biased because I believe in the social model of disability and advocate that inclusive education should be about whole-school improvement in which a diverse range of students are empowered and engaged through meaningfully relevant forms of education. I also think that neo-imperialistic forces within the global movement for inclusion are harmful for the evolution of it in countries of the South. Further, my thoughts have been impacted by my belief that schools should aspire to instill "model" inclusive cultures, policies, and practices in which they continuously and contextually address their obstacles in a collaborative environment, where children are valuable stakeholders and speakers. These positions color my understanding of a school situation in any given context, including that of BRAC.

Several other biases influenced the way I view the data collected for my dissertation, including my emphasis on seeking out children's "likes" and "dislikes" and my need to search for links between that and Tagore's philosophy of education. I am also an ardent advocate of children's rights and voices. In addition, at every juncture of the data collection and analysis, I was confronted with my emotions, my ever-changing relational status with the children, and my not-always-clear understanding of the extent of my own "reflexive" limitations. All of these points influenced how I interpreted the data during my largely phenomenological process of analysis. This is especially the case because phenomenological analysis is a procedure that breaks the flowing and organic forms of thinking required by reflexivity into one that calls for a series of neutral, mechanical, and decontextualized procedures that keep the issue of generating themes at the forefront. In other words, the principal concern of phenomenology is that "how knowledge is acquired, organized, and interpreted is relevant to *what* the claims are" (Altheide and Johnson 1994, p. 486, as cited in Mauthner and Doucet 2003, p. 416).

Concluding Comments: Reflexive Memoing as a Tool in PAR

PAR for me, as explained by Baum, MacDougall, and Smith (2006), "is collective, self reflective inquiry that researchers and participants undertake so that they can understand and improve upon the practices in which they participate and the situations in which they find themselves" (p. 854). Hence, reflexivity and PAR go hand in hand, as reflexivity is the tool through which researchers can address integral, significant, and internal research issues honestly with authenticity in order to improve the research process. Further, they can better understand their own place in the research process and those of the participants. Although I conducted mostly self-reflexivity in my research, reflexivity can extend to participants too when they are asked to reflect on their biases and understandings on the research process, especially within the PAR framework. This would definitely be an interesting and ground-breaking study of the use of reflexivity in PAR. This is something I could have conducted more in my own work.

Further, memoing is a tool that is very malleable in terms of its applicability to research, as it generally is just thoughtful reactions and write-ups to research episodes, and reflexivity can (or cannot) be kept in mind while memoing. I purposely kept reflexivity in mind as I worked, and I hope that in this chapter I have been able to illustrate that process successfully. It is a definite strength in conducting PAR in the Global South, where research worldviews, methodologies, processes, and meanings are still in continuous transition and formation.

Notes

1. I had other research questions that are not mentioned here as they were irrelevant to my reflexive process.
2. Why did I choose these specific two pieces? After combing the data, I realized that several quotes stated more than "likes" and "dislikes." I chose these two perspectives specifically because they were the most coherently written reflections/poems—that is, in full sentences without blanks or repetitions and with the least amount of side notes on my part. For the reflexive discussion, I wanted to pick the quotes that were the closest to representing the children's most authentic voices (and that needed the least amount of syntax interventions). Also, I wanted to pick two different types of data, each generated through a different activity and representing a different school. Moreover, this discussion is carried out to illustrate my thought process about the spaces between "likes" and "dislikes." It is to emphasize that I was aware of the complexity of the data. Due to the limitations of my dissertation—length, space, and word count—such a discussion on additional pieces of raw data was not feasible.

References

Ahsan, M. (2009). The potential and challenges of rights-based research with children and young people: Experiences from Bangladesh. *Children's Geographies, 7*(4), 393. doi:10.1080/14733280903234451.

Arora, R. P. (2012). *Discovering the postmodern nomad: An artful inquiry into the career stories of emerging adults transitioning under the Caribbean sun.* Unpublished doctoral dissertation, McGill University Faculty of Education, Montreal, Quebec.

Baum, F., MacDougall, C., & Smith, D. (2006). Participatory action research. *Journal of Epidemiology and Community Health, 60*(10), 854–857. doi:10.1136/jech.2004.028662.

Birks, M., Chapman, Y., & Francis, K. (2008). Memoing in qualitative research: Probing data and processes. *Journal of Research in Nursing, 13*(1), 68–75. doi:10.1177/1744987107081254.

Butler-Kisber, L. (2010). *Qualitative inquiry: Thematic, narrative and arts-informed perspectives.* Thousand Oaks, CA: SAGE.

Mauthner, N. S., & Doucet, A. (2003). Reflexive accounts and accounts of reflexivity in qualitative data analysis. *Sociology, 37*(3), 413–431.

Case Study 3

One Moment of Participatory Data Analysis

Meagan Call-Cummings

As I worked through a long-term youth participatory action research (PAR) project and reflected on the collective nature of aspects of it, I became acutely aware that as practitioners of PAR, we seem to give a great deal of attention to participation while we decide on a research focus, gather data, and present our findings, but we often neglect meaningful participation in data analysis. The purpose of this short description of one moment of participatory data analysis is to add to the growing body of PAR literature that explores the doing of PAR as opposed to its theoretical underpinnings. It is critical to discuss not only the *why* of authentic participation but the *how* as well, so that as researchers and practitioners committed to building and supporting transformational opportunities in the work we do, we can follow examples of success while avoiding the pitfalls of previous lessons learned.

M. Call-Cummings (✉)
George Mason University, Fairfax, VA, USA
e-mail: mcallcum@gmu.edu

Context

This PAR project was collectively designed and carried out by a core group of 25 researchers, including: myself, then a university graduate student; a high school teacher; and 23 high school students. The teacher, Mrs. Christine James,[1] and I both identify as female and White. All the students self-identify as Latino/a; 12 self-identify as female and 11 self-identify as male. Many of these students also self-identify as "undocumented," meaning they do not have the required documentation to be considered legally living in the United States.

In October 2012, we decided as a group that we wanted to create a research project that helped us understand more about racism at the students' school in rural Idaho, United States. In particular, the students asked, "Why are our teachers racist?"[2] Over 18 months, we conducted several rounds of data collection in various creative ways; also, while our overarching question remained the same, these modes of data collection led us to various subquestions and topics. Data analysis was fluid and ongoing and often blurred with moments of data collection.

One of the creative ways we engaged in this blurred data collection and analysis was through Theatre of the Oppressed (Boal 1985). Mrs. James and I wanted to help the students explore the research question in a way that would give them the opportunity to articulate and examine their racialized interactions with their White teachers. By creating the space to make their own and their teachers' perspectives more explicit, we thought we might be able to pursue a more nuanced research agenda. We thought Theatre of the Oppressed would allow us to do this.

Theatre of the Oppressed was created by Augusto Boal (1985) as one way of doing pedagogy of the oppressed as articulated by Paulo Freire (2006). From Boal and Freire's points of view, liberating people from oppressive relationships required people working together. Boal suggested through his Theatre of the Oppressed that even the smallest gesture could help us learn about oppressive relationships. He also argued that our awareness of oppression can shift—can be made more inclusive or wider, in a sense; we can experience moments of consciousness raising and discover the wisdom to act and live in new ways by using theater to explore social events and issues (Dennis 2009). By finding new ways of acting, we could find new ways of being in this world, and by being different, we would free ourselves from the oppressive relationship (Dennis 2009).

One subcategory of Theatre of the Oppressed is Cops in the Head, which refers to the influential voices we hear—both consciously and subconsciously—telling us what we should do, think, and feel (Dennis 2009). Often these voices are given to us through socialization, but they can remain with us as a kind of oppression. Through Cops in the Head, we have the opportunity to bring these oppressive voices to the surface. We can raise our consciousness of them. In this way, we can confront and challenge assumptions, norms, and other mechanisms of oppression that often go unnoticed in everyday interactions (Dennis 2009).

Our group was excited about this creative opportunity to work together to reach a more nuanced and explicit understanding of what racism is and what it looks like in each of our everyday lives, for we all experienced and understood it differently. Over three days, Mrs. James and the student coresearchers recorded in their class journals everyday experiences they had had with racism. They then took time to share these with the rest of the class on a volunteer basis. The group then chose a few to act out as scenes, opening the scenes up to comment and questions from the rest of the group.[3]

THE SPECTRUM OF RACISM: TELLING AND HEARING STORIES AS DATA ANALYSIS

After our collective attempt to make sense out of our feelings of frustration and confusion about racism at this school through Theatre of the Oppressed and other approaches and techniques, including a Photovoice exhibit[4] and interviews with White and Latino/a teachers, and because I felt that some of those attempts failed to achieve authentic participation,[5] I explicitly sought out ways we could achieve a sense of balance within our collective as we continued our exploration of racism. One issue that kept coming up in discussions with both Latino/a students and White teachers was a sense that racism was messy and blurry. No one was ever sure what to call racism, and if it wasn't racism, then what was it? Mrs. James and I called this messy, blurry space "the Spectrum of Racism,"[6] and one day during class, we drew a big, horizontal line on the whiteboard at the front of our collective's classroom. (See Photo 1.)

Photo 1 The Spectrum of Racism, as created by the research collective

We started by collectively identifying each end of the spectrum and then we filled in the middle with positive and negative stories and experiences from the students' lives. We took several days to tell and hear these stories and to decide where they should be placed on the spectrum and why. An example of one such discussion from the Monday Class Discussion on October 2013 follows.

> *Mrs. James:* So, can you think of other examples of behavior that would be just like a little awkward and not right, or a little like it's okay but it's not totally accepting? Or, this would be totally accepting? Somebody treated my dad like this and he didn't understand and it was perfect, wonderful, it was accepting. Or, somebody treated my dad like this and he never went there again they were just the most awful people in the whole world. Or my mom had this happen to her when she was in Arizona. So, we want an example that is good or bad. Do you have an example?
>
> *Sebastian:* Yeah, there was this one time we were at Mandarin House [a Chinese restaurant] we left because we didn't like the food because it was rotten like the meat was like, smelly, you know.

Mrs. James: Uh-huh.
Sebastian: And we were, I was just like, and I didn't know like I was totally like eight and he [the waiter] was like yelling at us and I was like hey try something else.
Mrs. James: So was that racist?
Sebastian: I don't know why he was yelling at us, it was like a long time ago.
Mrs. James: Okay, so, so yelling at you, where would that fit? If someone yells at you and you're not sure why?
[Class discussion about where it goes on the spectrum.]
Wilfred: Because you don't know why, in the first place, you can't just say "Oh that's racist."
Mrs. James: So should we put it like, right where bullying is? Or should we put it—
Meagan (Author): Sebastian, how did it feel to you?
Sebastian: I don't care.
Meagan: So, at that point in your life, where would you have put that? Did it feel like racism to you? Did it—
Mrs. James: How did that feel, on the continuum?
Sebastian: Bullying.
Mrs. James: Where would you have put it, at eight?
[Class discussing where to put it.]
Mrs. James: Tell me this, tell me where to stop. [Mrs. James points a marker at the spectrum line and, starting at the far left of the line, moves slowly toward the right end, maintaining eye contact with Sebastian.]
Sebastian: Right—
Mrs. James: Here? [Stopping her marker.]
Sebastian: Yeah.
Mrs. James: So, yelling. [Makes a mark on the spectrum with her marker.]
Sebastian: Well, I hate getting yelled at.
Meagan: Me too.

In this example of participatory analysis, everyone was meaningfully involved in this exploration into what racism is and how we individually experience it. Sebastian told his story. Mrs. James and I prodded him to tell more and to identify what felt like racism and how it felt to him. The class joined in the conversation about "how" racist the yelling was—where it fell on the spectrum. No one told Sebastian he was wrong. Sebastian started out saying the incident didn't really matter: "I don't care," he said. But with a bit of encouraging support, he quickly moved to "Well,

I hate getting yelled at." Clearly the event meant something to him and was important enough for him to share it. His feelings and his analysis of the situation were simply yet necessarily validated—through collective—and supportive—analysis of that particular life experience.

REFLECTIONS ON PARTICIPATORY DATA ANALYSIS

Nind (2011) wrote: "As data analysis is central to knowledge construction, if there is to be participation or collaboration anywhere then for emancipation it must be here: it is through active participation in understanding the world through research that participants benefit from a transformative experience" (p. 354). If we as practitioners of participatory research are to claim goals of emancipation and transformation for ourselves and our coresearchers, then we must seek them in every aspect of the research process, not just in those aspects that are easy or that are naturally participatory. The analysis of data is essentially made up of moments of knowledge construction, and those moments must be fully democratic and participatory in order to be counted as valid participatory research. These moments do not have to be formal or set aside as dedicated to analysis only. As is obvious in the examples in this chapter, data collection and data analysis occurred simultaneously, for our collective both uttered and made some sense of these experiences with racism. This example illustrates that as PAR practitioners, we must engage in strong and continuous reflexive practice to maintain our awareness of the participatory nature of every moment of our work.

But these experiences were not perfect, nor were they exempt from the limitations that often trouble PAR collectives. For example, I was not able to be on-site at the coresearchers' school continuously. I made several trips (six weeklong trips over the course of 18 months) and in between connected with our group via phone, email, and Skype. Reflecting on this, I see these circumstances as simultaneously limiting and emancipating. It was limiting in that I often felt like I was not a full participant in the process or that I would get the rest of the collective really excited about the project and its potential, then leave them "on their own" in the field. This often led to concerns about their vulnerability, as I had the freedom to come and go as I pleased, stirring the pot, as it were, and then leaving the coresearchers to navigate the consequences of that in their everyday lives. I asked myself, for example, how I could help these students raise questions and concerns about their own teachers acting in racist ways and then leave them to sit in those teachers' classes and be subject to racial microaggressions. This was unfortunately something I had to accept as a part of the process.

This forced separation was emancipating, however, in that I simply could not "oversee" or "control" the process. I had to take steps back—literally. I was forced to take a backseat at times, to encourage the coresearchers to take a leadership role, to not depend on me as "expert," which is how we as university-based researchers or outside "knowers" are often automatically positioned, whether we want to be or not. But because I could not be in the field continuously, the coresearchers, so often positioned in their lives as "nonexperts" or "nonknowers," became the experts and knowers. So, for example, while I was physically present, we talked about how to code effectively and how to conduct a thematic analysis. But they were the ones who, after I left the space, adapted my methodological training to their own needs and understandings and carried that work out. They presented their findings over Skype to me, but they actually conducted some of this analysis themselves.

Distilling the findings from our data collection and analysis followed a similar process of me working closely with the coresearchers when I was physically present and then them forming a "research committee" to work together during lunches and after school on how they would present their findings to groups and organizations within their committee. This led to their decision to present to the local school board their stories of racialized experiences they had had in their community as a way to start a conversation that had for too long gone unspoken. To me, these moments of insider coresearchers taking the lead in moments of data collection, analysis, and presentation of findings truly fulfilled the promise of PAR: to allow those historically marginalized by traditional research processes to produce authentic knowledge based on their own life experiences and, at the same time, to decide what/whose knowledge is and should be valued and valuable.

Notes

1. This is a self-selected pseudonym, as are all names of coresearchers here.
2. Full details of this project, "Why Are Our Teachers Racist?," can be seen at www.researchforempowerment.com
3. A more comprehensive discussion of this process, the students' reflections on it, and my own concerns about it, can be seen at www.researchforempowerment.com/theatre-of-the-oppressed/ or in the Call-Cummings and Martinez (2016b) publication cited in the references.
4. See Wang (2006), for a complete description of Photovoice. See www.researchforempowerment.com/photovoice/ for a full description of this process and our group's findings.
5. See Call-Cummings and Martinez (2016a) for a discussion of potential unintended consequences associated with Photovoice.
6. See www.researchforempowerment.com/spectrum/ for a visual exploration of this process as well as recordings of the stories we placed on the spectrum.

References

Boal, A. (1985). *Theatre of the oppressed*. New York: Theatre Communications Group.

Call-Cummings, M., & Martinez, S. (2016a). Consciousness-raising or unintentionally oppressive? *The Qualitative Report, 21*(5), 798–810. Retrieved from http://nsuworks.nova.edu/tqr/vol21/iss5/1.

Call-Cummings, M., & Martinez, S. (2016b). "It wasn't racism; it was more misunderstanding." White teachers, Latino/a students, and racial battle fatigue. *Race Ethnicity and Education*, 1–14.

Dennis, B. K. (2009). Acting up: Theater of the oppressed as critical ethnography. *International Journal of Qualitative Methods, 8*(2), 65–96.

Freire, P. (2006). *Pedagogy of the oppressed* (30th Anniversary ed.). New York: Continuum.

Nind, M. (2011). Participatory data analysis: A step too far? *Qualitative Research, 11*(4), 349–363.

Wang, C. C. (2006). Youth participation in photovoice as a strategy for community change. *Journal of Community Practice, 14*(1–2), 147–161.

Case Study 4

Shikshagiri: Including Marginalized Children in Policy and Praxis of Education

Anusha Chandrasekharan and Pradeep Narayanan

INTRODUCTION

In India, where every development indicator hints at widespread disparity based on gender, caste, tribe, class, and religion, the importance of education as an inequality leveler cannot be stressed enough. The vision of education for all was emphasized in the first National Education Policy (1968) and the subsequent one (1986), but the concept of common school system presented decades ago was never implemented.[1] The exodus of upper- and middle-class children to expensive private schools reduced the quality of monitoring of government schools. It created a parallel system, wherein the rich go to quality schools while the poor, especially those belonging to scheduled castes and scheduled tribes, receive education from the oft-neglected government schools.

The stated aim of the government of India in bringing a new education policy is to meet the changing dynamics of the population's needs with regard to quality education, innovation, and research, aiming to make India a knowledge superpower.[2] As part of this process, a five-member committee headed by former Cabinet secretary T.S.R. Subramanian submitted its two-volume report.[3] The ministry then uploaded a concise document

---

A. Chandrasekharan (✉) • P. Narayanan
Praxis Institutue of Participatory Practices, New Delhi, India
e-mail: communications@praxisindia.org; research@praxisindia.org

on their website, seeking public feedback.[4] Although the Subramanian committee and the ministry held consultations to seek large-scale public opinion, there was one big gap. These consultations and opinions were sought from a range of stakeholders, yet the primary beneficiaries of the policy—children and, among them, children from marginalized communities—were largely left out. Clearly one reason for their omission is the lack of space in policy making and implementation for their needs.

Policy Expertise in Education that Is Often Ignored: Experiences of Marginalization

An important feature of conventional policy making is the constitution of high-level panels of experts. The expertise within these panels comes from erudite learning and a lifetime of knowledge building but rarely from experiences of marginalization, which pose barriers to achieving the outcomes the policies set out to achieve.

Shikshagiri was an attempt to make the "experience of marginalization" a form of expertise essential for policy making.[5] Who else but children, especially those who have dropped out or been discriminated against in school, can explain what kind of education system India needs? Shikshagiri is a ground-level platform for children's participation. It brings together 16 children[6] from diverse backgrounds and different education experiences: girls; boys; Dalits;[7] members of denotified tribes;[8] Muslims; Hindus; Christians; children from different parts of the country; children with disabilities; children from government, private, and open schools; and some students who had dropped out. They met over four days to provide comments on the draft New Education Policy.

The Process: Creating a Safe Space for Children to Voice Opinion on the Draft National Policy

The panel, exclusively of children from 10 to 18 years of age, deliberated on their experiences of education; interacted with stakeholders, such as teachers, parents living in homeless shelters, representatives of nongovernmental organizations, and school management committee members; and came up with some time-bound recommendations for the policy makers. Ultimately, the panel presented its recommendations before an audience comprising people from different sectors and age groups.

The process followed by the children over the four days (indicated by four shades) is described in Fig. 1.

The children's panel initiated the Shikshagiri process by getting to know each other through ice-breakers, designed so that the panelists reflected on their own skills, strengths, likes/dislikes, and experiences. The discussions that followed involved aspiration mapping, card sorting,[9] prioritization tools, role-plays, debates, and presentations.

The second day, panelists met different stakeholders. (See Photo 1.) They participated at Raahgiri,[10] an event where they sought the opinions of middle-class people of what they wanted in the new education policy. Later, they formed smaller groups among themselves and met approximately 50 opinion makers (who can influence educational experiences), such as teachers, representatives from nongovernmental organizations, parents of homeless children, and members of a school management committee.[11] To seek opinions from these stakeholders, they used a participatory tools set they adapted from the processes from the first day, including problem tree analysis, card sorting, and the 10 circles image exercise.

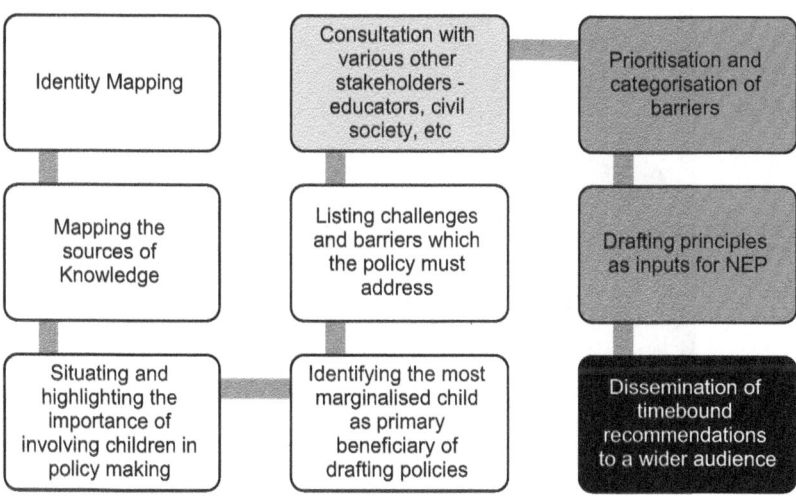

Fig. 1 Process map of Shikshagiri

Photo 1 Children interact with the public at Raahgiri as part of Shikshagiri

CASE STUDY 4 **259**

The panelists, brimming with knowledge from different quarters, developed a detailed analysis on the third day to come up with their recommendations.

Understanding Exclusion in Education

Taking child participation to the next level, panelists looked at those who tended to fall out of the planning frame by identifying different scenarios related to accessing education. These are outlined in the five images in Photo 2.

Case 1: Children are interested but there is no school
Case 2: Children who dropped out before completing education

Photo 2 The five images reflect five cases, or scenarios, related to education that the children analyzed

Case 3: Children who can attend but have been denied access to schooling or enrolment

Case 4: Youth who are able to access education and complete schooling but are unable to find relevance to education

Case 5: People who are able to receive education, find a job, and make a decent living.

The panelists deliberated on these scenarios and concluded that any policy on education must focus on children belonging to the first four categories. They wrote down names of children they knew in each respective scenario, applying a face to the vulnerability. They pictured two of the most marginalized *children* (see Photos 3 and 4) and then listed the identities these children hold. The panelists reiterated that policies should focus on such children, reaffirming the talisman[12] shared by Mahatma Gandhi, which spoke about this very aspect of introspection on the impact of one's action by keeping in mind "the poorest and the weakest."

Photo 3 Gandhi Talisman 1: Panelists draw Chotu, a child involved in labor at a roadside eatery. The employer asks him to come and wash the plates of the entire country. In the image, the children pledge to stop child labor

Photo 4 Gandhi Talisman 2: Panelists draw the photo of a snake charmer to represent extreme marginalization. The snake charmer belongs to a denotified tribe and does not have any means of alternate employment. Children from such families are exposed to poverty, according to the panelists

The panel members recognized that the education system actually leaves behind more children from particular backgrounds—Dalits, tribals, girls, the homeless, ragpickers, denotified tribes, religious minorities, and *sewerage workers* (see Photo 5). After interacting with teachers, they subsequently added children of sex workers and HIV-affected children.

Photo 5 Exclusion. Panelists list different categories of vulnerabilities to identify the target of any policy

Understanding Challenges Faced in School

Through card sorting, panelists listed the challenges children faced at stages of enrollment and schooling and the discrimination encountered there. On the basis of these experiences, the panelists summed up their single most important expectation: free schooling for all.

At each stage, from enrollment, to classrooms, to midday meals, to sanitation, to after dropout, the children expressed a sense of "othering." They have been called names by students, teachers, and the school administrationnames such as Kabadi,[13] Madaari,[14] and caste names. For a boy living in a shelter for homeless persons in Delhi,[15] education should not be denied due to absence of an identity or proof of residence. After all, "Being homeless is the biggest discrimination that we face," he said. Another panelist pointed out wisely, "When I am standing in front of you, what value will a piece of paper add?"

A 15-year-old visually challenged girl from West Bengal explained why having separate schools for children with disabilities is a form of exclusion. She outlined the need for special educators in all schools where children could learn to be empathetic toward each other and children with disabilities could receive the best learning opportunities. The absence of inclusive schools means a disabled child has to travel farther to study. *A Class 9 panelist from Rajasthan illustrated what education means to him* (see Photo 6). He explained, "Even after getting independence in 1947, the country is still not free; uneducated children are caged birds who need to be freed; just the way nature doesn't lay restrictions on who should drink its water, education shouldn't be restricted on the basis of caste or gender."

Children rarely drop out. They are pushed out by discrimination in schools or pulled out by families because of poverty's burden, among other issues. The children raised a pertinent question: "*Mantri ka beta aur chaprasi ki beti—ek hi school mein kyun nahin pad saktey* (Why cannot a minister's son and a peon's daughter study in the same school)? If you want the school to be a place where rich and poor study together, make education free for everyone, including the rich."

Photo 6 Nandkishor. Illustration by a panelist that explores the realities of India and its education system

Unpacking the Education System

With support from facilitators, all the children identified a "question" whose answers they wanted to explore. (See Fig. 2.) They spoke to various stakeholders and deliberated in groups to seek responses. They used participatory tools, such as card sorting, root cause analysis, participatory theater, and illustrations to explore the questions.

For children, education goes beyond schooling. They devised "sources of knowledge" as varied as parents, books, society, school, elders, rivers and trees, friends, computers, television, and the internet. Some innovative sources of knowledge included animals, farming, nature, and sorrow and failure. Panelists regarded sports as fundamental for children and wanted them to be indispensable components of school curricula. Many children who cannot enter neighborhood parks can play only in schools; therefore, school playgrounds are essential. Although participation in play is a child's right, many are either deliberately left out (girls) or there are design barriers to some children (those with disabilities). Consequently, the children raised the need for inclusive playgrounds.

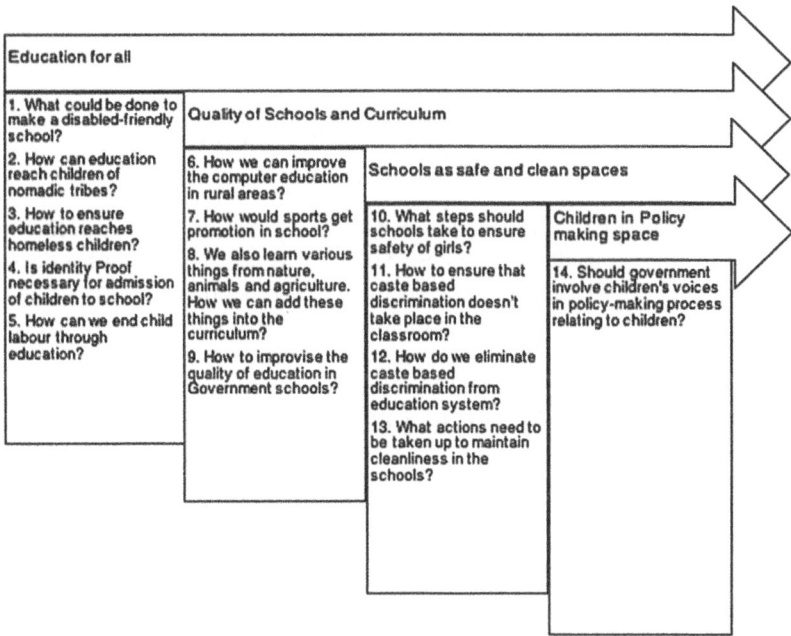

Fig. 2 Key questions raised by panelists

Table 1 Priorities evolved by children's panel from discussions

Priorities	Allocation of Resources (%)	Desired Timeline
Free education for all up till Class 12	18	2017
Secure access to education for children of nomadic and denotified tribes	16	2018
Education system that is inclusive of children with any form of disability	15	2018
Curriculum that includes sports, agriculture, culture, and heritage	15	2018
Same quality education for children irrespective of tribe, gender, religion	14	2018
Education curriculum that breaks gender stereotypes and discrimination	8	2017
School enrollment regardless of availability of identity documents	8	2018
End to all forms of discrimination and harassment in schools	7	Immediate

The panelists revisited some of the issues that came up in discussions during the first two days among themselves and with the stakeholders. They collectively analyzed the recommendations that emerged and prioritized them using different types of ranking and scoring. (See Table 1.)

KEY PRINCIPLES OF CHILD PARTICIPATION IN POLICY MAKING

This panel, besides being made up exclusively of children, is different from any other consultation process. First, it was not an extractive process but one in which children gathered information among themselves and sought information from others, analyzed the data, and then made inferences about key issues. Therefore, they were analysts.

Second, the participants did not represent particular constituencies, although they held multiple identities. They analyzed based not only on their experiences but on experiences of fellow participants and others whom they talked to or met throughout their lives.

Third, the process was facilitated by a group of three facilitators in the first session. After that, the facilitators largely withdrew after creating a space where children spoke to each other rather than to facilitators.

Finally, the panelists were 16 individuals with diverse opinions, opinions that were transformed during their interactions. Each sought the opportunity to expand the theme with which they identified. Creating consensus of the group's standpoint was attempted but not ensured as the children's opinions were informed by their diversity and a unanimous opinion was not the desired aim.

The challenge for the facilitators was to keep in mind three unwritten norms:

1. *Autonomy.* Ensure children have the autonomy to engage, interact, analyze, and form opinions.
2. *Transformation.* There was a need to introduce children to contemporary debates on issues—and for the children to form new opinions on issues related to education.
3. *Protection.* There was the need to remember that the children would return to their own environments, where their new set of opinions might not be supported to the extent that they were in the safe space of the panel.

On the fourth day, when panelists presented the process to a wider audience, their views were not unanimous and also were not "acceptable" to many. For example, children were against the no-detention policy (i.e., not failing students). (Although the current policy says there should be no detention until Class 8, the draft policy suggests reducing the limit to Class 5.) Having discussed this issue during their deliberations, they summarized that this aspect of the policy should be removed, as it tended to make students wanting and teachers less accountable. Similarly, one child wanted to do away with coeducation to prevent gender violence while other panelists disagreed.

Overall, the process provided children a platform where they could share their experiences of education. The process reiterated the position that all stakeholders, especially the primary beneficiaries of any policy, must be involved in the decision-making *and* policy design stages, not just in the implementation or monitoring stage, to inculcate a sense of ownership, accountability, and sustainability of the policies.

Notes

1. A concept recommended by Kothari Commission in 1966. D.S. Kothari, *Education and National Development: Report of the Education Commission (1964–66)*; (Delhi; Government of India, 1964–66).
2. About New Education Policy Consultation; website of the Ministry of Human Resource Development, Government of India: http://mhrd.gov.in/nep-new

3. This can be accessed at http://www.nuepa.org/New/download/NEP2016/ReportNEP.pdf
4. Ministry of Human Resource Development, Government of India, "Some Inputs for Draft National Education Policy 2016." http://mhrd.gov.in/sites/upload_files/mhrd/files/Inputs_Draft_NEP_2016.pdf
5. "Shikshagiri" is a neologism conveying empowered action on education and draws from the Hindi word for education—*shiksha*.
6. The children were identified through partner organizations working on issues of exclusion, education, and child rights based on a set of criteria including: understanding of a common language, experience of marginalization, and a balanced gender mix. Most were from northern India to ensure they did not miss out on too many days of school. A panelist list can be accessed here: www.shikshagiri.in
7. Dalits are a social group who fall outside the Indian caste system and have been marginalized and discriminated against for centuries.
8. In a peculiarly Indian context, denotified tribes are tribes that originally were listed under the Criminal Tribes Act of 1871 as "addicted to the systematic commission of non-bailable offences." Although the term "criminal tribes" was dropped over time, the historic association with crime has stigmatized the community to the extent that the traditional occupations they followed, such as snake charming, have been outlawed.
9. Card sorting is an exercise detailing everything shared in a group discussion on cards and involves the contributors rearranging the cards to organize them into categories.
10. Raahgiri started out as a temporary closure of a network of streets to vehicular traffic so that they become "open" to people. Children and adults are invited to bike, skate, run, and walk; partake in community leisure activities; and come together as a community and celebrate life. Read more at http://raahgiriday.com
11. Section 21 of the Right to Education Act (2009) mandates the creation of school management committees in all government, government-aided, and special category schools. The composition of committees includes parents (of whom 50% will be women), teachers, local authorities, academicians, and students.
12. Talisman refers to a totem or magic charm. In this context, Gandhi's talimsan refers to a piece of advice shared by father of the Indian nation, Mahatma Gandhi, which reflects his vision for the country's progress. He said: "I will give you a talisman. Whenever you are in doubt, or when the self becomes too much with you, apply the following test. Recall the face of the poorest and the weakest man [woman] whom you may have seen, and ask yourself, if the step you contemplate is going to be of any use to

him [her]. Will he [she] gain anything by it? Will it restore him [her] to a control over his [her] own life and destiny? In other words, will it lead to swaraj [freedom] for the hungry and spiritually starving millions? Then you will find your doubts and yourself melt away."
13. *Kabadi* is person from the ragpicker community who collects recyclable waste and sells it to make a living. The term is used in a derogatory way for children whose parents are ragpickers, likening them to the waste.
14. *Madari* is a juggler or street performer, a person from a denotified tribe, who is often discriminated against because of the association of the community with crime. (See note 8 for details.)
15. Shelters are provided by the government for people who have been displaced by development projects, disasters, and the like. This particular shelter houses many people who were evicted from their slum dwellings during the Commonwealth Games in 2010.

Conclusion

Reading and Rewriting South Asia

Erik Jon Byker

INTRODUCTION

This conclusion summarizes the themes related to participatory action research (PAR) that emerged from the chapters in this volume. Additionally, this conclusion looks to the future of PAR in South Asia with recommendations for a future research agenda. Throughout the volume, much has been written about the possibilities for PAR in South Asia. The authors provided descriptive accounts of PAR-related research in Bangladesh, India, Nepal, and Sri Lanka. Research methodologies were diverse, as the authors investigated PAR using case studies, ethnography, mixed methods, and quantitative research designs to frame their chapters. The varieties of PAR research designs encompassed in this volume are indicative of the flexibility of PAR as a participatory method of research. Robin McTaggart (1991), though, warned that such flexibility can often lead to the dilution of PAR. Hence, he emphasized that researchers should not lose sight that the very core of PAR is about authentic participa-

---

E.J. Byker (✉)
University of North Carolina at Charlotte, Charlotte, NC, USA
e-mail: ebyker@uncc.edu

© The Author(s) 2017
H. Kidwai et al. (eds.), *Participatory Action Research and Educational Development*, South Asian Education Policy, Research, and Practice,
DOI 10.1007/978-3-319-48905-6_14

tion, "which means sharing in the way that research is conceptualized, practiced, and brought to bear out on the life-world. PAR is also about ownership—the responsible agency in the production of knowledge and improvement of practice" (p. 171). Participatory action in the construction of knowledge *by the* community and *in service* to the community is what distinguishes authentic PAR. Although malleable in research design, PAR remains grounded in action research to build greater awareness and to spur on changes in the community. PAR's action orientation through the construction and ownership of knowledge echoes what Paulo Freire (1970, 1994) described as development of conscientization. Freire explained that conscientization is part of education's emancipatory purposes in which people are able to "read the world" (Freire 1970, p. 14) and "rewrite the world" (Freire 2001, p. 91). The chapters in this volume captured ways that stakeholders across South Asia are "reading and rewriting" their world through means of the participatory and empowering practice of action research. Several themes emerged across the chapters. Here we revisit three themes in particular: identity through voice, collective empowerment, and transforming the community.

Identity Through Voice

Representations of voice and identity were common threads across the chapters and case studies in this volume. In the introduction, Huma Kidwai and Radhika Iyengar established the overall purposes, which was to bring together the voices from the South Asian region in order to better understand how PAR is being conceived and practiced in the region. They further explained that this volume is long overdue since there is a dearth of PAR research and studies specific to South Asia. The chapters illuminate the relationship between identity and voice vis-à-vis data collection methods like Photovoice. Indeed, Photovoice was a popular method for connecting to PAR, as the volume includes chapters and case studies focused on Photovoice as a PAR method. Photovoice offers many opportunities. First, it is a "participatory tool that puts cameras in the hands of people with the belief that they have something important to say" (Wang 1999, p. 186). Photovoice is an identity tool as the participants capture what is important about their lived experiences. Mary Vayaliparampil illustrated the power of using Photovoice in Chap. 8 on parents' perceptions of India's Education for All policy. The pictures that the parents captured morphed into personalized policy platforms, which the parents used as evidence for voicing their concerns to district authorities. Second, as Vayaliparampil explained, Photovoice fostered a deeper connection between the policy targets and policy makers. The effect of such a connection is that it starts a grassroots and holistic transformation of the policy process as community members start to identify with their role in shaping policy. Third, Photovoice helps to create dialogue. In Case Study 1, which discussed the Kasturba Gandhi Balika Vidyala school in the Indian state of Gujarat, Payal Shah discussed the dialogical possibilities with Photovoice. As Shah explained, Photovoice created a space for school participants to identify and share about their constructions of reality. Their photos led to group discussions and dialogues about shared identities. Shah further shared how the project increased school participants' confidence and ability to reflect on their future identities.

Caroline Wang and Mary Ann Burris (1997) contended that Photovoice is an action-oriented method that helps to "promote critical dialogue and knowledge ... and to reach policymakers" (p. 370). Certainly the chapters and case studies in this volume echo that notion. Yet there are challenges with using Photovoice for PAR. In Case Study 2, for instance, Tahiya Mahbub discussed Photovoice-related obstacles in two PAR-related case studies in Bangladesh. The obstacles included issues with camera hardware and equal access to cameras. Other Photovoice-related challenges include material cost, image clarity and processing, and the issue of interpretation of voice. In their chapter, Rohit Setty and Matthew A. Witenstein identified the issue of interpretation as the challenge of filtering. Even with a PAR-oriented research design, the photos captured by participants might be filtered or narrated by the researchers or might be taken by participants to appease researchers. All of these challenges are important for PAR researchers to acknowledge and account for when using Photovoice as a data collection method. Although there are limitations, Photovoice is a powerful participatory method for enabling participants to visually capture their identity and voice.

Empowering the Collective

Empowering the collective was a second theme throughout this volume. Many chapters provided evidence and findings to exemplify how the PAR methodology empowered participants. This was evident in both small sample sizes and large-scale data sets. The Northern Education System Review in Sri Lanka—described by Meera Pathmarajah and Nagalingam Ethirveerasingam—highlighted the possibilities of PAR at the state level.

Their chapter showed how the program review was implemented on a small budget but with a large vision for empowering the people of northern Sri Lanka. The implementation process was a collective experience where citizens were encouraged to share their opinions and viewpoints simply because they were invited into the review process and were asked. With large-scale studies, PAR may seem something of a misnomer. However, the findings of Pathmarajah and Ethirveerasingam in this volume show the possibilities for PAR empowering a whole region of people.

Chapter 5 by Neha Migalini, Jayasree S., and Vishnuteerth Agnihotri, is another example of a study that employed the PAR methodological framework to interpret the findings from a large-scale, multiphase study in the South Asian context. Centered on evaluating the implementation of activity-based learning in several Indian states, the authors found few instances where the practices were being consistently adopted and practiced by teachers. These findings reflect the realities of employing participatory practices like PAR on a large scale. The lack of teacher buy-in is even more reason to embrace the participatory action research and implementation model that Pathmarajah and Ethirveerasingam argued for in their chapter. The implementation of PAR on a large-scale regional or state level needs considerable buy-in, it seems, in order for it to be a collective empowering experience. In education and school, evidence of buy-in includes teachers being prepared to participate in researching their own practices as well as practices in the schools where they are situated. Action research is at the heart of such preparedness. Chapter 3 by Suman Bhattacharjea and Erik Jon Byker provided a case study of how teacher candidates are being prepared for participatory and action-oriented teacher practices.

Empowering the collective through teacher preparation happens through the use of PAR-focused instruments like the Annual Status of Education Report (ASER) Translating Policy into Practice (TPP) tool. Chapter 3 provided evidence for how educators and teacher candidates are being empowered to collect data for "evidence-based action" (Byker and Banerjee, 2016, p. 5) through the use of a PAR-focused tool. For example, the TPP survey tools have been used for over a decade by everyday citizens in India to collect information on children's foundational learning abilities for ASER. In turn, ASER findings help India's policy makers and government leaders assess the impact of education-related policy. Additionally, ASER influences how India's educators, leaders, and policy makers argue for and shape future education-related policies. The power of the TPP toolkit is that it is action-oriented yet simple to administer.

The PAR-related features of the toolkit prepare and empower teacher candidates to begin engaging in their communities of practice. In addition, the toolkit is flexible enough to suit a range of contexts as it is utilized by teacher candidates, education policy makers, and everyday citizens.

Technology also has an important PAR role. Chapter 6 by Rajashri Singh, Neha Sharma, and Ketan Verma on Hybrid Learning showcased the relationship between tablet computer technology and PAR. The Hybrid Learning model adopts many features of PAR to address two obstacles to quality learning in rural areas of India: poor access to materials and the absence of learner-centric pedagogies. The model empowers the collective through the use of digital devices. It focuses on the ways children utilize tablet technology to improve their educational competencies. When children have a participatory role in the design and implementation of educational technology, they do not merely have access to computer hardware. Rather, the Hybrid Learning model is about how children participate in the educational uses for tablet technology. Such participatory design encourages discovery-based learning among the children. Digitally equipped discovery is a form of PAR as children participate in asking questions, posing problems, working in groups of their choice, selecting the pace of learning as they wish, getting their communities involved in their learning, and communicating with the Hybrid Learning team about what is working and what is not. The Hybrid Learning model is another example of collective empowerment as children fully participate in the uses and evaluation of tablet technology. Indeed, the PAR-oriented initiatives and tools have a great impact on many segments of South Asian communities.

Transforming the Community

Transforming the lives of people and communities is the third theme that chapters in this volume share. Many chapters discussed the possibilities of PAR as a way not only to empower but also to transform. Before highlighting the possibility of transformation, it is important to revisit the questions that Setty and Witenstein posed in Chap. 1:

1. What is the work involved in enacting PAR?
2. What kinds of opportunities might researchers face and what kinds of problems will they need to solve?
3. What would it take to solve the problems and leverage the opportunities in a way that promotes social justice and transforms the context and the players?

The volume's chapters and case studies speak to all these questions but largely concentrate on the first two through a focus on PAR-related work and opportunities in the South Asian context. The third question remains a critical one: to identify ways in which PAR promotes transformative social justice. Transformation is deeply embedded in the PAR methodology. Orlando Fals-Borda (1977), for instance, aptly and succinctly defined PAR as the process of "investigating reality in order to transform it" (p. 1).

What PAR-related transformations did the volume uncover? It depends. The volume captures research and projects that show the promise of transformation but not, perhaps, transformation in its entirety. That is because community transformation is a dynamic, ever-evolving process that takes time to unfold. Thus, transformation seems to be best captured with a longitudinal methodical research lens. A PAR-focused longitudinal study was not one of the research designs in this volume. Such a study, though, is a necessary part of a future research agenda. The chapters and case studies in this volume report on transformative slices that illustrate the characteristics and features of how community participants engaged in PAR methodology to make inroads into transforming their communities.

Commitment to the community is one feature of a transformative slice of PAR. Chapter 7 by Shabnam Koirala-Azad about the PAR youth project in Nepal provides an example of such commitment. The political backdrop of Nepal forms the chapter's setting as the country moves from a dictatorial monarchy to a republic that is rife with instability. Nepal's recurring natural disasters and economic troubles also frame the setting of the chapter. Yet it depicts how a group of committed young people utilized the PAR methodology to take grassroots action about such issues as caste-based discriminatory practices in schools and the challenges of meritocracy. The participants' actions included speaking before Nepalese education ministers about these issues and providing recommendations for policy changes. In discussing the relationship of PAR with transformation, Koirala-Azad and Fuentes (2010) cautioned that too often PAR is synonymous with sweeping social transformations for the greater good of all involved. What is often truer is that PAR makes a small impact and difference among a committed group of people. Like a ripple in water, these small differences can lead to larger community transformations—over a period of time.

The volume's case studies highlight inclusivity as another PAR feature of transformation. In Case Study 3, Meagan Call-Cummings explained that the purpose of case studies is to explore the doing of PAR rather than just focusing on PAR's theoretical underpinnings. Indeed, community transformation happens in the actual doing of PAR. Case Study 1 by Payal Shah illustrates an example of inclusivity through Photovoice. Shah explained that Photovoice provided a platform for student participants to have an important voice as social actors regardless of their age. Case Study 4 about Shikshagiri, as described by Anusha Chandrasekharan and Pradeep Narayanan, provided another example of the inclusivity of PAR in order to transform the lives of children. The Shikshagiri program guides policy makers in understanding the lived experiences of marginalized children. The case study included 16 diverse children who share their firsthand accounts of being discriminated against or eventually dropping out of school altogether. The authors emphasized how important inclusivity was to the transformative work of PAR as Shikshagiri included all stakeholders in decision making and crafting of policy.

Connecting to one's praxis is the final transformative feature of PAR. Paulo Freire (1970) identified praxis as the connection between "reflection and action on the world in order to transform it" (p. 28). Community transformation is often forged by committed people who are dedicated to their praxis, which is informed action based on critical reflection. Fran Baum and her colleagues (2006) explained that praxis is part and parcel of PAR because "when action and reflection take place at the same time they become creative and mutually illuminate each other" (p. 857). In this volume, an example of praxis is captured in Case Study 2, by Tahiya Mahbub, on the importance of memoing as a PAR-related research habit. The author shared how she used memoing as way to reflect and improve on the practices in which she participated. Memoing forms a PAR practice to authentically capture the voices of participants.

Conclusion: Future Research Agenda

In the introduction to this volume, Huma Kidwai and Radhika Iyengar asserted that PAR is an appealing methodology for education researchers and practitioners. PAR's appeal is tied into the three themes that emerged throughout this volume: (1) identity through voice, (2) collective empowerment, and (3) transforming the community. These themes reflect the larger emancipatory purpose of education (Freire 1970, 2001). The features of PAR also connect with development of praxis as one begins to engage in the process of reading and rewriting the world. This volume shows that there is not a one-size-fits-all PAR methodology; nor is PAR methodology confined to one state or region. The volume investigates PAR in the context of South Asia and shows the benefits of employing PAR for the betterment of people and communities.

Next we turn to future research recommendations for practitioners and researchers.

1. More PAR-related research is needed across all the countries that make up South Asia.
2. Comparative research can be quite instructive. A future research agenda would also include comparative research findings that compared and examined PAR in the context of two regions, such as South Asia and Central America.
3. A future research agenda related to PAR in South Asia should investigate PAR in the elementary and secondary schools as well as in higher education. Many chapters in this volume focused heavily on adult participants and included children somewhat at the periphery. The Shikshagiri case study provides a strong example for what PAR research with young people.
4. More longitudinal research into PAR is needed to measure and assess its transformative power. The transformative slices theme may be a promising avenue of study for long-term research.

In sum, PAR research designs hold great possibilities to engage and empower communities. This volume has highlighted ways that is happening in Bangladesh, India, Nepal, and Sri Lanka.

References

Baum, F., MacDougall, C., & Smith, D. (2006). Participatory action research. *Journal of Epidemiology and Community Health, 60*(10), 854–857. doi:10.1136/jech.2004.028662.

Borda, O. F. (1977). *For praxis: The problem of how to investigate reality in order to transform it.* Symposium on Action Research and Scientific Analysis, Cartagena, Colombia.

Byker, E. J., & Banerjee, A. (2016). Evidence for action: Translating field research into a large scale assessment. *Journal of Current Issues in Comparative Education, 18*(1), 1–13.

Freire, P. (1970). *Pedagogy of the oppressed.* New York: Continuum.

Freire, P. (1994). *Pedagogy of hope.* New York: Continuum.

Freire, P. (2001). *Pedagogy of freedom: Ethics, democracy, and civic courage.* Lanham, MD: Rowman & Littlefield.
Koirala-Azad, S., & Fuentes E. H. (eds.) (2010). Activist scholarship: Possibilities and constraints of participatory action research. *Social Justice, 36*(4).
McTaggart, R. (1991). Principles for participatory action research. *Adult Education Quarterly, 41*(3), 168–187.
Wang, C. C. (1999). Photovoice: A participatory action research strategy applied to women's health. *Journal of Women's Health, 8*(2), 185–192.
Wang, C. C., & Burris, M. (1997). Photovoice: Concept, methodology, and use for participatory needs assessment. *Health Education and Behavior, 24*(3), 369–387.

Name Index[1]

A
Ahsan, Monira, 53, 54, 65, 67–70, 236
Altbach, Philip, 194

B
Barvelas, Alec, 106
Baum, Fran, 52, 244, 277
Boal, Augusto, 248
Brydon-Miller, Mary, 17, 19, 24, 38

C
Chakrabarty, Dipesh, 62
Chambers, Robert, 3, 30–2, 43n1
Collier, John, 20, 21, 24, 231
Corey, Stephen, 22, 23

D
Dewey, John, 20, 33, 34, 131
Doucet, Andrea, 243, 244
Du Bois, W.E.B., 50, 54

F
Fals-Borda, Orlando, 14–18, 24, 25, 110, 119, 186, 187, 276
Feyerabend, Paul, 32–5
Freire, Paulo, 4, 16, 24, 25, 36, 42, 98, 130, 131, 162, 166, 192, 207, 248, 272, 277

G
Giorgi, Amedeo, 53

H
Hall, Budd, 15–17, 24, 130, 166, 169, 174, 176

K
Kaluram, 24, 25
Kumar, Krishna, 92, 118, 131

[1] Note: Page number followed by 'n' denote notes.

L
Lewin, Kurt, 4, 20–2, 24, 106, 167

M
MacDougall, Colin, 244
Mauthner, Natasha, 62, 243, 244
McTaggart, Robin, 26, 31, 83, 90–3, 119, 153, 167, 174, 194, 232, 271

R
Ruby, Jay, 207

S
Smith, Danielle, 244
Stenhouse, Lawrence, 23, 24
Subramanian, T.S.R., 255–6

T
Tandon, Rajesh, 16, 24, 166, 167, 173, 185

Y
Yin, Robert, 29, 83–5

Subject Index[1]

A

Abdul Latif Jameel Poverty Action Lab (JPAL), 94n4
ABL. *See* activity based learning (ABL)
action research, 2, 4–6, 9, 17, 19–27, 31, 106, 107, 133, 135, 166–7, 272, 274
activist research, 109, 187
activity based learning (ABL), 7, 8, 130, 133–7, 155n3, 155n8, 155n10, 155n12, 156n13, 156n15, 274
addas, 62–3, 65, 69
Agenda for Sustainable Development, 205
Annual Status of Education Report (ASER), 75–94, 162, 175, 180n4, 274
anti-colonial, 191
ASER. *See* Annual Status of Education Report (ASER)

B

Bhoomi Sena, 24, 25
blueprints for change, 195
BRAC. *See* Building Resources Across Communities (BRAC)
bringing participation into research, 166
Building Resources Across Communities (BRAC), 50, 51, 57, 61, 67, 70, 71n2, 235, 238, 241, 243, 244

C

card sorting, 10, 257, 262, 265, 268n9
case study(ies), 6, 7, 9, 10, 29, 78, 83–5, 89, 98, 209, 229–33, 235–45, 247–54, 255–73, 276
caste(s), 9, 10, 143, 187, 188, 193, 195, 201, 208, 222, 230, 233n2, 233n3, 255, 263, 268n7, 276

---

[1] Note: Page number followed by 'n' denote notes.

child-centered classrooms, 8, 130, 133, 134, 147, 148, 152
child-centered education, 7, 129–34, 142–4, 146, 150, 152, 153
child-centered reform, 7, 130, 133, 138, 139, 152
citizen led assessments, 81, 82
collaborative reflection, 59, 108
collaborative research, 175, 233
collective, 8, 9, 11, 22, 25, 26, 32, 52, 53, 91, 92, 108, 166, 185, 187–202, 207, 224, 244, 247–50, 252, 266, 273–4
  analysis, 186
  empowerment, 272, 275, 277
  negotiations, 186
Community-led Monitoring and Evaluation, 3
Community-Led Total Sanitation (CLTS), 3
Conceptual contexts (of PAR), 15–19
conflict and post-conflict societies, 98
culture of measurement, 81

D
Dalit(s), 195, 196, 201, 256, 261, 268n7
data analysis, 10, 32, 41, 54, 65, 85–6, 130, 143, 147, 210–21, 237–9, 243–4, 247–54
data construction, 37–8
democratic, 1, 21, 106, 119, 130, 131, 137, 152, 163–5, 180n6, 185, 187, 190, 191, 202, 206, 221, 252
DIET. *See* District Institute of Education Training (DIET)
distributing power, 197
District Institute of Education Training (DIET), 6, 75–7, 83–5, 88, 89, 94n1, 135

E
educational rehabilitation programs, 98
Education for All (EFA), 9, 100, 206, 208, 255, 272
education policy, 10, 78, 81, 91, 99, 100, 132, 205–26, 255–8, 275
EFA. *See* Education for All (EFA)
empower(s), 9, 64, 79, 92, 94, 174, 177–8, 207, 275, 278
equal partnerships, 175
evaluation, 7, 75, 81, 85, 87–9, 94n4, 115, 129, 130, 132–3, 136–7, 138, 139, 142, 144, 146, 147, 152, 155n1, 155n6, 155n10, 205–26, 275
evidence based action, 75–94, 274

F
Farmer Participatory Research, Participatory Geographic Information Systems (PGIS), 3
first-person research, 27–30, 38, 39

G
girls' education, 196, 229–33

H
historical context, 19–26
humanizing relationships, 192
Hybrid Learning, 8, 161–80, 275
Hybrid Learning program, 8, 162, 164, 167–74, 175, 179

I
identity through voice, 11, 272–3, 277
inclusive, 9, 50, 51, 56, 57, 59, 61, 71, 137, 142, 143, 156n14, 167, 175, 206, 221, 222, 238, 241, 243, 244, 248, 263, 265

SUBJECT INDEX 285

independence, 22, 60, 99, 125n5, 144, 163, 263
Integrated District-level Planning, 3
Integrated Pest Management (IPM), 3
intelligent programming and design (IPD), 165, 166
Internal Learning System (ILS), 3

K
Kasturba Gandhi Balika Vidyalaya (KGBV) Program, 230–2, 233n2, 273
KGBV. *See* Kasturba Gandhi Balika Vidyalaya (KGBV) Program
knowledge economy, 163, 174
knowledge generation, 42, 174, 185

L
local participation, 98, 107

M
marginalized communities, 9, 83, 167, 222, 223, 256
memoing, 10, 64, 235–45, 277
methodology(ies), 3, 5, 13–17, 19, 20, 22, 24, 26, 28, 30, 35–7, 41, 42, 50, 52, 54, 55, 59, 62, 68, 69, 83, 84, 107, 130, 146, 149, 155n10, 166, 172, 174, 179, 186, 189, 199, 206–8, 209, 221, 222, 226, 229, 231, 245, 271, 273, 276–8
method selection, 27
midday meal, 208, 210, 212, 213, 215, 217, 262
milestones, 10, 138, 142, 144, 236–9

N
National Curriculum Framework (NCF), 87, 130, 133
National Education Policy, India, 255, 268n4
NCF. *See* National Curriculum Framework (NCF)
neoliberal agenda, 189
NESR. *See* Northern Education System Review (NESR)
new neocolonialism, 194
NGO. *See* non-governmental organizations (NGO)
non-governmental organizations (NGO), 3, 50, 71n2, 75, 79, 82, 180n1, 208, 209, 213, 238, 256, 257
Northern Education System Review (NESR), 7, 98–100, 108–13, 116, 119, 120, 122–4, 273

P
PAR. *See* participatory action research (PAR)
PARI. *See* participatory action research and implementation (PARI)
participation, 1, 2, 4, 7, 8, 14, 16, 19, 20, 26, 30, 38, 40, 52, 54, 59, 66, 71, 81, 87, 88, 91, 93, 94, 97–9, 106–8, 119, 121, 129–56, 163–8, 172, 173, 175–6, 185, 202, 205–7, 224, 225, 247, 249, 252, 256, 259, 265, 271
participatory, 1–3, 5, 7–10, 23, 34, 52, 56, 70, 91, 93, 97–125, 129–31, 133–5, 143, 147, 148, 151, 152, 163–5, 172, 179, 188, 191, 206, 207, 221, 229, 233, 247–54, 257, 265, 272–5

Participatory Action and Learning System (PALS), 3
participatory action for policy development, 9, 108
participatory action research (PAR), 1–11, 13–43, 49–72, 75–94, 98, 106–8, 122, 130, 153, 161–80, 185–202, 205–26, 229–32, 235–45, 247, 248, 252, 253, 271–8
Participatory Action Research and Implementation (PARI), 7, 98, 99, 106–13, 119, 122, 274
participatory education, 129, 137–51, 153
participatory learning and action (PLA), 3
participatory research (PR), 3, 7, 24, 87, 91, 98, 99, 106, 107, 109, 166, 167, 186, 188–91, 252
participatory rural appraisal (PRA), 3
People's Action for Learning Network (PAL), 82
people's science, 186
phenomenology, 19, 39, 52, 54–7, 61, 65, 238, 239, 244
photo(s), 56, 59–61, 63, 65, 70, 72n6, 102, 210, 212, 214, 216, 218, 219, 229, 231, 238, 241–3, 250, 259–63, 265, 273
Photovoice, 9, 50, 59–61, 65, 205–10, 214, 215, 220–6, 229–33, 249, 254n5, 272, 273, 277
post-conflict participatory research, 109
post-war development efforts, 98
PR. *See* participatory research (PR)
Pratham, 8, 75, 78, 79, 81, 84, 91, 162, 167–9, 171–3, 175, 177, 178, 180n1, 180n4, 180n8, 180n13

Praxis Institute for Participatory Practices, 10
problem tree analysis, 257
program design, 8, 107, 174, 233

Q
qualitative research, 15, 27, 39, 55, 60, 222, 236, 237

R
racism, 10, 248–52
rapid rural appraisal (RRA), 3
reading the world, 272
reflect, Stepping Stones (SS), 3
reflexivity, 5, 6, 10, 51, 53–4, 61, 64–71, 230, 235–7, 239, 243–4, 245
re-writing the world, 272, 277
Right of Children to Free and Compulsory Education Act (RTE), 76, 86–90, 130, 133
Rishi Valley Institute for Educational Resources (RIVER) model, 138, 139, 142, 149, 155n10
RIVER. *See* Rishi Valley Institute for Educational Resources (RIVER) model
RTE. *See* Right of Children to Free and Compulsory Education Act (RTE)

S
Sarva Shiksha Abhiyan (SSA), 9, 208–10, 213–15, 217, 219, 221–4
school management committee, 77, 86, 87, 256, 257, 268n11
shifting power, 197
Shikshagiri, 255–69, 277, 278

SUBJECT INDEX 287

social change, 1, 14, 17, 18, 24, 51, 52, 59, 83, 167, 175, 202
SSA. *See* Sarva Shiksha Abhiyan (SSA)
Stipend for Girls, 208, 221
student participation, 149, 277

T

teacher participation, 130, 143–7, 155n4
teacher preparation, 274
teacher professional development, 4
Theatre of the Oppressed, 10, 248, 249
theory development, 14, 20, 24
TPP. *See* Translating Policy into Practice (TPP)

transforming the community, 11, 272, 275–7
Translating Policy into Practice (TPP), 6, 75–94, 274
tribe(s), tribal, 10, 21, 24, 135, 208, 222, 230, 233n3, 255–6, 261, 268n8, 269n14

V

Village Swaraj, 163, 180n10
voice(s), 5–9, 11, 14, 18, 19, 30, 49–72, 87, 109, 133, 146, 163, 164, 166, 187, 189, 192, 193, 221, 226, 230, 231, 233, 239, 243, 244, 245n2, 249, 256–9, 272–3, 277

Place Index[1]

A
Andhra Pradesh, India, 134, 136, 139, 140, 142, 146, 150, 155n6, 155n11

B
Bangladesh, 5, 25, 49–72, 235, 241, 271, 273, 278

F
Faridabad, India, 75, 84

G
Gujarat, India, 9, 134, 136, 140, 144–6, 150, 151, 155n3, 155n5, 155n10, 229–33, 273

I
India, 7–9, 16, 24, 29, 78, 79, 81, 85, 91, 93, 129–56, 162–4, 167–9, 174–6, 179, 180n1, 180n5, 180n8, 208, 219, 221, 224, 229–3, 255–6, 264, 267n1, 267n2, 268n4, 268n6, 271, 274, 275, 278
Haryana, 6, 75, 84
New Delhi, 10, 75, 81

J
Jaffna, Sri Lanka, 104, 105, 109, 110, 112, 116, 118, 124, 125n5
Jharkhand, India, 134, 136, 140, 155n12, 212, 216

---

[1] Note: Page number followed by 'n' denote notes.

K

Karnataka, India, 129, 132–4, 136, 140, 144, 145, 150, 151, 155n2, 155n3, 155n5, 219
Kathmandu Valley, Nepal, 188, 197

L

Lagankhel, Nepal, 188
Lamangaon, India, 172

M

Madhya Pradesh, India, 134, 136, 140, 142, 144–6, 150, 151

N

Neemtikar, India, 172
Nepal, 8, 9, 26, 107, 186–9, 191–6, 198, 199, 201, 202, 271, 276, 278
New Delhi, India, 10, 75, 81
Northern Province, Sri Lanka, 97–125

P

Pakistan, 26, 81

R

Rajasthan, India, 134, 136, 139, 140, 142–4, 146, 147, 150, 151, 155n5, 164, 168

S

South Asia, 2, 5, 10, 13–43, 57, 94, 206, 222, 225, 226, 271–8
Sri Lanka, 7, 97–125, 271, 273, 274, 278

T

Tamil Nadu, India, 133, 134, 136, 140, 142, 144–6, 150, 151, 155n2, 155n10

U

USA, 10, 21, 23, 54, 113, 188, 189, 248

The manufacturer's authorised representative in the EU is Springer Nature Customer Service Centre GmbH, Europaplatz 3, 69115 Heidelberg, Germany. If you have any concerns regarding our products, please contact ProductSafety@springernature.com

Printed and bound by CPI Group (UK) Ltd, Croydon, CR0 4YY

23/03/2026

02076674-0010